The Economic History
of
NEWPORT RHODE ISLAND

From the Colonial era to beyond the War of 1812

KENNETH WALSH

authorHOUSE®

AuthorHouse™
1663 Liberty Drive
Bloomington, IN 47403
www.authorhouse.com
Phone: 1-800-839-8640

Published by AuthorHouse   10/23/2014

ISBN: 978-1-4969-3543-4 (sc)
ISBN: 978-1-4969-3544-1 (e)

Library of Congress Control Number: 2014915870

Contents

Abstract.. vii

Introduction ix

Chapter 1   The Economy of Newport
            in the Time before George III.. 1

Chapter 2   The Economy of Newport after George II....................... 22

Chapter 3   The British Occupation of Newport............................... 49

Chapter 4   Analysis of Post-Occupation Economy (1779 – 1800)..... 65

Chapter 5   Politics, Issues,
            and the Impact of the War of 1812 93

Chapter 6   Rhode Island's Economy
            from the War of 1812 to the Civil War 106

Epilogue..121

Chapter 7   Analysis, Summary, and Conclusions............................ 123

Appendix A.. 143

Appendix B..179

Bibliography.. 187

Index..197

Abstract

Newport, Rhode Island, at the start of the reign of George III (1760) was one of the major international maritime trading centers on the eastern seaboard of British North America. Newport was expanding its maritime commerce. One hundred years later, Newport's maritime commerce had suffered a catastrophic loss and Aquidneck Island was becoming a summer vacation destination for the wealthy American industrialists. This book seeks to explain the changes that occurred in Newport's economy in those years.

Newport, Rhode Island was founded in 1639, and the Colony was chartered by King Charles II of England in 1663. Due to the efforts of the Rev. John Clarke and Roger Williams, the Colony became the first nonsectarian state of its time. Because of its religious freedom, Newport became home to a host of enterprising merchants such as Aaron Lopez, a Jew from Portugal, and Quaker Thomas Robinson

During the American Revolution Newport was occupied by the British (1776) and besieged by the Colonials and the French in August of 1778. The British destroyed much of the city's housing and caused a large depression in its economy. They left in 1779, taking a number of prominent Tory merchants with them to New York City.

The French arrived in Newport in 1780, bringing hard currency with them, whereupon some of the Colonial merchants returned. Newport's economy then began to recover as the maritime merchants started to trade with the Baltic countries and China; however, the events leading up to the War of 1812 and the actions of Britain during the Napoleonic Wars again suppressed trade. The loss of the majority of the major maritime merchants through death or retirement, and other events related to the Industrial Revolution in Rhode Island, put Newport into a decline once again. With Providence flourishing as an industrial and trading center, Newport found itself unable to compete effectively. By the mid-nineteenth century, Newport was relying increasingly on tourism and manufacturing to survive.

None of the literature reviewed to date has provided a comprehensive description of the economic structure of Newport and a detailed analysis of the various adverse impacts of events to say with certainty which factors caused Newport's maritime shipping economy to eventually decline. In most cases scholars pointed to the British occupation. There is enough information in the researched material, however, to demonstrate that this was not the case. An analysis of the events after the American Revolution indicates that Newport had fully recovered by 1800 and was doing a profitable maritime trade.

This study made use of detailed tax records kept by the Newport Historical Society; Rhode Island census records; the Historic Newspaper Archives, which includes the *Newport Mercury, Newport Gazette* and the *Providence Gazette*; first-hand accounts of events in Newport during and after the Revolution; maps from the Clements Library at the University of Michigan and the British War Department; and land records at City Hall in Newport and Town Hall in Portsmouth. It also used Microsoft Excel and MATLAB to analyze the available data.

Introduction

Newport, Rhode Island, at the start of the reign of George III (1760) was one of the major international maritime trading centers on the eastern seaboard of British North America. At this point in time, Newport was expanding its maritime commerce. One hundred years later, Newport's maritime commerce had suffered a catastrophic loss and Aquidneck Island was becoming a summer vacation destination for the wealthy American industrialists. This work seeks to explain the changes that occurred in Newport's economy in those years.

To assess Newport's ability to recover economically from two wars (the Revolution and the War of 1812) and at least one natural disaster (Great Gale of 1815) required a numerical analysis not provided in the available literature. The numerical data needed for the analysis was obtained from shipping records and advertisements in the *Newport Mercury* (1762-1763), and tax records for the years 1772 and 1774.[1] Census reports through 1875 provided data on the Rhode Island economy after the War of 1812. Newspaper accounts provided information on merchant activity before, during, and after the British occupation of Newport.[2]

Did the occupation of Newport by the British during the Revolutionary War put Newport in a position where it could not recover economically? What, if any, were the other factors that led to the eventual decline in Newport's maritime trading economy?

The thriving trading economy of Newport with its good harbor suffered a severe blow from the British occupation but started to recover under the French deployment after 1780. There was an eventual decline, but there has been no definitive proof that the decline was caused by the events of the Revolution. There are indications that the decline was related to events associated with the War of 1812, to the death and retirement of most of the major merchants, from damage due to hurricane weather, and

---

[1]   Information obtained from the Newport Historical Society document collection.
[2]   Historic newspaper database available on-line through the McKillop Library, Salve Regina University, and published with permission of Readex.

to shifts in the technologies and economic forces due to the Industrial Revolution in Rhode Island.

The detailed analysis showed that Newport's prosperity was critically affected by:

1. Personnel--The availability of talented and focused people.
2. Geography--Newport is centrally located, has a great harbor and temperate climate.
3. Technology--The Industrial Revolution introduced major changes in Rhode Island.
4. Politics--Relations with the British Crown and two wars with England.

Sources

The primary sources are listed in the Bibliography. The tax records, newspaper accounts, advertisements, and census reports have detailed information from the time of the events under study. However, many of the claims may be wrong due to careless reporting or deliberate deception in the case of customs records. For example, smuggling appears to have been very widespread in Newport, especially after the British increased taxes in the 1760s. Aaron Lopez, the leading merchant in Newport, had chests of tea and bolts of duck[3] shipped to Surinam.[4] From there he had his ships pick the cargo up and take it to Newport tucked between hogsheads of molasses.[5] The Vernons of Newport sent their ships to Gothenburg, Sweden, for cargoes of hemp, textiles, and East India goods which they passed off as a shipment of herring for the West Indies.[6] Spanish wines from Barcelona and Madeira along with silk were shipped concealed in shipments of salt from Lisbon.[7] The Newport rum industry used 14,000 hogsheads of molasses yearly, yet the custom records indicated that only 2,500 hogsheads were from the British Islands and no duty was paid for the remainder. This discrepancy prompted the British to assign the *H.M.S. Squirrel* to patrol Narragansett Bay in the winter of 1763-1764.[8]

In the *Newport Mercury* of September 1765, it was reported that an armed mob surrounded the Customs House and with great threats

---

[3] Duck is sail cloth.
[4] A Dutch colony on the north coast of South America.
[5] A Hogshead was a large barrel used for shipping liquids.
[6] Carl Bridenbaugh, *Cities in Revolt, Urban Life in America 1743-1776* (New York: Knopf, 1965), 259.
[7] Ibid.
[8] Ibid.

demanded the person of Benjamin Wickham, His Majesty's Customs Collector. When they could not see him, they went to the house of the Comptroller. This resulted in the shutdown of the tax collection until protection could be arranged for the Customs Collector.[9]

This defiant attitude toward the British continued. In July of 1766, the *Newport Mercury* reported that a Captain Hackett on a British cutter captured a large smuggling ship filled with brandy and brought it into Newport. Twenty-eight smugglers came at noonday, attacked the British crew, took the brandy and carried it away on their horses. This event was evidently not considered newsworthy because it was published several days later and took only ten lines of print in one column.[10] In this lawless environment, it is difficult to assess the true economy of Newport without the proposed in-depth and detailed analysis of all the available data.

Methods

By careful analysis and cross-checking, an accurate picture emerged. A review of the secondary literature in the bibliography has revealed a number of facts and details. There is no one document that is detailed and comprehensive enough to demonstrate that the claims are valid. Many of the conclusions drawn on incomplete sets of data may be faulty.

A significant amount of information about Newport is available in the timeframe of the American Revolution. Much of it comes from the *Newport Mercury*, the *Newport Gazette*, and the *Providence Gazette,* which are now accessible online. The amount of detailed information in the historic newspapers would not be accessible without the digitized systems offered through the McKillop Library at Salve Regina University. The newspapers are stored as images, and the search engine is image-based. Without these technologic tools the information would be too time-consuming to retrieve.

There is also a significant amount of information from city tax records and court records that is reliable. There are letters between the merchants and their agents and ship captains, customs reports, and auction advertisements. Some of this information is less accurate because of the efforts of local merchants to evade British tax and customs collections. Information about the siege of Newport in 1778 is available from memoirs and interviews with Colonial and British officers directly involved with

---

9   *Newport Mercury,* September 9, 1765.
10 *Newport Mercury,* July 1766.

the events, as well as from detailed maps obtained from the Middletown Historical Society.

A detailed, analytical approach is taken to examine pre-Revolution Newport and the robustness of its economic enterprises to determine where the vulnerabilities existed. It is also used to examine the effects of the British occupation (1776 to 1779) and the siege of Newport (August 1778) on the people of Newport and its infrastructure. Newport merchants tried to recover after the French arrived in 1780 and continued to make an effort through the following years. The analysis methods are applied through this timespan to develop an understanding of this recovery process. No one has yet tried to apply these techniques to the questions surrounding Newport's economic changes.

Computer based analysis was essential to the examination of the mass of data available from various sources. The Newport tax data (Appendix A) was input into Microsoft Excel then sorted into ordered files. Some plots (graphs) were made directly from Excel, but in cases where a more sophisticated statistical analysis was required, the Excel data were imported into MATLAB which is a product of The MathWorks Inc. of Natick, Massachusetts. It is proven analysis software used in the engineering field for over thirty years. A combination of Excel, POWERPOINT and MATLAB was used to produce the figures. In the case of some of the maps, Corel's Paintshop 5 was used to handle the large image files.

Organization

The first chapter covers the events in Newport up to the death of King George II in 1760. This was a turning point in the relationship between Britain and the Colonies. At this point the analysis seeks to establish a detailed baseline. Newport's economy consisted of a limited number of very capable merchants who developed trading networks that included a number of ships and crew, as well as agents in foreign and domestic ports that handled the local deals. They also had local networks which distributed the trade goods along the Colonial coast. There was a set of second-tier merchants who made profits in Newport's retail market, but on a smaller scale than the major merchants. All traders functioned in the various markets. In some cases several of the smaller merchants would form a joint venture to gain access to one of the larger, higher risk markets. Newport had direct trade with the West Indies, exchanging manufactured goods, livestock and salted fish for sugar, molasses and letters of credit from Britain. The letters of credit were used in the trade with Britain for manufactured goods. Food and livestock were exchanged in the coastal trade for imported manufactured goods.

The most profitable and riskiest trading loop was the Triangular Trade. Livestock, trade goods and rum were exchanged on the West African coast for gold and slaves. Most of the slaves were transported to the West Indies and sold. Some of the more promising slaves were taken to Newport where they would bring a better price than if sold as a field hand. A cargo of sugar and molasses was purchased in the Caribbean and transported to Newport where the molasses was sold to the rum distillers and as a sweetener in the Colonial trade.

In addition to the merchants, there was a significant amount of local industry. The rum distillers were a major employer of local labor at the height of the Triangular Trade. There was also a large shipbuilding industry. In both cases the customer was the local merchant who would sell the rum and the ship as an export. There was also the usual support economy such as the butchers, bakers, and candlestick makers. In addition, there were carriage makers, cabinet makers, blacksmiths, masons, carpenters, fishermen, doctors, and lawyers. This complex economic network was running at a good pace and resisting the British government's restrictions and taxes.

The time from 1760 to 1776 (Chapter 2) is concerned with the impact of George III and the British efforts to get money out of the Colonies. George III could have benefited from the advice given by Niccolò Machiavelli when he wrote *The Prince* in 1513.[11] In chapter 17 Machiavelli advises the Prince to avoid the hatred of his subjects. To do this he should abstain from taking the property of his citizens. When it is necessary for him to take the life of someone, he must do it with proper justification and for manifest cause, but above all things he must keep his hands off the property of others, because men more quickly forget the death of their father than the loss of their patrimony. When George III settled the Seven Years War with France, he took a number of French possessions and left France in a condition to recover and provide both covert and overt help to the American Colonies. When the British placed taxes on the Colonial commerce, they were attempting to take the property of the Colonies with nothing given in return. When the British tried to enforce their control by military actions, there was an open rebellion. At the start of the Revolution the British occupied the town of Newport.

---

[11] Niccolò Machiavelli, *The Prince*, trans. W. K. Marriott, eBooks@Adelaide. 2002, (accessed October 11, 2012).

Chapter 3 considers the impact of the British occupation. In 1775 two British warships attacked Prudence Island, which is in the bay to the northwest of Aquidneck Island. This precipitated a major exodus of people from Newport. In the following year the British landed 6,000 troops and occupied Newport and the rest of Aquidneck Island. This force did considerable damage to Newport's infrastructure.

In 1778 a combined Colonial and French force tried unsuccessfully to dislodge the British. This was the first multinational military effort of the revolution. The Colonials and the French engaged the British and their Hessian mercenaries. In the following year, orders came from the British headquarters in New York for the troops in Newport to move to New York and participate in campaigns in the South. The British moved their cannon to an artillery park, dismantled their forts and redoubts and evacuated Aquidneck Island for New York. The British took a number of prominent merchants who were Tory sympathizers with them. This further reduced the pool of skilled merchants available for Newport's economic recovery.

The post-Revolution recovery (Chapter 4) started with the French arrival in 1780. They brought money with them and were good customers for the Newport economy. Returning merchants and local people found a local market with available hard cash. This started the Newport economy toward recovery. Advertisements were placed in the *Newport Mercury* in both English and French. Newport merchants began trading with the Baltic countries, with China, and with the French and the rest of Europe after an agreement with Napoleon. The actions of the U.S. government to limit international trade with the Embargo Act of 1807, and the impending war, convinced many Newport businessmen to retire or sell out and go elsewhere.

The events leading up to the War of 1812 and the impact of the War on the Newport economy are covered in Chapter 5. The time from 1800 to 1812 was dominated by four political entities. The French and English were engaged in the Napoleonic Wars. In the United States, the Federal Government, which was dominated by Southern landowners, did not have a firm grasp of international commerce. The Northeastern merchants as neutrals were making profits by trading with both sides of the Napoleonic War. In this chapter the interaction of these four entities will be examined, along with the unintended consequences of the Federal Government's actions.

The events after the War of 1812, including the Industrial Revolution in Rhode Island, are examined in Chapter 6. The Industrial Revolution became important as it shifted the source of manufactured goods from

England to Providence. This had a high impact on the value of English imports. The transportation networks that developed between Boston, Providence and New York had an adverse impact on Newport's coastal trade. A detailed analysis of Newport's maritime trade and the causes for its extinction are provided in Chapter 7.

Appendix A is comprised of various tables—tax records, shipping data, census information—on which much of the analysis is based. This data will facilitate fact checking and hopefully lead to further research in this area. Two software programs have been used in the analysis. Microsoft Excel was used in organizing and tabulating the data sets as they were acquired. In the situations where a more complex analysis tool was required, MATLAB software was employed.

Appendix B contains the MATLAB files used in the analysis.

Fundamentals of Analysis

There are no infallible sources, although some are better than others. As an example: Dr. Roderick Terry, who during the 1920's was the historian at the Newport Historical Society, dedicated a redoubt on Vernon Avenue in Middletown as a British fort. The account of this effort by Dr. Terry was documented in the *Newport Historical Bulletin*. Terry's information was meager, and he was under pressure to find a British fort. Over the next forty years, a large amount of solid data arrived at the Newport Historical Society. In 1976, a paper published in the *Newport Historical Bulletin* provided proof that the fort on Vernon Avenue was built in 1780 by the Rhode Island Militia and the French for the St. Onge Regiment. Through a combination of geometry, surveying and analysis, the probability of error was calculated to be less than one in one million. The information has been available at the Newport Historical Society and the Newport Public Library for the last thirty-six years. Yet, there are recently published books and web sites that still refer to it as a British fort. The moral of this tale: take no publication or expert statement at face value unless hard, reliable, data are presented with it.

The research in this effort requires the establishment of a concrete baseline for Newport's pre-Revolution economy. If Newport recovered, this baseline must be exceeded. A detailed examination was conducted for the time between 1780 and 1844. These dates were chosen because the French arrived in Newport in 1780 and the city's last merchant prince went bankrupt in 1844.

The ability to analyze Newport's economy in detail depends on the available information sources. When analyzing a sequence of events in time, the Nyquist sampling criterion requires at least two data points in the smallest time interval considered.[12] The *Newport Mercury* provided information on a weekly basis. Tax and census records provided yearly data. Eyewitness reports provided random data points throughout the time of interest. With these data sources, the trends on a bi-weekly basis would be the shortest useful interval. In the time interval from 1780 to 1844, the major adverse event was the War of 1812 and its precursors. The secondary but more lasting economic event was the expansion of trade, transportation, and manufacturing in northern Rhode Island. The available data sources will allow a robust analysis of the Newport economy.

The first process to consider in the methods used is moving the data from its original form into that which can be manipulated using available software. Most of the data comes in the form of images stored as JPG files. These files come from images imported from online newspaper articles or scanned images from printed reports. OCR (Optical Character Recognition) software in association with Microsoft Word is used to translate the images in the JPG files into text files. The text files must be carefully reviewed, because some of the colonial printed characters do not translate well. For example, image quality can cause an 8 to be translated as a 3.

The text files were imported into Microsoft Excel which was used to sort the data into various patterns. The results were plotted which make the trends more apparent. This level of analysis shows the trends well enough to determine the degree to which Newport recovered after the Revolution.

The second part of the problem is to determine the cause of the demise of Newport's maritime trading businesses. The method chosen required the modeling of the Newport taxpayers' trends and the merchants' trading methods and facility. This provides information on the sensitivity of the merchants' business processes to changes in the environment. This analysis requires software that is more capable than Excel.[13]

The choices outlined by the economist Paolo Brandimarte are FORTRAN, C++, and MATLAB. FORTRAN is a compiled scientific

---

[12]   Harry Nyquist and Claude Shannon sampling theorem. Alan V. Oppenheim, and Ronald W. Shafer with John R. Buck, *Discrete-Time Signal Processing* (Upper Saddle River NJ, Prentice Hall, 1999), 146.

[13]   Paolo Brandimarte, *Numerical Methods in Finance and Economics 2nd ed.* (Hoboken, NJ: John Wiley and Sons, 2006). Dr. Brandimarte is a Full Professor at the Polytechnic University in Turin (Politecnico di Torino) and the author of numerous books on finance and analysis.

language that was used by the early computer systems. It is powerful analysis software, and is still in use in some legacy systems. C and C++ superseded FORTRAN when the personal computers became available. C and C++ are compiled languages, which are the preferred options for problems that require high speed and complex processing. These languages are employed extensively in Engineering and Computer Science curriculums; however, they are more complex than what is required for this analysis. The best choice for this level of analysis is MATLAB. It is an interactive language, which means that it can be easily modified. This is an important consideration when the analysis involves exploring options. Brandimarte favored MATLAB for the analysis of finance and economics, and it is currently being taught by the Salve Regina University Mathematics Department.[14]

Analysis

In developing an understanding of Newport's economy from 1700 onward, it is necessary to understand the people involved and the dynamics of the economic environment as it changed over time. The period from 1700 to the early 1800s was a time of relative stability in the technology of the Newport merchants. After the War of 1812 there was rapid technological change in Rhode Island and change in the international environment in which Newport did business. Wooden sailing ships had been replaced by steam ships and railroads, and the Industrial Revolution had transformed Providence into one of the great industrial centers of the world.

The Newport merchants provided a strong focused leadership in managing their businesses which included the wharves, warehouses, ships, crews, clerks, and factors needed to be successful. One such factor was a businessman in a foreign port that handled the sale of delivered materials and arranged for a return cargo for the home-bound ship. Without this strong, focused leadership, the business would drift along, not adapt to changing conditions, lose money and go out of business.

Another consideration for a strong economic environment is the availability of the resources that are necessary for the business. At the start of the Industrial Revolution in Rhode Island, Slater Mill was built in the Providence area. A similar mill could not be operated in Newport because there are no strong rivers on Aquidneck Island, and the steam engines that would later be used to power the mills in Newport were not available at that time.

---

[14] Ibid.

A strong local economy must be able to survive the fluctuations in the general environment in which it exists. Most businesses will do well in a strong overall economy, but when there is a downturn, the marginal businesses will fail first. If an environment becomes hostile to a particular type of business for a long enough period of time, that type of business will eventually disappear and something else will take its place. As the 19th century progressed, Newport became the vacation spot for the rich and famous.

Approach

A classic book that includes analysis, *A Study in Scarlet* published in 1887, should be considered. The author, Sir Arthur Conan Doyle, has Sherlock Holmes saying: **"It is a capital mistake to theorize before one has data. It biases the judgment."**

The first step was to identify the things and conditions required to operate a successful business in Newport in the time just before the American Revolution. The next step was to assess the impact of three years of British military occupation and look at the results of the recovery effort. After 1800 three cascading circumstances impacted Newport. The first was the Napoleonic Wars in Europe, the second was the actions of the U.S. government and the War of 1812, and the third was the Industrial Revolution in Providence and its environs.

The analysis method chosen was first to obtain as much hard data as was available and then employ computer-processing techniques to examine the trends. This provided a reasonable assessment of the relative impacts of the British Occupation, the risks due to the Napoleonic Wars, and the adverse actions of the U.S. Government and the British navy without the bias of personal viewpoints.

Data

There is a large amount of reliable information available from the period just before and after the American Revolution. The most important to this effort were the Newport tax records which are housed at the Newport Historical Society Research Library. The tax records provided a name and the amount of the tax paid which was based on an assessment of the person's wealth. Some of the post- Revolution tax records indicated the value of the assessed wealth upon which the tax was based.

The *Newport Mercury* was the local newspaper before and after the Revolution. During the British Occupation of Newport, the *Newport Gazette* was published by James Howe, a Tory from Halifax, Nova Scotia.

The volume of advertisements and what was being sold provided insight into the retail mercantile economy. The shipping news in both newspapers provided information on how many ships were coming and going from Newport. The shipping news also listed the ports that the ships came from or were listed as a destination.

The state and federal census records provided extensive information on the people, industry and wealth of Rhode Island. Other sources were used to assemble a timeline of local and world events that would be expected to have an impact on the economy of both Newport and Providence.

Investigating the data associated with the economic history of Newport without the enabling technology would be frustrating, error prone, and time consuming in the extreme. For the reasons stated in the beginning of this chapter, two pieces of software were used in the analysis. The first is Microsoft Excel which was used to examine the tax data. Excel has some limitations when processing data so MATLAB was used to do some of the detailed sorting and data matrix manipulations. The data was imported into Excel, processed, and transferred to MATLAB for more processing and sorting. The results of the analysis were plots and tables that allowed a qualitative look at Newport's economy.

In the time between 1800 and 1811, the Newport merchants involved in maritime trade died, or decided to retire, or took their capital elsewhere. A Bayesian computer model of the international merchants' trading system was written by the author using MATLAB.[15] It allowed for the evaluation of the various parameters related to the merchant's performance. The parameters examined included but were not limited to the profits from successful voyages and the loss of ships to the French and English and their associated privateers.

The combination of large amounts of raw data and the availability of computer processing and modeling software offered significant insights into the Newport economy.

Plots of the wealth of Newport from the Newport tax reports conformed to the expected exponential form but had a higher rate of change near the start of the plot than expected. To explore this, several MATLAB based simulations were used. A model using 1,000 merchants was used to establish a 1,000 venture baseline. To get a fit to the empirical data, the

---

[15]   Thomas Bayes law was refined by Pierre Simon Laplace in 1812. It describes how the likelihood of an event A is influenced by the knowledge that an event B took place. $P(A/B)$ means the probability of A given B. $P(A)$ is the probability of A. $P(B)$ is the probability of B. Then $P(A/B) = (P(B/A)*P(A)/P(B))$.

capabilities of a segment of the merchants was gradually increased and the fit to the data examined. This model provided a reasonable explanation for the shape of the empirical data.

Another model was used to examine the robustness of the Newport merchants in the face of adversity. The MATLAB program provided information as to which were the important characteristics of the Newport merchant that allowed him to profit in the face of adversity.

In particular, the model assessed the impact of loss of the merchant's ship to foreign navies or privateers. The parameters that were used in the analysis were profit and risk. It was expected that in high-risk situations where the profits were high that the Newport merchants could manage their businesses to make money. This type of analysis provided a means to examine the tradeoff between wartime risk and the impact of government interference, e.g., the Embargo Act, on the Newport merchants.

The consideration of Newport history was approached in a manner and with the philosophic outlook described by Thomas Kuhn in his studies of the history of science.[16] An investigator never believes he is correct in an absolute sense. He believes that his current approximation is a good fit within the limits of the ability of the past researchers to uncover information. The conclusions of past studies may have been the best conclusion based on the available information at that time. When new information comes to light those conclusions may change. The methods used in this study depend on recorded facts to the greatest extent possible, and then extrapolations from those facts to obtain a picture of the historic events and to avoid the trap of going with popular opinion and conventional wisdom.

---

[16] Thomas S. Kuhn, *The Structure of Scientific Revolutions* 3ed (Chicago: University of Chicago Press, 1996), 4, 5.

CHAPTER 1

The Economy of Newport in the Time before George III

Overview

Newport functioned as an independent colony up to the death of George II of England in 1760. When George III became king there was a shift in thinking about the role of the colonies in the British Empire. This chapter will cover the time up to 1763 and provide background for the years just before the American Revolution.

English Economy

The financial well-being of England in the European community of nations depended on maintaining a trading economy that could support its army and navy. England had no reserves of natural resources such as gold or silver mines and depended on maintaining a favorable balance of trade that could be taxed to provide for its military.[17] The conventional wisdom of the time was that there was a limited amount of trade available and, to be successful, England had to acquire as much of it as possible.[18] England imported raw materials and exported manufactured goods. The English colonies acted both as a source of raw materials and a market for the manufactured goods. The Navigation Acts, enacted by Parliament in 1651, were designed to shape the relationship between England and the Colonies into a self-sufficient one that would enable England to succeed in the world's economic and military competition.[19] In the time before 1763, the Navigation Acts provided a workable system of mutually beneficial trade patterns which were successfully evaded by the Colonials when

---

[17] Thomas Barrow, *Trade & Empire, The British Customs Service in Colonial America 1660 – 1775* (Cambridge: Harvard University Press, 1967), 1.

[18] Ibid., 1.

[19] Ibid., 2.

they were inconvenient.[20] The Colonial merchants may have objected in principle to the Navigation Acts, but since they were not enforced before 1763, they made little complaint.[21] Documentary evidence was sent from the British Customs service to England showing the "infamous practices of the Colonials."[22] Through the use of bribery and fraudulent papers, the Colonials had been effectively evading English law and trading with the French colonies.[23] Up until 1760, Newport's economy had no practical constraints placed upon it.[24]

Newport's Economy

To build a baseline for Newport's economy, it is best to start at the beginning and build it in layers as it evolved from 1663 to 1760. The charter granted by King Charles II for the Colony of Rhode Island and Providence Plantations had a clause suggested by the Reverend John Clarke of Newport that made the Colony the first secular entity of modern times.[25] The unique characteristic of religion in Rhode Island was the absence of a religious hierarchy. There was no state-supported religious authority to intrude in the lives of the inhabitants. The English government was far away and the Navigation Acts were not enforced. This allowed the expansion of a secular state and a "laissez-faire" economy.[26] The phrase indicates a trading economy free from government interference such as restrictive regulations, taxes, tariffs and enforced monopolies. A pure laissez-faire economy never existed in England, but in Newport, far away from any effective interference, something close to it developed.[27]

---

[20] Ibid., 3.

[21] Ibid.

[22] Quoted in Barrow, 173.

[23] Ibid.

[24] It was unconstrained by any effective law; i.e. "laissez-faire."

[25] Carl Bridenbaugh, *Fat Mutton and Liberty of Conscience* (New York: Atheneum, 1974), 5.

[26] The term "laissez-faire" was reputed to have been first used by a group of French merchants in a meeting with the French finance minister, Jean-Baptiste Colbert, in about 1680. It was recounted in an article by Rene de Voyer published in *Journal Oeconomique* in 1751.

[27] Barrow, 62.

Early Newport

Early in the history of the Colony, trade became important. Not trusting the people of Boston, Newporters did most of their trading on Long Island Sound with the towns along the Connecticut coast and New Amsterdam (renamed New York in 1665). Livestock and corn were shipped to Barbados, and in 1649 trade was initiated with the Guinea Coast using the *Beginning*, a 40-ton vessel.[28]

William Withington was one of several Newport merchants who obtained English goods through Boston. Bills of Exchange were traded for tobacco grown on Aquidneck Island and used to purchase the imported goods. By 1657 Rhode Island was producing a surplus of agricultural products. These products were sent in Newport-owned vessels to New Amsterdam, Salem, and Boston.[29]

Quakers, who were banned from Massachusetts and Connecticut, established themselves on Aquidneck Island and were protected by the Rhode Island Colonial government. The Quakers had a network for religious activity which also provided trade information throughout New England, the Caribbean, and England. This allowed them to deal directly with England. Boston could be bypassed.[30]

Livestock flourished on Aquidneck Island. After 1670 salt pork was being sold locally at £4 a barrel and was also exported to Barbados.[31] Cattle were plentiful on the Island as well, and were also traded to Boston and Barbados. In 1654 England placed a duty on all horses exported from England. This made the market for Aquidneck Island horses economically sound in the other Colonies and the islands of the Caribbean.

By 1690 the Quakers had gained control of the agrarian production and the local, coastal, and foreign trade.[32] There were about 40 of them of considerable estate (Major Farmers) that also functioned as merchants. Newport had become an important seaport doing considerable trade with the other colonies, the Caribbean Islands, and England.

The relationship among the Colonies, England and the rest of Europe in the 17th century laid the framework for the American Revolution and the War of 1812. There was peace for only eight years of the 17th century in Europe. Peace was just a rest period between wars. During these years

---

[28] Bridenbaugh, 24.
[29] Ibid., 26.
[30] Ibid., 69.
[31] Ibid., 41.
[32] Ibid., 71.

England engaged in two revolutions and nine foreign wars, and faced economic competition from Spain, Holland and France.[33]

English Viewpoint

Money was required to wage war. England had no source of gold or silver except for revenues obtained from a favorable balance in foreign trade. This trade was taxed to provide the funding to support the fleet and the army which was used for projection of force on foreign soil.

The economic potential of the Colonies did not go unnoticed by the British. There were two factions in England that were particularly interested in the Colonies. The first was the Crown and its supporters, in and outside of Parliament, who saw the Colonies as a source of tax revenue. By regulating trade, extra profit could be made by British interests. The second group consisted of the major British merchants who were dealing with the Colonies as profitable trading partners.

The viewpoint of the Crown and its supporters toward the Colonies in the 17th century was one of disinterest. Their attention was focused on their European competition: the Dutch, Spanish, and French. In the early time of colonization, the Colonies were to supply the raw materials and Britain would provide the manufactured goods. This symbiotic relationship would put England in a good position for international commerce.[34] The Navigation Acts had been intended to shape the way trade was conducted but were not as concerned with raising revenue.[35] This set of laws would focus most trade through England and require those goods to be transported in English ships. The merchants and factors were required to be English citizens.[36] No sugar, tobacco, cotton-wool, indigoes, ginger, fustic or other dying wood of Colonial production could be shipped to any country other than England.[37] An English-built ship was defined as one built in England, Ireland, Wales, Guernsey, Jersey, Berwick, or the English possessions in Asia, Africa and America.[38] By 1673 it was recognized by the English Parliament that the New England colonies were the least useful to England and the most likely to become a competitor.

---

[33] Lawrence Harper, *The English Navigation Laws* (New York: Octagon Books Inc., 1964), 9.

[34] Barrow, 2.

[35] Ibid., 7.

[36] A factor was an agent of a merchant that expedited trade in foreign ports.

[37] Barrow, 5.

[38] Harper, 389.

In May of 1678 King Charles II named Edward Randolph the collector, surveyor, and searcher of the customs in New England.[39] Randolph found that the courts, governor, and inhabitants all obstructed the British customs collectors.[40] Randolph commented upon visiting Newport that there was "neither law nor Government."[41] The city had become a major port and there was much illegal trade occurring there.[42] Ships from New England were buying goods in Holland and France and distributing them throughout the Colonies without a stopover in England as required by the Navigation Acts.[43]

The Colonial governments were not enforcing the Navigation Acts. Therefore, in 1673 the King appointed the first Customs Officer for the Colonies.[44] The English Parliament also authorized the Royal Navy to arrest smugglers. This produced jurisdictional conflicts with the local customs officials. In addition, there were not sufficient agents to cover all the ports in New England. In Newport, the local courts were used to harass the custom officials. In many cases, if a smuggler was caught and brought to trial, the witnesses disappeared along with the evidence and the smuggler was found not guilty. Oftentimes, if the custom official did not keep to the letter of the law, he was arrested and found guilty.[45]

Most of the colonial trade with Europe was through England. The colonists' dealings with Holland were minimal.[46] The colonial merchants traded with England due to the economic advantages rather than the existing laws. When it was profitable, the Navigation Acts were evaded with relative ease. The result was a general disrespect for the English law and the custom service.[47]

This illegal trade could not be stopped as long as the Colony retained its charter privileges.[48] This ineffective administrative system for customs remained in place with little change from 1710 until George III became king.[49] The Acts of Trade, passed by the English Parliament, were not stringently enforced, and the illicit traders increased in numbers, wealth

---

[39] Barrow, 16.
[40] Ibid., 43.
[41] Ibid., 47.
[42] Ibid., 9.
[43] Ibid., 15.
[44] Ibid., 13.
[45] Ibid., 86.
[46] Ibid., 151.
[47] Ibid., 152.
[48] Ibid., 71.
[49] Ibid., 72.

and wiles to the point where attempted enforcement in the 1760s and '70s helped spark the American Revolution.[50]

Newport Business Conventions

The common form of commercial organization was the partnership.[51] The junior partners (young men) contributed labor, while older partners contributed capital. According to the merchant's ethical code, the cardinal sin did not lie in slaving, or smuggling, or privateering, or even in piracy and murder, nor did it lay in dishonest dodges devised to cloak such practices. Rather it was not delivering on promises. The merchant's word was his bond.

1) Debts were paid when due.
2) Goods of the required quality were delivered on time.
3) A note endorsed on behalf of a fellow merchant was honored.

Partners were selected for ability, not kinship. At home the merchant supervised the clerks, draymen, truckers, coopers, warehouse men, shipwrights, sail makers, watchmen and many others.[52]

In foreign trade there were:

1) Supercargo, the owner's representative on the ship. He received a 2% commission, or a salary and two tons of cargo space for his personal use.
2) If no supercargo was on board, captains sometimes acted as owner's representative. They would receive salary and cargo space and were responsible for navigation. They were eligible for a bonus for a profitable voyage.
3) Agents, factors, and correspondents. These salaried men were sent ahead to assemble cargo in a foreign port.

Factors expedited trades in a foreign port, provided business intelligence, and paid port-related fees. Correspondents supplied specialized financial services. They honored drafts of other houses and supplied credit to merchants of equal standing. There was a penalty of 10% damages on bad paper. It was only in an extreme case that there would be a default. Business ventures could have between 2 and 20 partners to spread the risk.

---

[50] Ibid., 159.
[51] Peter J. Coleman, *Transformation of Rhode Island 1790 –1860* (Westport, CT: Greenwood Press, 1985), 26.
[52] Ibid.

Molasses Act

In 1763 the planters of the West Indies successfully lobbied the English Parliament to impose a tariff on molasses from foreign colonies (the Molasses Act). The motive behind this was to stop New England ships from trading with the French Islands where they could buy molasses for about half the price that it was selling for in the British West Indies. After an initial period of enforcement, things returned to their lax state.[53]

Maritime Commerce, Newport 1762-1763

By the early 1760s, Newport had developed a maritime trading economy. The details of this economy can be reconstructed from accounts in the *Newport Mercury*. Fortunately, the newspaper is available through the Salve Regina Library and the on-line database of America's Historic Newspapers. The search engine that supports the database has a provision to search for shipping news. It started indicating data in May of 1762. The data taken extended from May of 1762 to May of 1763.

The search engine passed over a number of issues in that time span which were checked and the shipping data was extracted manually. The "Shipping News" was a regular feature published in the *Newport Mercury*, usually on page three of the four page paper. The information regarding the ships entering and leaving Newport Harbor was provided by the British Custom House. The Shipping Data (Figure 1) was from the *Newport Mercury*.

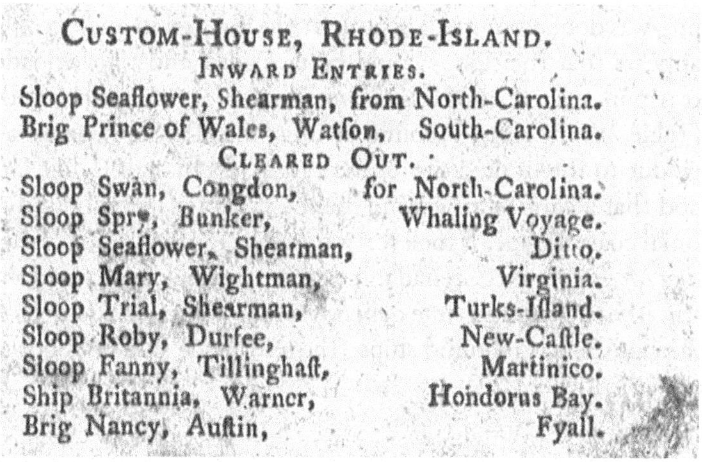

```
CUSTOM-HOUSE, RHODE-ISLAND.
           INWARD ENTRIES.
Sloop Seaflower, Shearman, from North-Carolina.
Brig Prince of Wales, Watson,   South-Carolina.
           CLEARED OUT.
Sloop Swan, Congdon,      for North-Carolina.
Sloop Spry, Bunker,            Whaling Voyage.
Sloop Seaflower, Shearman,              Ditto.
Sloop Mary, Wightman,                 Virginia.
Sloop Trial, Shearman,            Turks-Island.
Sloop Roby, Durfee,                 New-Castle.
Sloop Fanny, Tillinghast,           Martinico.
Ship Britannia, Warner,          Hondorus Bay.
Brig Nancy, Austin,                     Fyall.
```

Figure 1 Shipping Data *Newport Mercury* April 4, 1763

---

[53]   Barrow, 136.

Most of the data in Appendix A, Table A-2, was obtained using software for OCR.[54] The images from the *Newport Mercury* were converted to characters, and then put into an Excel Table. Considerable editing was required as the Colonial printing used a character that looks like an "f" but is an "s"; i.e., note Turks-Island and New-Castle in Figure 1. A shipping event in these tables is defined as an entry into port or a departure of a merchant ship. In either case cargo is moved across the Newport docks.

Between May 1762 and May 1763 there were sixty-eight brigs/snows, eighty-nine schooners, ten ships, 540 sloops and four pelliaieger entering or leaving Newport.[55] These numbers were provided to the *Newport Mercury* by the British Customs office. They represent a lower bound on the commercial shipping since the smuggling traffic would not be included.

There were almost five hundred ship events associated with trade within the Colonies in this period (Table 1). This provided the raw material for the international trade, which consisted of two markets. The Caribbean colonies were the main ports, primarily Jamaica and Barbados. The trading included ports on the north coast of South America such as Surinam and the Musquito-Shore.[56] Twelve ships left for West Africa on slave trading ventures. This amounts to a little less than 2 % of the total shipping but it was a high risk and high profit business. The trading with England and Europe was for wine, brandy, and manufactured goods, which would be used in the Colonial and Caribbean trade. The ships that cleared for the Canadian Maritime provinces most likely put into Halifax where they could trade for English goods. Only three ships cleared for whaling and just one for fishing. Most of the fishing was done from small boats that did not sign in and out.

It appears that the sloops could be unloaded and then reloaded for the next trip in seven days or less. *Sloop Africa, Sloop King-Bird,* and *Sloop Betsey* (Table 2) were turned around in this time. The short turnaround is probably due to the limited size of the cargo, less than 100 tons, and the likelihood that a cargo was waiting for the sloop for its outbound trip in the colonial coastal trade. It took forty-two days to load cargo for the *Sloop Charming Molly* going to Grenada. It took forty nine days to load the *Brig Sea-Horse.* The turnaround time depends on the ability to assemble a cargo from warehouses and inbound ships. The size of the ship does not appear to have been critical.

---

[54] Optical Character Recognition software by Nuance coupled to Microsoft Word 2007.
[55] Pelliaieger is a small cargo carrier.
[56] Named after an Indian tribe, not the insect.

Table 1 Shipping events by location of source and destination

104	Philadelphia	42	Jamaica	12	Africa
82	New York	20	Barbados	6	Madeira
69	North Carolina	8	Antigua	3	Amsterdam
49	Maryland	8	Guadeloupe	3	Gibraltar
46	South Carolina	8	Havana	2	Bristol
44	Virginia	8	Martinico	2	London
39	Boston	6	Casco-Bay	1	New Castle
12	New London	5	St. Christopher's	1	Lisbon
8	Falmouth	4	New Providence	1	Hamburg
7	Georgia	4	Turks Island	31	Total
6	Amboy	3	Granada		
5	New Haven	3	Leeward Islands		
5	Piscataway	2	Grandterre		
4	Connecticut	2	Musquito-Shore	3	Whaling Voyage
3	Nantucket	2	Tenerife	1	Fishing Voyage
2	Cape-May	1	Martinis	4	Total
2	Egg-Harbor	1	Nevis & St. Martins		
2	Fayal	1	Dominica		
2	Hull	1	Dominique	10	Nova Scotia
2	Long Island	1	Surinam	3	Halifax
1	Salem	1	West- Indies	2	Newfoundland
494	Total	1	Honduras Bay	15	Total
		1	Isequcbo		
		133	Total		

Total events 677

The cargo for a brig is three to four times larger than that of a sloop, yet the time to unload and load an outbound cargo was only 16% longer. The trip time appears to be determined by the ability of the merchants to organize a cargo in the foreign port for the return trip. The sloop would have an advantage dealing with the smaller ports in the Caribbean where the facilities are limited.

The following round trip times are from data in Table 2:

Round trip to	Philadelphia	(Brig)	28 days
Round trip to	Turks Island	(Sloop)	42 days
Round trip to	Virginia	(Sloop)	46 days
Round trip to	Philadelphia	(Brig)	58 days
Round trip to	South Carolina	(Brig)	79 days
Round trip to	Maryland	(Schooner)	84 days
Round trip to	South Carolina		98 days
Round trip to	North-Carolina		133 days

Turks Island in the southern Caribbean is the longest distance. The dominant factor in the round trip time is the in-port time while delivering cargo and waiting for the return cargo. Note there was a difference of thirty days in the round trip time for the two brigs that sailed to Philadelphia. If the sailing time for the brigs was approximately the same, then the lack of organization by the merchant at the port of Philadelphia would be the likely cause of the extra port time.

Table 2 Ship Trip Data

Ship	Master	Ports		Days	
Brig *Sea Horse*	Clarke	New Providence	Feb. 14, 1763 out		
Brig *Sea-Horse*	Clark	New-Providence	Dec. 27, 1762 in	49	Turnaround in Newport
Brig *Defiance*	Duncan	South Carolina	Jan. 3, 1763 out		
Brig *Defiance*	Duncan	South Carolina	May 16, 1763 in	164	Round trip to South Carolina
Brig *Freelove and Nancy*	Burdick	Jamaica	Dec. 13, 1762 out		
Brig *Freelove and Nancy*	Burdick	Musquito-Shore	May 23, 1763 in	161	Round trip to Caribbean
Brig *Hope*	Cowdry	Philadelphia	Nov. 29, 1762 out		
Brig *Hope*	Cowdry	Philadelphia	Dec. 27, 1762 in	28	Round trip to Philadelphia
Brig *Nancy*	Stetson	Philadelphia	Nov. 13, 1762 out		
Brig *Nancy*	Stetson	Philadelphia	Jan 10, 1763 in	58	Round trip to Philadelphia
Brig *Prince of Wales*	Watson	South Carolina	Jan. 3, 1763 out		

Brig *Prince of Wales*	Watson	South Carolina	Apr. 11, 1763 in	98	Round trip to South Carolina
Schooner *Abigail*	Church	Maryland	Dec. 13, 1762 out		
Schooner *Abigail*	Church	Maryland	Mar. 7, 1763 in	84	Round trip to Maryland
Sloop *Africa*	Hammond	Viginia	Dec. 13, 1762 in		
Sloop *Africa*	Hammond	Viginia	Dec. 20, 1762 out	7	Turnaround in Newport
Sloop *Africa*	Hammond	Virginia	Mar. 7, 1763 in	46	Round trip to Virginia
Sloop *Betsey*	Parker	Connecticut	Oct. 26, 1762 in		
Sloop *Betsey*	Parker	New London	Nov. 2, 1762 out	7	Turnaround in Newport
Sloop *Charming Molly*	Arnold	South Carolina	Nov. 13, 1762 out		
Sloop *Charming Molly*	Arnold	South Carolina	Jan. 31, 1763	79	Round trip to South Carolina
Sloop *Charming Molly*	Arnold	Granada	Mar. 14, 1763	42	Turnaround in Newport
Sloop *Fancy*	Gould	Philadelphia	Oct. 19, 1762 out		
Sloop *Fancy*	Gould	Philadelphia	Dec. 6, 1762 in	48	Round trip to Philadelphia
Sloop *King-Bird*	Allan	North-Carolina	Dec. 27, 1762 out		
Sloop *King-Bird*	Allen	North-Carolina	May. 9, 1763 in	133	Round trip to North-Carolina
Sloop *King-Bird*	Allen	North-Carolina	May. 9, 1763 out	<7	Turnaround in[57] Newport
Sloop *Sally*	Grinnell	Turks Island	Apr. 4, 1763 out		
Sloop *Sally*	Grinnell	Turks Island	May 16, 1763 in	42	Round trip to Turks Island

Some of the goods that were imported from Europe are listed in the *Newport Mercury* advertisement (Figure 2).

---

[57] Sloop King-Bird was in and out in the same week, and both events were reported in the same "Shipping News".

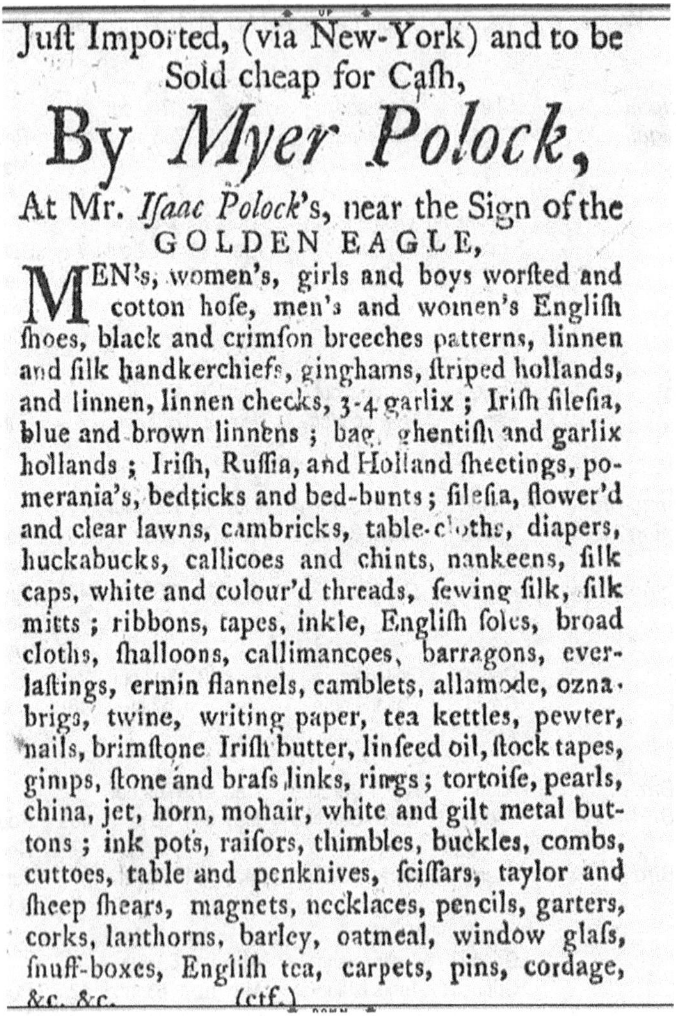

Juſt Impoʻted, (via New-York) and to be
Soid cheap for Caſh,

By *Myer Polock,*

At Mr. *Iſaac Polock*'s, near the Sign of the
GOLDEN EAGLE,

MEN's, women's, girls and boys worſted and
cotton hoſe, men's and women's Engliſh
ſhoes, black and crimſon breeches patterns, linnen
and ſilk handkerchiefs, ginghams, ſtriped hollands,
and linnen, linnen checks, 3-4 garlix ; Iriſh ſileſia,
blue and brown linnens ; bag, ghentiſh and garlix
hollands ; Iriſh, Ruſſia, and Holland ſheetings, po-
merania's, bedticks and bed-bunts; ſileſia, flower'd
and clear lawns, cambricks, table-cloths, diapers,
huckabucks, callicoes and chints, nankeens, ſilk
caps, white and colour'd threads, ſewing ſilk, ſilk
mitts ; ribbons, tapes, inkle, Engliſh ſoles, broad
cloths, ſhalloons, callimancoes, barragons, ever-
laſtings, ermin flannels, camblets, allamode, ozna·
brigs, twine, writing paper, tea kettles, pewter,
nails, brimſtone Iriſh butter, linſeed oil, ſtock tapes,
gimps, ſtone and braſs links, rings ; tortoiſe, pearls,
china, jet, horn, mohair, white and gilt metal but-
tons ; ink pots, raiſors, thimbles, buckles, combs,
cuttoes, table and penknives, ſciſſars, taylor and
ſheep ſhears, magnets, necklaces, pencils, garters,
corks, lanthorns, barley, oatmeal, window glaſs,
ſnuff-boxes, Engliſh tea, carpets, pins, cordage,
&c. &c.   (ctf.)

Figure 2 Advertisements in the *Newport
Mercury* on June 6, 1763

The items include a variety of cloth, writing paper, tea kettles and tea, knives and razors. The printed character that looks like an "f" in "Cafh" and "Ifaac" is an "s" as in Cash and Isaac.

Only one ship came directly back from West Africa during this time period. The arrival in Newport by the Brig *Royal Charlotte* was followed by the following advertisement in the *Newport Mercury* (Figure 3).

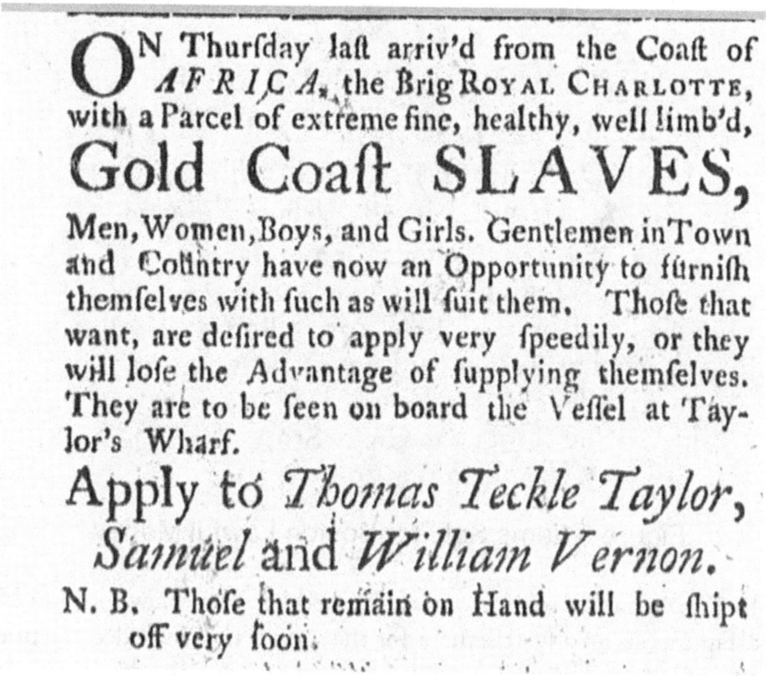

O N Thurſday laſt arriv'd from the Coaſt of
AFRICA, the Brig ROYAL CHARLOTTE,
with a Parcel of extreme fine, healthy, well limb'd,

Gold Coaſt SLAVES,

Men, Women, Boys, and Girls. Gentlemen inTown
and Country have now an Opportunity to furniſh
themſelves with ſuch as will ſuit them. Thoſe that
want, are deſired to apply very ſpeedily, or they
will loſe the Advantage of ſupplying themſelves.
They are to be ſeen on board the Veſſel at Taylor's Wharf.

Apply to *Thomas Teckle Taylor*, *Samuel* and *William Vernon*.

N. B. Thoſe that remain on Hand will be ſhipt
off very ſoon.

Figure 3 *Newport Mercury* June 6, 1763

Advertisements for cargo and passengers were also placed in the
Newport Mercury. Figure 4 is an advertisement for cargo and passengers
for London by Aaron Lopez. Lopez's organization and management skills
resulted in his becoming the wealthiest man in Newport by 1774.

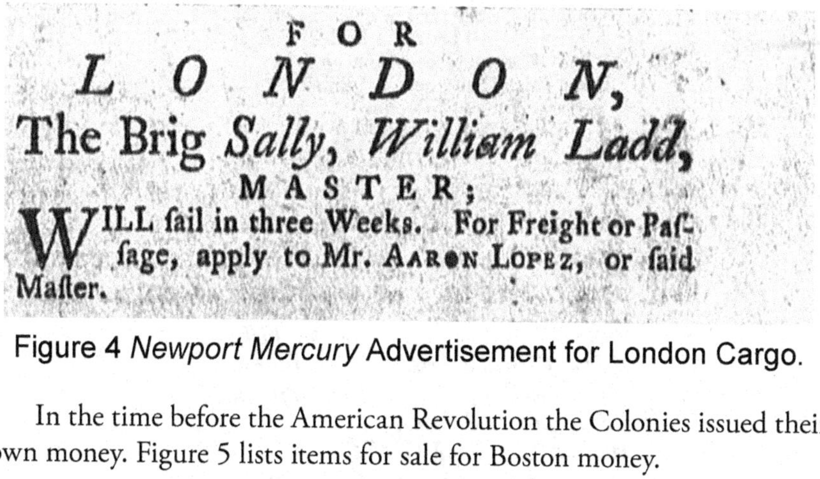

FOR
LONDON,
The Brig *Sally*, *William Ladd*,
MASTER;

WILL ſail in three Weeks. For Freight or Paſ-
ſage, apply to Mr. AARON LOPEZ, or ſaid
Maſter.

Figure 4 *Newport Mercury* Advertisement for London Cargo.

In the time before the American Revolution the Colonies issued their
own money. Figure 5 lists items for sale for Boston money.

To be SOLD
At PUBLIC VENDUE, by
JAMES KEITH,
On Thursday the 18th Inftant,
A Few Hogfheads, Teirces, and about 50 Barrels of choice Mufcovado Sugar. The Conditions of Sale for Bofton Lawful Money, to be paid on Delivery of the Goods.
The Sugars are in a Store near the Ferry Houfe on the Long Wharf.

Figure 5 Items Sold for Boston Lawful Money.

In 1762 a packet service was established between Newport and New York. Figure 6 is an advertisement for the service that included the prices.

THAT Benjamin Blagg, of New-York, and William Richards, of Newport, have provided, and properly fitted two Sloops, to go between New-York and Newport, as Pacquets, to tranfport Paffengers and Merchandize; the Rates mentioned at Foot; to fail the one from New-York, every Friday, and the other from Newport, every Thurfday, Wind and Weather permitting. The Mafters to be fpoke (when in Port) from 12 to 1 o'Clock, at the Coffee Houfe. All Letters to be delivered at the Poft-Office, at 4d. each Letter.
Every Cabbin Paffenger, one Piftole.
Steerage, Ditto, two Dollars.
New-York Currency.

Cafk Goods,	32s. per Ton.
Bar Iron,	16s. per Ton.
Pigg Iron,	10s. per Ton.
Cordage,	24s. per Ton.
Molaffes and Rum,	8s. per Hogf.
Candles,	9d. per Box.
Butter,	9d. per Firk.
A Two Wheel Carriage,	one Piftole.
A Horfe or-Cow,	one Piftole.

All Baggage as Cuftomary.
Half per Cent. for MONEY.

Figure 6 New York Packet Prices.

Note that the prices are in New-York Currency. The symbol d is for pence, and s is for shillings. To transport a two-wheel carriage, a horse or a cow, the fee was a pistole. A pistole was a Spanish gold coin (doubloon) worth approximately eighty three percent of an English pound.[58]

From the advertisements in Figures 7, 8 and 9, the imported goods were those that were being manufactured in England and Europe and not otherwise available in the Colonies.

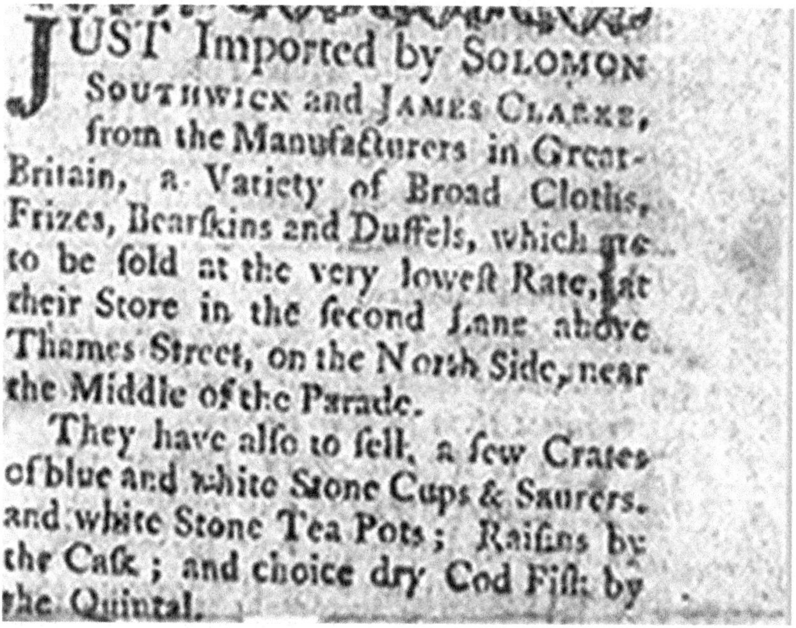

JUST Imported by SOLOMON SOUTHWICK and JAMES CLARKE, from the Manufacturers in Great-Britain, a Variety of Broad Cloths, Frizes, Bearſkins and Duffels, which are to be ſold at the very loweſt Rate, at their Store in the ſecond Lane above Thames Street, on the North Side, near the Middle of the Parade.

They have alſo to ſell, a few Crates of blue and white Stone Cups & Saucers, and white Stone Tea Pots; Raiſins by the Caſk; and choice dry Cod Fiſh by the Quintal.

Figure 7 Advertisement for Cloth and Dishes *Newport Mercury* February 9, 1762

58 University of Virginia at Wise, "People," University of Virginia at Wise, http://people.uvawise.edu/runaways/currency.html (accessed June 19, 2012).

To be SOLD by
Benj. Willbor,
At the Widow Willbor's, on the Wharf adjoining to Capt. John Brown's,
CHOICE 6 by 8, 7 by 9, and 10 by 12 Crown Sheet Glaſs, by the Box or ſmaller Quantity.

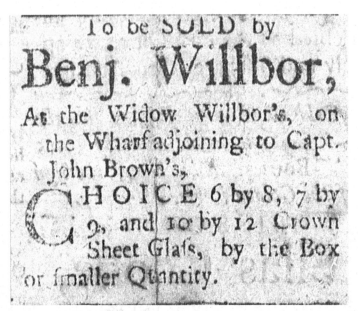

Figure 8 Window Glass *Newport Mercury* February 2, 1762

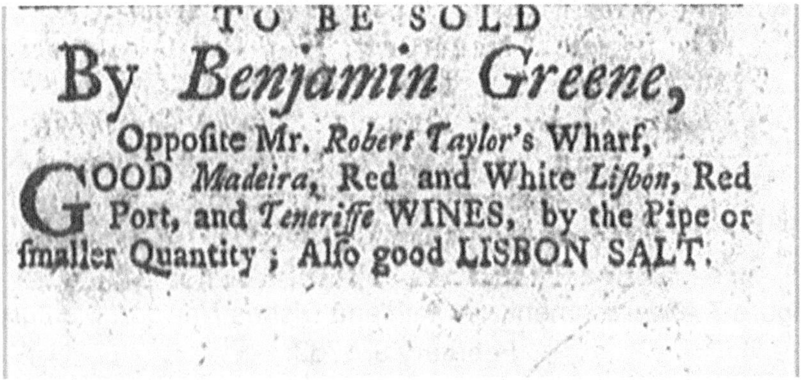

TO BE SOLD
By *Benjamin Greene*,
Oppoſite Mr. *Robert Taylor's* Wharf,
GOOD *Madeira*, Red and White *Liſbon*, Red Port, and *Teneriffe* WINES, by the Pipe or ſmaller Quantity; Alſo good LISBON SALT.

Figure 9 Wine for Sale *Newport Mercury* October 9, 1762

Newport merchants could export raw material such as wood and foodstuffs and acquire a cargo of manufactured goods such as cloth, tea pots, dishes, and pen knives for the return trip. They would then trade these products to the other Colonies for the raw material. The other trading loop was from Newport with rum and livestock to the African Gold Coast for gold and slaves, then to the Caribbean Islands to exchange the slaves for molasses, sugar, and letters of credit. In Newport the sugar was sold, the molasses was made into rum, and the letters of credit were used in the trade with England. Based on the volume of trade, Newport was doing quite well at this time.

In Colonial America, there was very little hard cash. Merchants extended credit to their customers and to each other in the form of letters of credit. Without this flow of credit the volume of Colonial trade could not have been sustained.

In 1766 the tariff on foreign molasses was reduced to 1 d/gal.[59] The molasses was primarily used in the production of rum. As the rum distillers were well established, the demand for molasses would have been constant. The imports listed as coming from the English islands fell from 326,675 gallons to 125,466 gallons, suggesting that an additional 201,209 gallons of molasses were being imported from foreign ports. But the foreign imports went from 2,824,060 to 4,878,794 gallons, indicating that the total molasses import was 3,150,735 gallons before the tariff reduction and 5,004,260 gallons after the tariff reduction. If the number of gallons of molasses required by the rum industry and that sold in the coastal trade as a sweetener was the same before and after the tariff reduction, then 1,853,525 gallons of molasses were not accounted for before the tariff reduction.[60] A simple explanation would be that false entry of customs data due to bribery was the likely cause of the differences rather than smuggling.[61] After the tariff reduction, it was likely cheaper to pay the tariff than bribe the custom collector.

Items traded to the Caribbean islands aboard a Newport ship might include, as an example: spermaceti candles, 6000 bricks, 11,000 shingles, 1000 barrel staves, 1100 barrel hoops, onions, cutlery, cheese, bread, beef and pork. The ship that transported the cargo was also for sale for the right price.[62]

One of the techniques for justifying Colonial trade with the French islands was the repatriation of French prisoners of war (POWs). A French POW was anyone that could speak French and was willing, for a fee, to make the trip. Under a flag of truce, one French POW and a large cargo could be transported. In a period of 18 months, 60 vessels with one POW each sailed from Newport to the French islands of the West Indies.[63] It is

---

59   1 Pound Sterling (£) was equal to 20 Shillings (s) or 240 Pence (d) or $4.87 dollars U.S. in 1800. Foreign molasses was from the French Islands in the Caribbean.

60   Barrow, 142.

61   Ibid., 143.

62   Ibid., 150.

63   Ibid., 161.

likely that the same "POW" was repatriated a number of times. Another method was to sail to the Spanish port on the island of Hispaniola and have a Spanish crew take the ship into a French island port. At one point Monto Christi on Hispaniola was declared a free port by Spain. There was no port as such but the Colonial ships often met the French ships there and exchanged goods.

The most feasible method of assessing the economic worth of Newport is to do a detailed analysis of the written records available from that time. This type of analysis can be illustrated by specific examples. First, there is the case of the Triangular Trade from Newport which can be understood by examining letters between the brig *Ann* captained by William English and the ship's owners Jacob Rivera and Aaron Lopez of Newport.[64] The ship left Newport in 1772 and arrived at Ilse de Los off the coast of Guinea 40 days later, having made a speed of about 4 knots. The cargo consisted of about 201 hogshead (i.e., a wooden barrel containing 63 gallons) of rum, letters of credit for 27 male and 13 female slaves owed to the owners from a previous trip, and some livestock. Upon arrival, Capt. English delivered 27 sheep, 16 geese, 12 ducks, and 5 turkeys. Only 30 of the 40 slaves needed were available at the first location. The demand for slaves was high, therefore the delays were long. There was much competition from other ships. By shopping down the coast at various slave dealers, Capt. English acquired 65 more slaves at a cost of about 201 hogsheads of rum and departed for the West Indies. Six slaves died in transit to Jamaica. The slaves that survived were sold and 127 hogsheads of molasses were purchased for the return to Newport. There was insufficient information to determine what the profit was for the trip, but it appears to have been a marginal venture because Captain English continually apologized to Aaron Lopez in his progress reports. Other recounted ventures were worse. The snow (a type of brig) named *King of Prussia* was taken by a French privateer, resulting in a total loss to the owners. On another ship there was a slave rebellion and the captain and crew were killed. In a third incident a privateer chased a merchant ship into shallow water. The ship hit a reef and disintegrated.

---

[64] Bertram Lippincott, *Indians, Privateers and High Society* (New York: J. B. Lippincott Co., 1961), 125-131.

Characteristics of Ships in the Colonial Trade

The ships used in the colonial trade were crafted based on years of experience and not a design process.[65] Fredrik Henrik af Chapman[66] provided the data for forty merchant vessels of various types and sizes.[67] From this data the following was obtained (Figure 10):

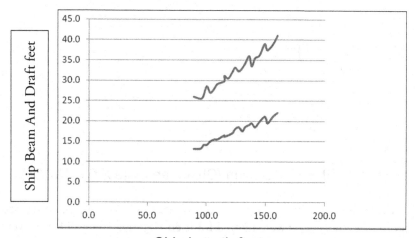

Ship Length feet
Figure 10 Ship Dimensions

For the ship data provided, the length varied from 89 feet to 160 feet. The ratio of the length to the beam was 3.84 with a standard deviation of 0.162. In modern ships this ratio varies between 4 and 10.[68] The ratio of the draft to the beam was 0.537 with a standard deviation of .0192 (Figure 10).[69] Chapman conducted tests with shaped towed bodies which indicated that a body with a blunt nose and a tapered tail was the best performer.[70] A standard deviation is a measure of the displacement of samples from a mean value. For large numbers of measurements, 68 % of the samples fall within +/- 1 standard deviation from the mean value of the group.

---

[65]   Fredrik Henrik af Chapman, *Architectura Navalis Mercatoria* (New York: Dover, 2006), Reprint from 1768.

[66]   Chapman was a Swedish ship builder and is considered the first naval architect.

[67]   Ibid., Index and description.

[68]   John P. Comstock, *Principles of Naval Architecture* (New York: Society of Naval Architects and Marine Engineers, 1967).

[69]   In modern ships between .555 and .25. Comstock, 44

[70]   Chapman, 132, Body No. 2.

The contours for the colonial merchant (Figure 11) are similar to those for a modern freighter.[71] The colonial merchant is a better hydrodynamic design for low speeds.

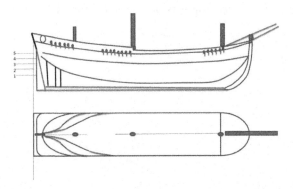

Figure 11 Ship Hull Design (Chapman Plate XXIV, No. 34)

The length of the various types of merchant vessels can be compared (Figure 12). The vessels were named for their rigging. The hull forms were very similar when scaled by the length of the vessel. Ships had three square-rigged masts. Snow and Brig had two masts. The Schooner had two masts, and the Sloop had one.

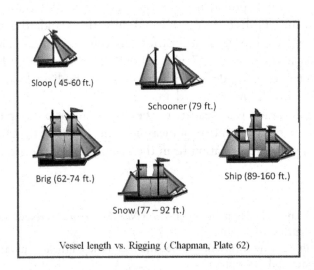

Sloop (45-60 ft.)

Schooner (79 ft.)

Brig (62-74 ft.)

Snow (77 – 92 ft.)

Ship (89-160 ft.)

Vessel length vs. Rigging (Chapman, Plate 62)

Figure 12 Ship Lengths Showing Masts and Rigging.

---

71   Comstock, 3.

The large ships, length greater than 150 feet, could carry cargo over 1000 tons. The smallest ship, 89 feet, could carry 244 tons. The Snow, Brig, and Schooner had cargo capacity of 316 to 89 tons. The Sloops could carry from 93 to 41 tons.[72]

In the 18th century the construction of a ship with good performance was a matter of chance. Without a good theory of ship design, there was nothing to guide the design but the trial and error approach of the past.[73] Chapman conducted a number of towed model tests in the 1760's that produced reasonable results.[74] The method of towing scale ship models is required even today as the computer-based hydrodynamic modeling is not detailed enough to produce sufficiently accurate and detailed data.[75] Modern studies of ship hydrodynamics indicate two forms of resistance to motion. The first is associated with the hull moving through the water (viscous drag). The second is the energy that is expended making the waves as the ship moves through the water. These two phenomena do not scale at the same rate. Ship models will always be a compromise.[76]

A ship of the optimum form to perform at its best must be well rigged, well stowed, and well worked by the commander and crew.[77] These considerations become important when analyzing the performance of the Newport merchants who may be using the same ship type but getting different performance to the same voyage destinations.

---

[72] Ibid., Index and Description.
[73] Chapman, 125.
[74] Chapman, 132.
[75] Bertram Volker, *Practical Ship Hydrodynamics 2 ed.* (Oxford, UK: Butterworth-Heinemann, 2012), 80.
[76] J. N. Newman, *Marine Hydrodynamics* (Cambridge: The MIT Press, 1997), 8.
[77] Volker, 127.

CHAPTER 2

The Economy of Newport after George II

Overview

King George II was succeeded by his grandson George III who ended the Seven Years War on terms that let the French rebuild their army and navy. The British wanted to have the Colonies pay for the war debts but the Newport merchants had developed extensive methods for cheating the British customs and were not interested in erasing the British debts.

Newport money-saving methods can be found by examining the customs reports on imported molasses. As free trade was a way of life in Newport, merchants were not about to pay duties if they could avoid them. An example is derived from the Official Report of Charles Dudley to the British for the quarter ending on October 10, 1769.[78] The report of ships for the quarter (Table 3) did not list the type of ship but listed the ship's name, the captain, and the owners.

Table 3. Ships Importing Molasses during the Quarter Ending 10 October 1769[79]

Ship	Type	Captain	Merchant	From	Notes
Sally	Brig	Smith	Not Listed	Surinam	
Ranger	Sloop	Cranston	Wanton	Hispaniola	
Recovery	Sloop	Rathbone	Thurston	Hispaniola	NM lists Capt. Sheffield
Industry	Brig	Peters	Lopez	Jamaica	
Betsy Sloop	Stanton	Cook	St Lucia		

---

[78] Edward Peterson, *History of Rhode Island* (New York: John S. Taylor, 1853), 86.

[79] Note: NM is *Newport Mercury*; Bliven was a local resident, not a Captain. Both the report and the *NM* information come from the Custom House.

Hope Brig	Gilbert	Pollock	Hispaniola		
Adventure	Sloop	Ladd	Champli	Hispaniola	
Diamond	Brig	Place	Collins	Hispaniola	
Nancy	Brig	Littlefield	Pollock	St Eustatia	NM Lists Capt. Rathburn
Pinnock	Brig	Palmer	Bowers Jamaica		
Abigail Sloop	Roland	Fletcher	St Lucia		
Speedwell	Sloop	Briggs	Reed	Jamaica	NM Lists Capt. Borden
Dolphin	Schooner	Thomas	Vernon	Hispaniola	
Polly	Brig	Bliven	Malborn	Jamaica	NM Lists Capt. Gardner
Polly	Brig	Stanton	Gibbs	Jamaica	
Dolphin	Brig	Weston	Wickham	Jamaica	

The type of ship was obtained from the shipping records published in the *Newport Mercury*.[80] The ships listed in Table 3 consisted of 9 brigs (200 to 300 tons each), 1 schooner (400 to 500 tons), and 6 sloops (25 tons each). The maximum carrying capacity of this group of ships was between 2,350 to 3,350 tons, where one ton is equal to 4 hogsheads. The maximum carrying capacity would be between 9,400 and 13,400 hogsheads. The molasses import per year was 79432 hogshead or 19858 hogsheads per quarter.[81]

As indicated in the previous chapter, Captain English brought back 127 hogsheads of molasses on his ship. If we take him as being typical, then the total for all of the Newport ships would come to 2032 hogsheads. However, Dudley's report stated that 3000 hogsheads were imported during that quarter. This is believable if the trading was bad, but if it had been good, it represents a discount of 85% off the customs duties. It is possible that between two and three quarters of the molasses was unloaded into coastal sloops at night or unloaded at points along the eastern shore of Middletown and Portsmouth and did not go through customs. There

---

[80] Occasionally ships used the same name. For example, *Polly* was duplicated but the ships could be distinguished by their captains. This worked well except that Bliven was not a captain but a local resident. The ship captain's name was Gardner.

[81] 79432 Hogshead = 5004220 gal. See page 35.

23

is insufficient information in the available literature to determine with any certainty if the custom report was a gross misrepresentation of the true value of imported molasses. Some simple analysis can indicate that the numbers given in the report are not realistic. The number of hogsheads is given as 3,000 for the quarter. This is from sixteen partially loaded ships which would make the number of hogsheads in each ship a random number. The probability that the least significant digit for the total number of hogshead is 0 is 0.1.[82] The probability that the second digit matches the first digit is .1. The probability that the third digit matches the second is 0.1. The chance of getting three zeros in a row if the numbers are random and uniformly distributed is .001, or 1/1000. If the British Comptroller was astute, his auditors would be on the next ship to Newport to check the books.

In 1766 the duty on molasses was reduced. From 1768 through 1772, half of the imported molasses sold in coastal trade was used as a sweetener, and half made into rum. Of the rum, 80% was consumed in the Colonies.[83]

Smuggling

Smuggling was a major endeavor of the Newport merchants. Aaron Lopez purchased land and buildings in Portsmouth in March of 1758. The property was located on Wapping Road just south of Braman Lane and situated at the top of a farm road down to the Sakonnet River between Black Point and Sandy Point. The road was two rods wide (19.4 feet) and suitable for transporting fire wood, or other materials, wares, or merchandise.[84] This was an ideal point to smuggle goods. Ships could unload goods in Lopez Bay (See Chapter 3), store them at the farm, and then bring them into Newport via Braman Lane and East Main Road as if they came over land from Boston. This must have been successful because Aaron Lopez expanded his holdings in 1770.[85] The British included Lopez's property in their defense line built in 1776 along the Sakonnet River.[86]

Under George III the British tried to stop the smuggling in Rhode Island. The custom revenues were less than the small port of New London.[87] The Collector of Customs, John Robinson, made $6000 from gratuities

---

[82] If the numbers are random, the least significant number could be any number from 0 to 9. P = 1/10.

[83] Bridenbaugh, 260.

[84] Town of Portsmouth Land Evidence Book Vol. 8, pages 203.

[85] Town of Portsmouth Land Evidence Book Vol. 6, pages 219 and 361.

[86] Chapter 3, Figure 28.

[87] Carl Bridenbaugh, *Cities in Revolt* (New York: Knopf, 1965), 259.

when his salary was £100 ($480).[88] The British navy started harassing the Rhode Island smugglers who had been landing goods on the Sakonnet River side of Aquidneck Island and carting the goods into Newport. [89] The smugglers became enraged at this assault on their profits. They burned the royal customs cutter *Gaspee* on June 10, 1773.[90] The response of the British was not effective. Business went back to normal

England exercised very limited control in the time between the populating of the Colonies and the American Revolution. A preoccupation with events in Europe and benign neglect of the American Colonies allowed the colonists to develop a laissez-faire economy that bypassed the English law whenever it was profitable. In each Colony the Americans sought to maximize income.[91]

A consumer-based economy developed in England. Wholesalers established themselves in the major cities that supplied goods to the retail markets in the smaller towns and villages. Unprecedented amounts of credit in the form of bills of exchange expedited the flow of goods throughout the network.[92] The exports from England to the American Colonies increased eightfold between 1700 and 1773.[93] To pay for these goods, the New England colonists relied on the West Indies trade. In the 1740's the colonial traders found the dominance of the English merchants limiting and began to develop their own merchant networks.[94] It is at this point that the detailed look at the Newport economy begins. There was a high volume of trade with England for manufactured goods. Most of what was sent to England consisted of raw materials and letters of credit obtained in the West Indies trade. In the 18th century there was not enough hard cash to support the volume of trade that was in progress. Merchants extended credit to their trading partners through a system of promissory notes called letters of credit. An example would be a Caribbean merchant accepting a letter of credit from an English merchant in payment for a cargo of sugar. The letter is exchanged for a shipment of livestock from Newport. The Newport merchant pays for a cargo of manufactured goods

---

[88] Ibid., Spanish dollars $4.8 to the £1.

[89] Ibid.

[90] Ibid.

[91] T. H. Breen, "An Empire of Goods: The Anglicization of Colonial America 1690-1776," *The Journal of British Studies* 25: 4 (October 1986): 474.

[92] Breen, 477.

[93] Ibid.

[94] Ibid., 491.

from England with the letter of credit. The manufacturer collects the value of the note from the purchaser of the original sugar. Letters of credit and a well-kept set of books allowed the merchants to conduct their business.

This analysis of Newport's economy is based on two major works in economics. The first is Robert Ekelund's *A History of Economic Theory and Method* which details the function and properties of the economic behavior of the 18th and 19th centuries. The second is by John von Neumann and Oskar Morgenstern, *The Theory of Games and Economic Behavior*. This work provides a mathematical approach to economic behavior. Additional background is provided by Gregory Clark's *A Farewell to Alms, A Brief Economic History of the World*.[95]

Newport's Human Resources

In order to establish an analysis, the general characteristic of the Newport economy needs to be outlined. The first step is to detail the commercial activity in type and quantity that was occurring in Newport before the Revolution. The merchants were a class of entrepreneurs that acquired merchandise at one location where it was plentiful and low in cost, and moved it to another place where it was scarce and more valuable. What was left over after the purchase, paying for the merchant's overhead, and the cost of moving the merchandise was the profit. The major merchants reinvested the profits in more transactions, building their businesses and their fortunes. These people would meet the definition of "barbarians" that Lawrence Miller outlines in his classic management text, *Barbarians to Bureaucrats*, detailing the styles of managers at various stages of their companies' development. [96] The first management stage is the inventor who is primarily concerned with his product. The second stage is under the control of the manager that produces the product and sells it to a wide population. This person Miller calls the barbarian. The successful Newport merchants fit this category.

There was very little technology to distract the merchant while he built his trading empire. Communication was by hand-carried letter, usually entrusted to a ship captain going in the direction of the intended recipient. The design of ships had evolved only gradually since the time

---

[95] Gregory Clark, *A Farewell to Alms A Brief Economic History of the World* (*Princeton*: Princeton University Press, 2007).

[96] Lawrence Miller, *Barbarians to Bureaucrats* (New York: Clarkson N. Potter, Inc., 1989), 2.

of the Minoans.[97] Letters of credit and bills of exchange were available in the time of the Greeks. Above all else the merchant's word was his bond. If he did not deliver on time and in good quality the goods for which he contracted, his fellow merchants would not deal with him and he would be out of business.

To the master merchant, for example Aaron Lopez, the business became the focus of his attention, and the execution of the tasks became the focus of his work. The mental and physical effort necessary to keep up with the details of the organization and markets required a dedication far beyond the ordinary. Only eight merchants were in the top 1% of the taxpayers in 1775 Newport. Lopez was the lead merchant with more than twice the wealth of the next nearest merchant.

Farming was considered the next wealthiest occupation because the land was taxed. The town of Middletown was formed in 1743 when the northern part of Newport was separated and the farmers formed their own town to avoid paying taxes which were spent on Newport streets and docks.[98]

There is a category of taxpayer that will be designated a craftsman. This person had the skills to develop a product and assemble a team to make it. Examples would be: distillery owner, shipyard owner, and cabinetmaker, sail loft owner, rope walk owner, candle maker, baker, fisherman, farmer, seamstress and blacksmith. The common characteristic of these businesses was a technical capability to produce a product that was then sold. The product could be sold to the local population or to a merchant who would ship it elsewhere and then sell it.

The next category of taxpayer included workers in the service industries such as tavern keepers, stablemen, doctors, lawyers, gardeners, and domestic staff. These are people who provided personal services for wages.

For the purpose of analysis, the merchant's team will include the ship captain (master) and crew, the dockworkers, warehousemen, shopkeepers, and a factor who represented the merchant in a foreign port. Each of the other types of workers will include their supporting staff as part of the analysis.

Newport had an unconstrained economy. There was neither master plan nor an overall controlling body. There were some trade groups such as a candle maker's organization. The Quaker religious network also acted

---

[97] The Minoans were a seafaring nation based on Thera and Crete about 2000 BC.

[98] State of Rhode Island, Town of Middletown/History, (http://middletownri.com/misc/history.php) (accessed February 27, 2012).

as a conduit for market information. Networks of family members and factors were built by major merchants such as Aaron Lopez and Abraham Redwood.[99] There were no large businesses with bureaucratic structures as is common today. Each of these enterprises was dependent on one or possibly two leaders that made the decisions upon which the business succeeded or failed. Newport's economy will be analyzed as an aggregate of mutually supportive, independent enterprises.

Newport merchants encountered three bureaucratic entities in the time from 1760 to 1815. The first was the British Government and its Customs Service, which the Newporters tried to avoid through widespread bribery, fraud, and smuggling. The second was the Colonial government which became the State government. The third was the United States Federal Government that was formed after the Revolution. Each of these had an effect, mostly adverse, on Newport.

Newport in Detail--Retail Activity

The activity of the retail merchants is an indicator of what was spent for luxuries and what was spent for necessities. The merchants of Newport placed paid advertisements in the *Newport Mercury*. By examining these ads, a baseline can be established for Newport's retail economy. The merchants that advertised are listed in the tables of Appendix A.[100]

There are available twenty-four issues of the *Newport Mercury* published in 1775. Each issue had between eight and sixteen ads, usually on the last page (Figure 13). The number of ads placed by each merchant indicates how much advertising his business was doing (Figure 14). The top fourteen advertisers are listed on Figure 14. If the merchants are ordered by the amount of advertising they used (Figure 14), the distribution is approximately exponential.

---

[99]   C.P.B. Jefferys, *Newport: A Short History* (Newport R.I.: Newport Historical Society, 1980) 13.

[100]   See Chapter 8, Table 8-2.

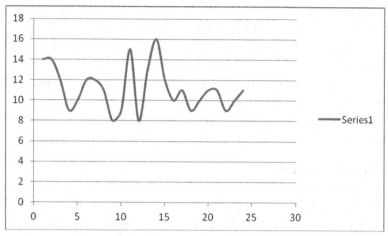

Figure 13 Number of ads/issue versus issue for the twenty-four relevant issues of the *Newport Mercury*. Note that the points are integers (ships) Indicating each point would make the graph less readable.

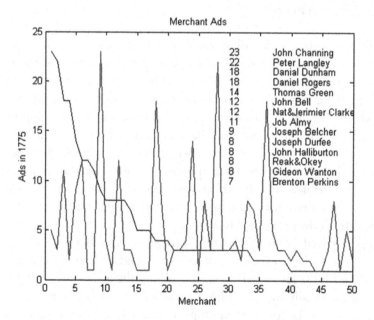

Figure 14 Number of Ads for Each Merchant.

This data on advertising will be used for comparison with similar data in assessing the economic situation during the British occupation and between 1779 and 1815. A comparison of the retail merchants with the major taxpayer list in Appendix A indicates that only six of the retail merchants were in the top tax brackets. It is likely that these six people were doing major wholesale trading and shipping, and as a side venture local retailing. It is also possible that these six merchants started as local retail and coastal merchants, and once they accumulated enough capital, successfully ventured into the international trade while maintaining the local retail business. It does not appear that large amounts of money could be made in the local retail business due to the limited population.

Major Merchants

The major merchants formed the backbone of the Newport economy. The members of this group paid more than $10 each in taxes in 1775 and controlled about 77% of the wealth of Newport. These people fit the description of Barbarians given by Miller.[101] The characteristics of a Barbarian style manager are:

1) A clear and urgent mission (build the trading empire)
2) They are in charge and very comfortable making decisions
3) Unlikely to consult associates in the decision making
4) Very action oriented.[102]

Albert Borgmann described focal things and focal practices. In the case of the Colonial merchants, there was no technology as we know it to distract the merchant from his focal thing which was his business.[103] However, there were the usual leisure pursuits available to the well-off everywhere. The focal practice was the strenuous exercise of the buying, selling and moving decisions that the organization's profits were critically dependent upon. The organization had to concentrate on getting and keeping satisfied customers. In the process of doing this the organization had to be flexible, disciplined, and responsive. Lopez was the classic example of the barbarian manager, and he became the richest man in Newport by performing in this way.

Lopez arrived in Newport from Portugal on October 13, 1752 at the age of 21. From 1752 to 1765 he developed a coastal trade with Boston, New York, Philadelphia and Charleston. In 1765, at the age of 34, he began to trade internationally by establishing a relationship with Henry Cruger of Bristol, England. Lopez sent five ships to England with goods for export,

---

[101] Miller, 34.
[102] Ibid., 40.
[103] Albert Borgmann is Regents Professor of Philosophy at the University of Montana.

and purchased English manufactured goods to sell in the Colonial market. Because of the European wars, the English market was depressed. The exported goods did not sell well in England and Lopez was in debt by more than £10,000 in 1767.[104] He then joined with Jacob Rivera in two West African ventures which produced marginal profits. His fortunes improved when he established Captain Benjamin Wright as his factor in Jamaica.[105] Wright established excellent business contacts with the planters and understood the trade. He lined up cargo so that Lopez's ships could sell their exports in Jamaica and have a return load waiting to take back to Newport. By being the first ships to return to Newport, their cargoes were sold at the best prices.[106] The economy of England and Europe improved after the end of the Seven Years War. Trade with Europe and South America became profitable, and by 1772 Lopez was the wealthiest merchant in Newport.

People of Lopez's talent were few in number and it took a long time for them to develop the knowledge and skills necessary to build a trading empire in the face of adversity. A large number of talented merchants evacuated Newport in 1775 due to the threatening actions of the British. The Revolution started in 1775, Newport suffered a major economic loss due to the shutdown of the port from 1776 to 1779, and the French arrived in 1780. The Revolution ended in 1783 with the Treaty of Paris.[107] The first tax in Newport after the Revolution was in 1785.

Taxes

The 1772 tax roll is a good indication of the status of a business in the time just before the Revolution. The items that were taxed were: land, dwellings, distilleries, sugar houses, ropewalks, warehouses, wharves, mills, spermaceti works, lime kilns, tan yards, iron works, pot ash and pearl ash works, slaves, trading stock, money, wrought plate, and livestock.[108]

The taxes in Newport were collected in British pounds before the Revolution. In the 1800's it was in dollars.[109] The Coinage Act of 1792

---

[104] Bruce Bigelow, "Aaron Lopez: Colonial Merchant of Newport," *New England Quarterly* 4:4 (October 1931): 746.

[105] A factor is a merchant's representative in a foreign port. The factor locates customers for incoming cargo and acquires cargo for the departing ship.

[106] Ibid., 764.

[107] See Appendix A.

[108] Elaine Crane, *A Dependent People* (New York: Fordham University Press, 1992), 29.

[109] Spanish 8 Reales coins and Mexican pesos were in circulation and considered equal to the American dollar and legal tender in Colonial America and the United States until 1857.

authorized the minting of silver coins, which were produced between 1794 and 1803. From 1528 into the 20th century, the British pound (£) was equivalent to 1 Troy wt. of silver. One British pound was the equivalent of 4.80 Spanish dollars (8 Reales) or Mexican pesos. The U.S. dollar was the equivalent weight of the average of a number of the worn Spanish and Mexican coins that were in use in the U.S. The British pound was equivalent to 4.87 U.S. dollars. The taxes collected in British currency were expressed in pounds, shillings, and pence. The taxes collected in U.S. dollars were expressed as decimals.

In the study of taxes the British money was converted to pounds in a decimal format.[110] It was then converted to U.S. dollars.[111] Estimates of wealth in British pounds were converted in the same fashion for ease of comparison. Before the Revolution taxes were assessed for a specific project. The taxes of 1772 needed £1200 for a project, and the 1775 project required £800. The tax assessors picked a number of taxpayers equal to the amount in pounds to be raised, 1200 and 800 in the above cases.

The taxes raised from 1772 to 1785 are shown in Figure 15. The major taxpayers (Figure 15) are listed in order of their worth. To get the total worth of all the taxpayers, each individual taxpayer's worth was estimated, then the estimates were summed. The tax goal (1200 or 800 pounds) was then divided by the total worth to get the tax rate. The tax on an individual was his estimated worth multiplied by the tax rate. The tax records for Newport in 1772, 1775, 1789, 1793, and 1801 are taken from the Newport Historical Society archive in Newport, Rhode Island, and are the source of the data tables in Appendix A. The values for taxes in Appendix A are given in U.S. dollars. Since both the English pound and the U.S. dollar were linked to a fixed weight of silver, the relationship was not changed by the effects of inflation.The 1774 census indicates that there were 1593 families in Newport. The occupations of some of the taxpayers were listed in the census report.[112] The taxes were assessed based on accumulated wealth rather than income. According to this criterion, the merchants and the farmers were the richest people in Newport. The high end taxpayers (Tax>£5) are listed by name and numbered in Appendix A.

---

[110] Tax (£) decimal = Value (£) + Value(s)/20 + Value(d)/240.
[111] Tax in U.S. Dollars ($) = Tax in Pounds (£)*4.87.
[112] See Table 4.

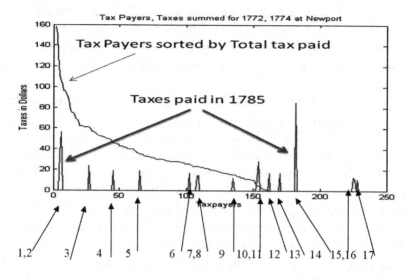

1) 'Jacob R. Rivera _187_5'
2) 'Samuel Dyre _81_6'
3) 'Henry Marchant _154_27'
4) 'Thomas Robinson _190_45'
5) 'Oliver R. Warner _241_65'
6) 'Simon Newton_167_102'
7) 'John Brown _31_108'
8) 'Jeremiah Clarke* _53_109'
9) 'George Champlin_43_135'
10) 'Nathanial Clarke_55_153'
11) 'Nathan Bebee_13_154'
12) 'William Atherton_7_162'
13) 'John Bofs_20_170'
14) 'Chace_47_182'
15) 'August Newman_166_225'
16) 'Beny Nicholas (Ferry man)_168_226'
17) 'John Oldfield_170_228'

Arrived after Revolution

Note that the first number is the position of the name as listed alphabetically in Appendix A; the second number is the position in the sorted graph.

Figure 15 Tax Base From 1772 to 1785.

The distribution of wealth in Newport just before the Revolution was exponential and relatively unchanged between 1772 and 1775. [113] There were a few very rich merchants and farmers, and a large middle class. The exponential distribution of wealth is related to the probability density of the rate of return.[114]

In the days of wooden shipbuilding, model ships were used to convince customers that the ships they were going to buy were seaworthy and properly designed. With the advent of modern computers, computer models are used for the same purpose. In this study stochastic models are used to explore the parameters that will impact the success of Newport maritime merchants. Stochastic modeling through the use of random variables is used to explore the behavior of dynamic systems.[115]

A relatively unconstrained capitalistic process is a mixture of skill and chance.[116] If the probability density for success is related to a normal distribution with a small positive mean value, then a group of 1000 merchants making 1000 deals will produce an outcome that is similar to the curve in Figure 16 generated by the following MATLAB program.

% Income Distribution

```
Mer = zeros(1000,1);
n = 1;
m = 1;
Ax = [0, 1000, 0, 1];
% randn has 0 mean, sd = 1;
PB = .1; %Profit Bias is 10% of 1 SD
```

---

[113] Having the form T = 186*e^(n/5) where 186 was the maximum tax fig 1-4, n is the number of taxpayers, e= 2.71828 (a natural constant), ^ means raised to the power of (n/5) in this case.

[114] Paolo Brandimarte *Numerical Methods in Finance and Economics 2ed* (Hoboken: John Wiley & Sons, 2006), 84.

[115] Barry L. Nelson, *Stochastic Modeling Analysis & Simulation* (New York: Dover Books, 1995), 23.

[116] Joseph A. Schumpeter, *Capitalism, Socialism, and Democracy 3ed.* (New York: Harper & Brothers, 1950), 73.

```
while(n<1001)
    while(m<1001)
    Mer(m) = (randn)+ PB + Mer(m);
        m=m+1;
    end
    m=1;
    n=n+1;
end
M = 1:1000;

% Sort ***********************************************
st = 1;
n=1;
while(st > .5) %Sort Taxpayers, high payers first
    st = 0;
    while n<1000
        if (Mer(n,1)<Mer(n+1,1));
            D = Mer(n,1);
            Mer(n,:)= Mer(n+1,1);
            Mer(n+1,1) = D;
            st=1;

        end
        n=n+1;
    end
    n=1;
end
NMer(1:1000) = Mer(1:1000)/Mer(1);
plot(M,NMer);
axis(Ax);
title('Wealth Distribution for 1000 merchants');
xlabel('Merchants');
ylabel('Wealth');
```

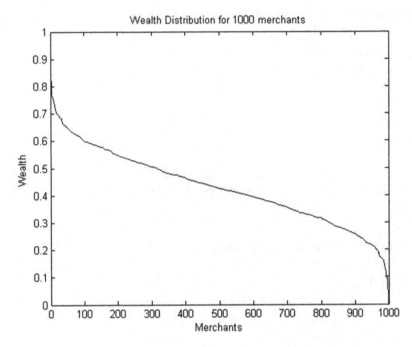

Figure 16 Distribution of Wealth Example (1000 Merchants X 1000 Deals).

The outcome in Figure 16 is expected if the merchants are equally talented with exactly the same knowledge and equipment. The outcome has been normalized by the value of the wealthiest merchant. The next step is to examine the outcome when some of the merchants are more proficient than the others. If 100 merchants are better than average, their methods will allow them to gain an increased wealth relative to the remaining merchants (Figure 17).

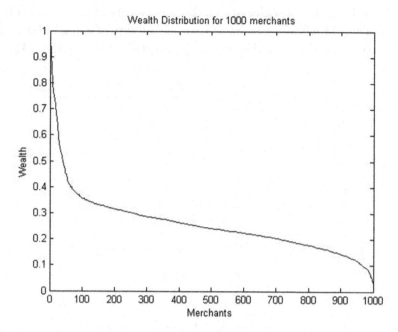

Wealth Distribution for 1000 merchants

Figure 17 Distribution of Wealth, 100 Smart Merchants (1000 Merchants X 1000 Deals).

When the merchants are not equally intelligent and the risks are not uniform, then a result similar to Figure 17 can be expected. In the calculation, the "while" loop was modified as follows:

```
while(n<1001)
    while(m<1001)
      if(m<100)
        PB = .1 +.3*((m^2)/10000);
      else
        PB=.1;
      end
      Mer(m) = (randn)+ PB + Mer(m);
      m=m+1;
    end
    m=1;
    n=n+1;
end
M = 1:1000;
```

If the Profit Bias is reduced to 0 for the majority of merchants (PB = 0) in the MATLAB, the merchants have a possibility of going below zero. This means that they would be bankrupt or deeply in debt (Figure 18).

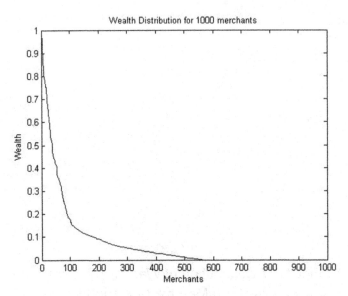

Figure 18 Wealth Distribution for PB = 0 Example (1000 Merchants X 1000 Deals).

Note that the distribution of wealth is similar to that in Figure 17, but with PB = 0, there is a chance of going below zero on the low end. From Figure 18, approximately 450 out of 1000 merchants would be in debt.

There may be some confusion with the term "randn". It is not a variable in the sense that A=1 and A is a variable always equal to 1. randn is a function, and each time it is called it returns a random number picked from a normal, zero mean distribution with a standard deviation of 1. The tax base comparison between pre-Revolution and 1785 indicates a reduction of major taxpayers from 150 down to twelve, with five coming in after the occupation. The pre-Revolution plot in Figure 19 was constructed by summing the taxes paid in 1772 and 1775, then sorting the taxpayers by the magnitude of the tax paid in these two years before the Revolution.

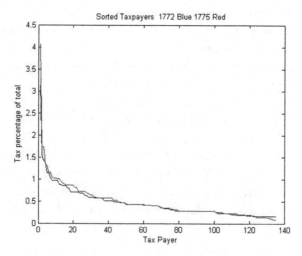

Figure 19 Taxpayers for 1772 and 1775 Sorted by Value Paid.

Aaron Lopez paid about 3.13% of the total tax in 1772 (Figure 20). The black line represents the taxpayers when ordered by magnitude. The distribution is in an exponential form. The top 9 taxpayers are listed in order. Note that Lopez was worth about twice as much as the next wealthiest taxpayer. In 1775 taxes were raised for an £800 project (Figure 23). George Rome and the Wanton brothers were still the second wealthiest, but at this point Lopez was 2.35 times wealthier.

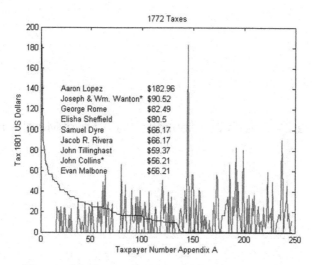

Figure 20 Taxes Paid in 1772 for a Project
Requiring £1200 ($5844.00).

Note the shape of the tax curve. It is similar to Figure 17 where there is a difference in intelligence among the merchants and an unknown risk factor involved in the venture.

The calculated curves still do not have the same peak and steep slope at the beginning as the tax curves. The difference can be simulated by inserting very smart merchants that make good decisions and decrease the risk for their ventures. Lopez did this by employing an excellent factor for the Caribbean end of his business. The model results in Figure 21 shows the peak due to the A+ merchants. Most Merchants are 'B', and only 10 of the 1000 merchants are 'A' level. Note that the slightly sharper rise at the beginning of the curve is similar to that of Figure 17. If the level is A+, then the curve in Figure 21 is similar to those in Figures 18 and 22.

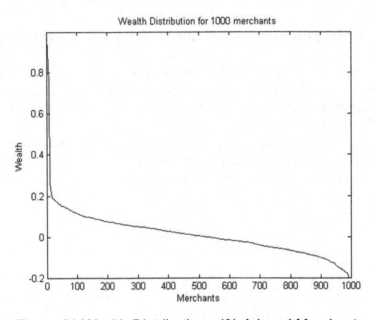

Figure 21 Wealth Distributions 1% A Level Merchants.

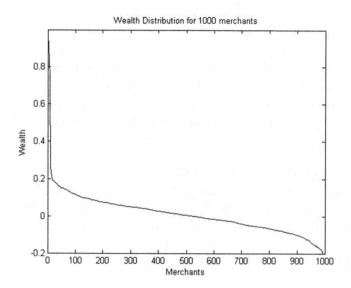

Figure 22 Wealth Distributions Where Most Merchants
are 'B', and 10 of the 1000 are 'A+' Level.

The wealthiest occupations were merchant, farmer, and distiller (Figure 23, Table 4).

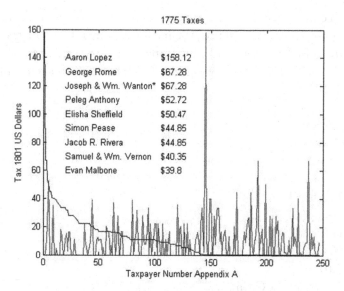

Figure 23 Taxes Paid in 1775
for a Project Requiring £800 ($3896.00).

41

The economy of Newport revolved around the merchant. Most merchandise moved in and out of Newport by water. Farm products, including livestock, were traded to England, West Africa, and the Caribbean by ship. Molasses was imported and rum was exported by ship both locally and to West Africa. All the occupations in the city of Newport depended on the ability of the merchant to make a profit and spend some of that money on local support personnel. If the merchants were inhibited, then the entire economy degraded.

Modeling Newport Merchants

To better understand the factors that influenced the merchant economy, a computer model was written with input parameters that could be adjusted to fit the Newport tax data. The tax data is an indication of the merchants' wealth.

```
% STPM Simulation of Newport Merchants
clc;
hold off;
n=1;
m=1;
k=2;
TPM = zeros(300,8);
People = 0;
% The table in Appendix A of tax information was saved as a text file and
when % going from Word to text, the file formatting is lost. The result is a
% column vector (Named John) containing the taxpayer first name and the
taxes % for each year. The following MATLAB converts this into a matrix.
Cit = zeros(1884,2);
Cit(:,1) = isnan(John);
Cit(:,2) = John;
while(n<1885)
    if(Cit(n,1)>.5)
        Cit(n,1) = m;
        TPM(m,1)=m;
        m=m+1;
        k=1;
    end
    if(Cit(n,1)<.5)
        TMP(m,k) = Cit(n,2);
        k=k+1;
    end
```

```
        n=n+1;
end
Mer = TMP;
% This MATLAB takes the 1772 tax data from the MATRIX and sorts
it by %magnitude.
% Sort ***********************************************
st = 1;
n=1;
while(st > .5) %Sort Taxpayers, high payers first
        st = 0;
    while n<255
        if (Mer(n,2)<Mer(n+1,2));
            D = Mer(n,2);
            Mer(n,2)= Mer(n+1,2);
            Mer(n+1,2) = D;
            st=1;

        end
        n=n+1;
    end
    n=1;
end
plot(Mer(1:141,2))
xlabel('Taxpayers in 1772');
ylabel('Tax $ at 4.87 dollars to the pound')
hold on;% This plots the value of taxes from highest to lowest and holds
the %plot for more curves
pause;


% This section of the MATLAB is a computer model of Newport commerce.
% Three parameters were adjusted to match the tax curve. They are: Profit
bias, merchant capability, and reinvestment.


% Income distribution

MerM = zeros(1000,1);
n = 1;
m = 1;
%Ax = [0, 150, -.2, 1];
% randn has 0 mean, sd = 1;
```

```
PB = .3; %Profit Bias is 10% of 1 SD
TF =1;
while(n<1001)
      while(m<1001)
          PB=.03; %Profit bias slightly better than even odds
          if(m<80)
              PB = .25-.25*((m^2)/(80^2));%a percentage of the merchants are
              %smarter than the majority


          end
          MerM(m) = (randn)+ PB +(MerM(m));
          m=m+1;
      end
      m=1;
      n=n+1;
end
M = 1:1000;
% Sort **************************************************
st = 1;
n=1;
while(st > .5) %Sort Taxpayers, high payers first
        st = 0;
      while n<1000
          if (MerM(n,1)<MerM(n+1,1));
             D = MerM(n,1);
             MerM(n,:)= MerM(n+1,1);
             MerM(n+1,1) = D;
             st=1;


          end
          n=n+1;
      end
      n=1;
end
n=1;
% This Trade Ratio represents the ability of the high end merchants to
%reinvest so that they can trade at a faster rate i.e. More ships at one %time.
TR = zeros(30,1);
while(n<20)
```

```
    TR(n,1) = 2/n;
    MerM(n) = MerM(n)*TR(n,1)+MerM(n);
    n=n+1;
end
ScaleAdj = .17;
NMer(1:1000) =ScaleAdj *MerM(1:1000);

plot(M(1:150),NMer(1:150),'x r');
title('Trading model vs. Taxpayer curve 1772')
text(50,50,'Solid Blue is Tax Data');
text(100,40,'Red X is Model Data');
```

By adjusting the model parameters, a good fit to the tax data was obtained (Figure 24). The parameters that allowed a good match between the model and the tax data are:

1) The merchants beyond the first 80 were modeled using a normal random process with a small positive mean value (Profit Bias PB in the model).

2) The merchants between 1 and 80 were modeled as having increased intelligence and a gradually rising profit bias (PB).

3) The merchants between 1 and 20 reinvested their profits in more ships and could trade faster than the other merchants. At his peak, Aaron Lopez had about 30 ships, with five on voyages at one time.

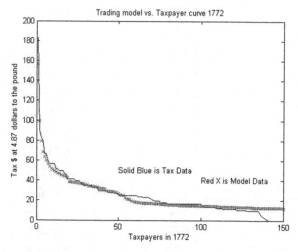

Figure 24 Plot of Computer Model data vs. Tax Data 1772.

In the Newport economy the merchants made the highest income and paid the highest taxes (Occupation number 24, Table 4), but most employed people paid some taxes.

Table 4 Tax by Occupation in Pre-Revolution Newport (£1 =$4.87 USD).

Occupation	Mean Tax USD	Percentage of Total Tax
1 Barber	$ 0.28	0.0073%
2 Boat Builder	$ 0.57	0.0146%
3 Butcher	$ 1.40	0.0359%
4 Broker	$ 1.14	0.0292%
5 Captain	$ 3.11	0.0798%
6 Carpenter	$ 0.51	0.0130%
7 Carter	$ 2.23	0.0573%
8 Comptroller	$ 5.60	0.1438%
9 Cooper	$ 0.57	0.0146%
10 Cordwainer	$ 0.96	0.0247%
11 Custom House Clerk	$ 0.28	0.0073%
12 Distiller	$ 4.14	0.1064%
13 Doctor	$ 6.84	0.1756%
14 Farmer	$ 16.27	0.4177%
15 Ferryman	$ 2.25	0.0578%
16 Goldsmith	$ 0.57	0.0146%
17 Gunsmith	$ 1.14	0.0292%
19 Hatter	$ 2.25	0.0578%
20 Inn holder	$ 0.57	0.0146%
21 Joiner	$ 1.50	0.0385%
22 Mariner	$ 0.36	0.0091%
23 Mason	$ 0.50	0.0128%
24 Merchant	$ 12.53	0.3217%
25 Miller	$ 0.71	0.0182%
26 Rope Maker	$ 1.14	0.0292%
27 Silk Dyer	$ 0.57	0.0146%
28 Tanner	$ 3.37	0.0865%
29 Taylor	$ 0.68	0.0175%
30 Watch Maker	$ 0.28	0.0073%

The bulk of the wealth and the highest tax payments came from the merchants and farmers (Figure 25).[117]

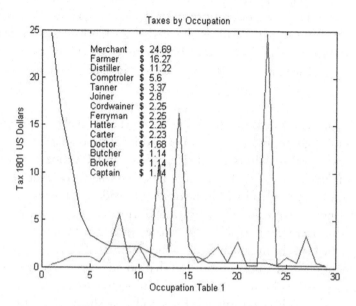

Figure 25 Taxes by Occupation.

Newport's Worth

There is no official record of the total worth of the city of Newport in 1775. An analysis of the wealth of several taxpayers that stayed in Newport through the British occupation and post-war recovery provided a rough estimate of Newport's worth in 1775.[118] The mean estimated worth was $1,087,658 with a standard deviation of $184,231.

Summary of Newport's Pre-Revolution Economy

Newport's primary business was national and international trade. There were no significant changes in the pattern of trade for the Newport merchants in the time leading up to the American Revolution.

There were three main international trade routes:

a) England exchanging raw material and letters of credit for manufactured goods.

---

[117] See Table 4.
[118] See Chapter 4, p133.

b) Caribbean islands exchanging food, livestock and manufactured goods for sugar, molasses, and letters of credit.

c) The Triangular Trade with West Africa and the Caribbean exchanging livestock and rum for slaves and gold in West Africa. The slaves were typically exchanged in the Caribbean for molasses and letters of credit issued by British merchants in their Caribbean trade. The molasses was then taken to Newport where it was made into rum.

Colonial trade was conducted from Newport and involved exchanging manufactured goods and rum for food and local products. By acting as wholesalers and distributors for the European and Caribbean markets, Newport merchants made substantial profits. The balance of trade between the Colonies and England was in favor of England. The balance of trade between England and the islands of the Caribbean was in favor of the islands. The balance of trade between the American Colonies and the islands in the Caribbean was in favor of the Colonies. This three-way trade arrangement reached an equilibrium so that no one entity went into debt.

The international trade ventures were vulnerable to interference from foreign and domestic governments. The stability of the trade relationships depended on England with its Industrial Revolution keeping its position as the only supplier of cloth and manufactured goods.

The technology associated with the transport of goods needed to be stable. If there developed a less expensive way to produce cloth and manufactured goods, or a less expensive method of transporting goods than by sail on the sea, the merchants of Newport would lose some of their competitive advantage.

After the merchants the next two wealthiest occupations were farming and rum distilling. Both of these occupations were critically dependent on the merchants to distribute their products. If the merchants were adversely impacted, then these occupations would also be adversely impacted.

CHAPTER 3

The British Occupation of Newport

Overview

In the previous chapter Newport was characterized as a prosperous port with a good harbor and a strong economy. As part of the effort to suppress the Revolution in the Colonies, the British occupied Newport, imposed martial law, and used the town as a base for blockading the East coast. The British military destroyed about 500 houses and some wharfs for firewood and material for fort construction. An attempt to dislodge the British in 1778 resulted in little damage to Newport. This chapter details the conditions in 1776 just before the British Occupation, during the Occupation, and immediately after they left in 1779.

Events Before the Occupation

The violent events in the beginning of the American Revolution were known in Newport in 1775. The *Newport Mercury* published in its August 3rd issue an article taken from a Philadelphia paper that quoted letters received from England. The letters dated the 5th and 10th of April stated that the brethren in America were to be "slaughtered by the large fleet and army that was ready to sail against them." An article in the *Newport Mercury* on September 4, 1775, describes General John Sullivan and 2,000 American troops digging in at Plough'd-hill (Breeds Hill) near Bunker Hill and notes that there was cannon fire. The British had a floating gun battery on the Mistick (Mystic) River which was sunk by the American troops.[119]

---

[119] General Sullivan started as a lawyer in New Hampshire. He became a major in the militia and was a delegate to the First and Second Continental Congresses at which he was made a Brigadier General in the Continental Army. In 1775 Congress promoted him to Major General. Washington had mixed feelings about him, describing him as both vain and popular.

The British

The Port of Boston was closed by the British in 1774 in the wake of the Boston Tea Party. The initial British strategy was to contain the revolutionary ports of the eastern seaboard. Open hostilities had occurred at Lexington in April of 1775. At Bunker Hill the British lost almost half of their troops.[120] There were 1,150 killed or wounded out of 2,400 troops (47.9%).[121] The British casualties would have been higher if the Colonials had not run out of ammunition.

In Newport during August of 1775 three British warships, the *HMS Rose, Swan,* and *King Fisher,* made preparations to cannonade Newport. At 9:00 PM the *Rose* fired her cannon with just gunpowder.[122] On December 11 at 1:00 in the morning a bomb-brig, a schooner, and two or three armed sloops left Newport Harbor and went to Conanicut Island and landed 200 marines at the East Ferry. The marines marched across the island and burned a number of houses.[123] It was reported that the *HMS Rose* and an armed schooner attacked Prudence Island. The ships landed men who destroyed a mill and a number of vacant houses. Prudence Island had already been evacuated.[124]

These actions by the British prompted a large percentage of the Newport population to leave for more secure locations. Aaron Lopez moved to Leicester, Massachusetts, a small town in Worcester County.[125] Joseph Anthony moved to Pennsylvania.[126] All in all, about 2000 people left Newport for safer places.[127]

In January of 1776, the cannons taken by Colonial General Henry Knox from Fort Ticonderoga on Lake Champlain, New York, arrived in Boston and were deployed on Dorchester Heights by the Colonials. This made Boston no longer defensible by the British. On the 17th of March the British, now under the command of Viscount William Howe, left

---

[120] Library of Congress, "The battle of Bunker Hill, Today in History: June 17," Library of Congress, http://www.memory.loc.gov (accessed July 1, 2012).

[121] British Battles,"Bunker Hill", http://www.BritishBattles.com/bunker hill.html (accessed July 1, 2012).

[122] *Newport Mercury* August 24, 1775, Issue 881, page 3.

[123] *Newport Mercury* December 12, 1775, Issue 901, page 2.

[124] Ibid., 2.

[125] Stanley Chyet, *Lopez of Newport* (Detroit: Wayne State University Press, 1970), 157.

[126] Joseph Anthony was a prominent Newport merchant and an associate of Aaron Lopez.

[127] Chyet, 159.

for Halifax, Nova Scotia.[128] In May of 1776 the British, under General Charles Cornwallis, made a failed attempt at capturing the capital of South Carolina, after which they sailed north to join General William Howe at Staten Island, New York.

Starting in August of 1776 Howe began a campaign that pushed Washington to the west of the Delaware River. On Christmas Eve of 1776 Washington, with 2,400 troops, captured 1,000 Hessian mercenaries at Trenton and then defeated the British troops at Princeton, forcing the British to move closer to New York.

The Occupation

The British arrived in Newport in early December of 1776. They occupied the island with 6,000 regular troops, 3,000 of which were Hessian. The British closed the port and put Aquidneck Island under martial law. Newport residents who spoke against the British were collected and put in a prison ship.[129] These ships were plagued with diseases and malnutrition.[130]

Military courts were used to adjudicate trivial offenses. On July 13, 1777, a Garrison Court Martial found Mr. Goldthwait (Merchant) guilty of insolent and public abuse toward Lieutenant Kersteman and fined him five pounds.[131] No civil government existed in the occupied areas. No freedom of speech was allowed, nor was the right to bear arms recognized. The British collected all the Newporters' firearms.

The incident between Mr. Goldthwait and Lt. Kersteman is an indicator of the tense relationship between the British military and the Newport population. The British officers were usually from the younger sons of wealthy, titled families. They would have little respect for merchants and tradespeople. If an arrogant lieutenant did not pay his debts on time as promised, it would be seen as a cardinal sin by a Newport merchant who lived and died by his word. The British interfered with all Newport's profit-making enterprises, causing great hardship for the population. Only the most hardened Tories found it acceptable.

---

[128] University of Houston "History," http://www.digitalhistory.uh.edu/database/article_display_printable.cfm?HHID=271 (accessed October 18, 2012).

[129] Frederick MacKenzie, *The Diary of Frederick MacKenzie.* (Cambridge: Harvard University Press, 1930), 198.

[130] Christian M. McBurney, *British Treatment of Prisoners During the Occupation of Newport* (Newport: Newport Historical Society, Newport History Vol. 79 Fall 2011.)

[131] Ibid., 309. Minor crimes were tried in Garrison Court Martial; Capital crimes were tried in General Court Martial.

The relationship between the Colonials and the British army was poor at best even when they were allied during the French and Indian War. The royal officers tended to be contemptuous of the professionalism of the Colonial officers, and the Colonials resented the loss of life in the battles caused by the incompetent and arrogant leadership of the British officers.[132]

In 1777 Howe's plan for an attack on Philadelphia was approved by the British Government, and was ordered to travel south from Canada down along the Hudson River to New York. The New England militia mobilized, and Major General John Burgoyne was stopped and captured at Saratoga along with his army of 5,000 troops on the 17th of October.[133] Because of the American victories, especially the triumph at Saratoga, France and Spain were considering to officially, overtly join the Colonials against the British.

British Forces on Aquidneck Island

In 1777 the British army and their German mercenaries were solidifying their positions on all of Aquidneck Island. Redoubts and gun batteries were placed at the ferry locations to control access to the island. Small warships were stationed on the Sakonnet River to the east of Aquidneck Island, and in Narragansett Bay's east and west passages.

The north end of the island, where ferries connected with Bristol and Tiverton, was fortified with redoubts and abbatis.[134] There were four redoubts between Bristol Ferry and Howland Ferry. An abbatis of brush and cut small trees (green) was used to protect the north end of the island. The east side near Fogland Ferry and Aaron Lopez's Portsmouth facility was also fortified (Figures 26, 27 and 28).

In addition to the fortifications at the north end and Fogland Ferry, the British built a second defensive line from the west end of Easton's Beach along the west shore of Easton's Pond, and from there along the ridge line to Two Mile Corner. The line then went from Two Mile Corner west to Tonomy Hill, then down to Coddington Cove (Figure 29).

By the spring of 1777 the British had the island under tight control. There was no travel on or off the island and boats, including fishing vessels,

---

132 British Battles,"American Revolution," http://www.britishbattles.com/american-revolution.htm (accessed 11/28/2011).

133 Burgoyne lost in part because he anticipated buying supplies as he traveled south and found out too late that the Americans would not sell to the British. This was a circumstance he had not encountered in European wars.

134 An abbatis was a barrier of cut trees and pointed branches.

could only leave port with the written authorization of the Commanding General. The *Newport Mercury* stopped publishing and a new editor, John Howe, began producing the *Newport Gazette* in 1777. At the start of the American Revolution Howe moved from Boston to Halifax. When the British occupied Newport, Howe followed them and established his newspaper.

The British were allowing items to be imported from New York. On February 20, 1777, James Moffatt was advertising goods from New York on sale at his shop at Thames and Church Lane. In July 1777 Howe was advertising stationery items and jack knives imported from New York for sale at his printing office on Thames Street.

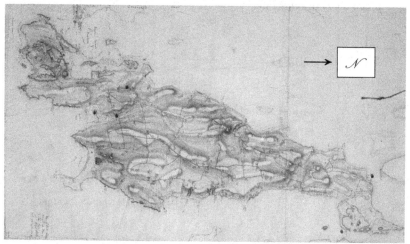

Figure 26 Map of Rhode Island surveyed and drawn
by Edward Fage, Captain of the Royal Artillery,
in the years between 1777 and 1779.[135]

Note that the colony name was Rhode Island and Providence Plantations. Rhode Island was the Island of Aquidneck.

---

[135] Map Images were provided by the Middletown Historical Society for use in Historic Research and published with permission of The Clements Library, University of Michigan, Ann Arbor, Michigan.

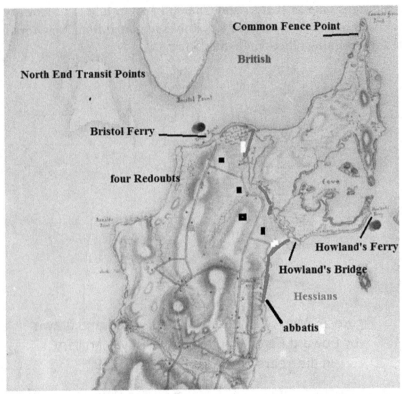

Figure 27 North End of Aquidneck Island. Edward
Fage's map with author's annotations

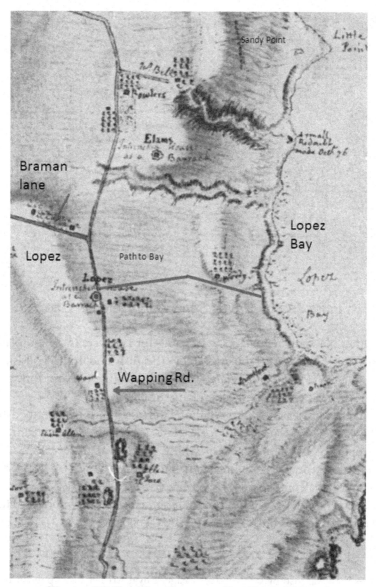

Figure 28 Fortifications on the East Side of
Aquidneck Island based on the Fage map.

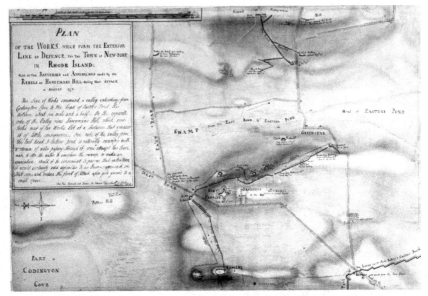

Figure 29 The British Secondary Defense Line.[136]

Other Newport merchants with goods for sale were Isaac and Nathan Hart, Agnes Nichols, Stephen Deblois (English and India goods), and James Center.[137] The Sloop *Happy-Couple* was sailing to New York with a British-escorted convoy and advertising for passengers.[138]

Caleb Gardner and John Malbone were selling food obtained from his Majesty's Vistulating Service in late July 1777.[139] Isaac Hart and Christopher Champlin were also selling goods in late July 1777. [140] In November Gardner was selling flour and codfish. The *Newport Gazette* was published from January 16, 1777 to October 6, 1779. From the advertisements in 1777 it appears that some of the Newport merchants were doing a limited business during the Occupation.[141]

---

136 This map was also by Capt. Edward Fage, Royal Artillery, and published with permission of The Clements Library, University of Michigan, Ann Arbor, Michigan.

137 Appendix A, Table A-1, number 41.

138 Captained by John Freebody.

139 For Gardner see Table A-1, number 97, and for Malbone see Table A-1, number 152.

140 For Champlin see Table A-1, number 45, and for Hart see Table A-1, number 113, and also footnote 46.

141 A listing of the merchants and the dates that they advertised in the *Newport Gazette* is provided in Appendix A.

In March General Clinton replaced General Howe as commander of the British forces, and the French fleet arrived from Toulon and anchored off the Delaware River. Between issues 21 and 22 of the *Newport Gazette,* in August of 1778 Newport was attacked by the Colonial Army under General John Sullivan operating in consort with the French fleet under the command of Comte d'Estaing. Newport was held by British forces under the command of Major General Robert Pigot. This was the Siege of Newport and the first joint military operation of the French and the Colonials during the American Revolution.

An insight into the economy of the population can be gathered from the number of newspaper ads. Just after the beginning of the British Occupation there were very few ads (Figure 30). Merchant activity picked up in 1778 (Figure 31) and then fell off in 1779 (Figure 32). The details on the merchants and ads are in Table 5.

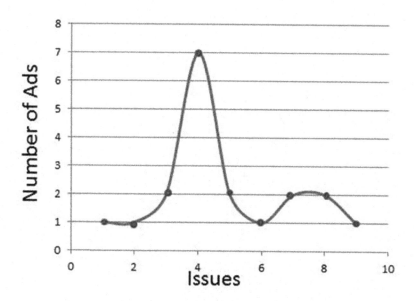

Figure 30 Merchant Ads in the Newport
Gazette vs. Issues in 1777.

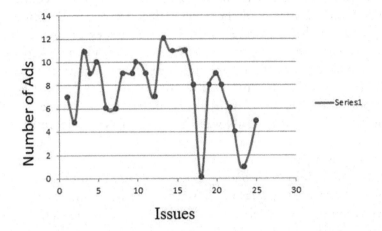

Figure 31 Merchant Ads in the *Newport Gazette* vs. Issues in 1778.

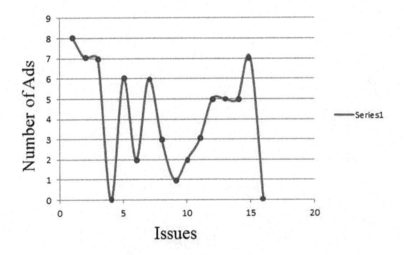

Figure 32 Merchant Ads in the *Newport Gazette* vs. Issues in 1779.

The merchants doing business in Newport during the British occupation are tabulated in Table 5. The number of advertisements placed by each merchant in each year is given in days.

Table 5 Merchants Doing Business in
Newport from 1777 to 1779.

Table of Advertizing days by year and the total

Merchant	1777	1778	1779	Total
James Arthur	0	3	0	3
John Askew (Privateer)	0	1	0	1
Stephan Ayrault	0	0	5	5
James Blackie	0	3	0	3
Bourk&Lawton	0	1	0	1
Alexander Bryson	0	16	0	16
Lewis Buliod	0	8	1	9
James Center	2	0	0	2
Christopher Champlin	0	0	0	0
Nat Chandler	0	3	0	3
William Clowet	0	0	1	1
Coddington	0	1	0	1
Silas Cooke	0	3	0	3
B.C. Cutler	0	2	0	2
Stephen Deblois	1	1	0	2
Charles Dunbar	0	3	0	3
Caleb Gardner	3	0	0	3
Samual Goldsbury	0	11	1	12
Samual Goldthwait	0	8	7	15
George Gracie	0	1	0	1
John Grayart	0	2	0	2
Joh Grozart	0	3	0	3
John Haliburton	0	1	0	1
George Hall	0	5	0	5
Isaac Hart	2	1	0	3[142]
Nathan Hart	1	13	3	17
Moses & Samuel Hart	0	8	1	9
James Hastie	0	3	5	8
James Henderson	0	0	2	2
Israel Hoursfield	1	0	0	1
John Howe	2	19	8	29

Jacob Isaacks	1	5	0	6
Alexander Johnstone	0	1	0	1
Bernard Kane	0	0	1	1
David Knox	0	0	3	3
Anthony Lechmere	1	4	0	5
John Malbone	3	0	0	3
James McCallum	0	2	0	2
Thomas McKie	0	5	0	5
James Moffatt	1	2	0	3
John Morrison	0	0	0	0
Edward Mumford	0	0	3	3
Thomas Pagan	0	1	0	1
Elizabeth Peckham	0	4	0	4
Moses Pitcher	0	1	0	1
Myer Polock	1	1	0	2
Thomas Powis	0	9	3	12
Philip Robinson	0	13	3	16
William T Robinson	0	5	0	5
William Ryson	0	2	0	2
Joshua St Croix	0	3	3	6
Miller & Sheaffe	0	0	1	1
John Simpson	0	0	3	3
Robert Spence	0	1	12	13
Robert Templeton	0	1	0	1
Charles Walker	0	1	0	1
William Wanton	0	2	0	2
John Watson	0	4	0	4
Thonas Wickham	0	1	0	1
James Wignell	0	0	1	1

---

[142] Isaac Hart was a Jewish Tory who stayed behind in Newport in October of 1779 when the British Army departed. While his brother left with the British, Isaac remained in Newport and was killed there by a mob on December 2, 1780. He was shot, bayoneted, and beaten. He died of his 15 wounds. William Pencak, *Jews & Gentiles in Early America* (Ann Arbor, University of Michigan Press, 2008), 109.

The Siege of Newport

In the summer of 1778 there were numerous events leading up to the siege of Newport. The Colonial army had control of the off-island side of the ferry landings at Bristol, Tiverton and Fogland.[143] On the 19th of July a French fleet of twelve Ships of the Line and four frigates were off the coast of Sandy Hook, New Jersey. This fleet was expected to attack Newport.[144] MacKenzie noted that unless the French fleet had the support of an Army of Colonials, it would not be effective against the English army. The fleet could, however, burn Newport and destroy the English ships.[145] Admiral John Byron was expected to arrive with a fleet of eleven Ships of the Line to join Lord Howe.[146] The gun batteries in Newport were being reinforced in anticipation of the French fleet. On the 29th of July the French arrived off Brenton's Reef. Guns were removed from the small warships at Newport and supplies were moved to more secure locations. The English troops were removed from Jamestown. The British burned their small warships stationed in the Sakonnet River when the French entered the river at Sakonnet Point. The French took Conanicut Island[147] on the 30th of July.[148] The British withdrew from the northern part of the island to the defensive line that extended from Easton's Beach to Tomini Hill and then to the Cove.[149] The French delay in attacking the island gave the British time to sink some large transports in the harbor between Goat Island and the shore to prevent the French from closing on the town by sea.

A British fleet of 31 ships, including 13 which had 50 guns or more, left Sandy Hook for Newport on the 6th of August.[150] They arrived off of Newport on the 10th of August and the French fleet left the harbor to engage them. A hurricane began on the 12th and lasted through the morning of the 14th. The Colonial Army under General Sullivan advanced to the top of Honeyman Hill opposite the British positions on the 15th.[151] The hurricane-damaged French fleet arrived off Newport on the 22nd of August. When they found that the British still held Newport, they went to Boston.

General Sullivan had been warned by General Washington that a British fleet was coming from New York to reinforce the Newport military.

---

[143] MacKenzie, 307.

[144] Ibid., 315.

[145] Ibid., 317.

[146] Adm. Byron was the grandfather of the poet George Gordon Byron.

[147] Jamestown, RI.

[148] MacKenzie, 322.

[149] Ibid., 323.

[150] MacKenzie, 323.

[151] MacKenzie, 353.

The British hoped to trap the Colonial army on the island. On the night of August 28th the Colonial forces began to evacuate the island. During the evacuation the Colonial regular troops acted as a rear guard while the militias evacuated first. Then the regular troops evacuated on the 31st of August. The clash between the British forces sent up the island to find the Colonials and the Colonial regulars, including the Rhode Island Black Regiment, was the Battle of Rhode Island. [152] At 10:00 on the 1st of September a British fleet of seventy ships arrived at Newport

General Sir Robert Pigot was called back to England and he departed on September 29, 1778.

General Richard Prescott took command of Newport.[153] Conditions were grim for those who remained on the island. There was a notice in the *Newport Gazette* that the British General had fixed the prices at which fish could be sold in Newport.[154] MacKenzie reported on the 24th of April that there had been no fish brought to the Newport market that season except perch. They had been caught in Easton's Pond. They were four to nine inches long and sold for twelve for 1s.[155]

Price fixing by a governing authority is a very good indicator that the local economy is seriously degrading. In the case of Newport during the British occupation the Commanding General limited the ability of the fishing fleet to fish. This reduced the income for the fishermen, who in turn raised their prices. The people complained to the General who imposed price ceilings. Once out to sea a large percentage of the fishing fleet went to some other port. This limited the fish supply in Newport to fresh water fish from the local pond. The unintended consequences of the British price controls were that the fishing fleet stopped fishing as the work was no longer profitable.

In March 1799, due to the increasing unrest among the civilians, General Prescott appointed Joseph Wanton, a prominent Tory, as Superintendent General of Police for the Island of Rhode Island.[156] The General hoped that Wanton would be able to pacify the Newport population.

British naval blockade activities limited the amount of flour available in Newport. The merchants then raised the price of flour. The cost to make bread consequently became higher. The bakers raised the price, the

---

[152] The Colonial Regulars were acting as a rear guard to protect the militia during the first part of the evacuation.

[153] MacKenzie, 399.

[154] *Newport Gazette*, April 22, 1779.

[155] MacKenzie, 270.

[156] *Providence Gazette*, April 3, 1779, Page 3.

population complained to the general, and he fixed the price at which bread could be sold in Newport. The bakers could not make a profit under the price controls, so they stopped baking. On the 11th of March, 1779, MacKenzie noted that the distress of the lower classes of Newport had become very great, particularly for provisions and fuel. The salted provisions that the British soldiers would not eat were eaten by these people.[157] Because of these shortages for the civilians, many had left the island before the winter of 1778.[158] In December 1778 the weather was very cold and there was heavy ice. A soldier was found dead of exposure on the 24th of December.[159] Flour was running out and more civilians were leaving the Island.

By the end of 1778 General Clinton held New York City and General Washington held the New York mainland. Heavy fighting had taken place in the South but nothing decisive had been accomplished.[160] General Clinton called the Newport troops to New York to support British operations in the mid-Atlantic and the South. John Howe, the Tory publisher, was forced to leave Newport in 1779 when the British evacuated the island. He returned to Nova Scotia and became a successful publisher.[161]

The British Evacuation

On October 16, 1779, Governor William Greene of Rhode Island issued a proclamation stating that, as the British appeared to be evacuating Newport, privateers were forbidden to land there or in Jamestown.[162] Having been ordered to New York, the British embarked on transports and their fleet sailed for New York on October 25th. Colonial troops occupied Newport the next morning.[163] Property damage to houses and wharves were estimated at £124,799.[164] About twenty-five of the Newport Tories left with the British, including William and Joseph Wanton, Thomas Bannister, and James Coggeshall.[165]

---

[157] MacKenzie,255.

[158] Ibid., 397.

[159] Ibid., 435.

[160] British Battles, "American Revolution," http://www.britishbattles.com/american-revolution.htm .6 (accessed November 28, 2011).

[161] Halifax Public Library, "John Howe", www.halifaxpubliclibraries.ca/research/topics/local-history-genealogy (accessed October 18, 2012).

[162] *Providence Gazette* October 16, 1779.

[163] *Providence Gazette* October 28, 1779.

[164] This is $607,771 in US 1801 currency, *Providence Gazette* October 28, 1779.

[165] Howard W. Preston, The *Battle of Rhode Island: August 29, 1778* (Providence: Rhode Island State Bureau of Information Historic Publication, 1928), 9,10.

After three years of British occupation, Newport had been heavily damaged. There were no British redoubts left standing on the west side of Valley Road, including Green End Redoubt. The British had dismantled all of their redoubts and taken their guns with them when they left. Of the sixty-one merchants that advertised in Newport during the Occupation, only eight had been Newport taxpayers either before or after the Revolution.[166] Stephen Ayrault and Christopher Champlin were the only merchants living in Newport before the Revolution and taxpayers after it ended. Four of the merchants came to Newport before the Revolution and three left with the British. They were Samuel Goldthwait, John Halliburton, and Nathan Hart. Three came during the Occupation and stayed. They were James Center, Stephen Deblois, and Edward Mumford. The remaining fifty-four merchants came after the British arrived and left before or at the same time that the British departed.

Newport suffered disruption of its commerce, destruction of its houses and wharves for firewood, and the departure of many of its most talented people. The attempt by a combined force of Colonials and French to dislodge the British in 1778, however, did little damage to the town of Newport. Most of the action during the Siege took place across Valley Road in Middletown and during the rear guard battle in Portsmouth.

In 1780, while Newport was trying to recover, General Cornwallis arrived at Charleston. Also in 1780 Benedict Arnold changed sides. He left behind General Clinton's Adjutant, Major John Andre, to be captured and hung as a spy. Newport was recovering slowly until the French fleet arrived in July of 1780. The British fought a series of battles in the South and arrived in Yorktown in July of 1781.

Summary of Conditions in Newport after the Evacuation

About 50% of the Newport infrastructure was destroyed by the British army during their stay in Newport. Houses and some wharfs were used as firewood and as building material for forts. The major merchants that were opposed to the British had departed the island and only a few would return. A limited number of merchants stayed through the Occupation and remained in Newport after the British left in October of 1779. The Tories left with the British army. The port facilities were damaged but serviceable enough for the British to use them during their evacuation.

---

[166] Appendix A.

CHAPTER 4

Analysis of Post-Occupation Economy (1779 – 1800)

The time from the arrival of the French in 1780 to 1800 was a period of recovery with some of the former merchants coming back and new businesses being established. As soon as the British evacuated Newport in October of 1779 the Colonial forces immediately moved in and occupied the town. The damage to Newport caused by the British forces while they were on the Aquidneck Island was estimated at £124,000 ($603,880), including the destruction of 500 houses.[167] The Colonials took steps to raise the British men-of-war and take possession of the houses of the Tories.[168]

The French

A French fleet made up of seven ships of the line, three frigates, one corvette (hospital ship), and thirty-two transports carrying 5000 troops departed from Brest and arrived in Newport in July of 1780. The fleet was under the command of Monsieur Charles Louis d'Arsac, Le Chevalier de Ternay, and the Army was under the command of Jean-Baptist Donatien de Vimeur, comte de Rochambeau. Rochambeau's headquarters was in Vernon House off Washington Square (Figure 33). Other houses used by the French can be seen on Washington Street (Figures 34 and 35).[169]

---

[167] Bayles, 267.
[168] Ibid., 266.
[169] Washington Street was named Water Street before the Revolution.

Figure 33 Rochambeau's Headquarters at Vernon House.

French Background

In the 17th century the relationship among the European states was a balance of power. The states would regroup to limit the influence of any one of them that was becoming too powerful for the others' comfort. The leading states were Spain, France, Holland, Britain, Prussia, and Russia. In the War of Austrian Succession, Britain and Russia combined to limit the expansion of Prussia. In the Seven Years War, it was Prussia and Britain defeating Austria and France.[170] The Peace of Paris in 1763, however, left France with the resources to rebuild its military. Learning from the losses in the Seven Year War, France instituted a number of sweeping changes in its army and navy.[171]

---

170 Some of the Seven Years War took place in America as the French and Indian War. It ended in 1763.

171 MIT, "The French Contribution to the American War of Independence," http://www.people.csail.mit.edu/sfelshin/saintonge/frhist.html (accessed March 3, 2012).

Figure 34 Robinson House.

Benjamin Franklin went to Paris in 1776 and acted as American Minister Plenipotentiary.[172] By playing off the French against the British, Franklin was able to negotiate loans from the French Government and use the money to purchase military supplies.[173] He then had the supplies shipped to Washington's army.[174]

---

[172] Franklin was granted this title by Congress in 1779.
[173] Franklin found merchants that would sell guns, uniforms, and shoes.
[174] Lisa Rogers, "Our Man in Paris How Benjamin Franklin Wooed the French to Win the War," http://www.neh.gov/news/humanities/2002-07/ourman.html (accessed March 2, 2012).

Figure 35 Warren House.

Franklin's approach was to make the French like him so they would become America's ally.[175] America needed the French ships and troops to offset the material and military advantages of the British.[176] Most of the muskets and cannon used in the victory at Saratoga, New York, in October 1777 were obtained from the French before a formal alliance was established.[177]

The French foreign minister, Charles Gravier, comte de Vergennes, delayed a treaty of alliance with the United States while he negotiated with the Spanish for their support.[178] After the victory at Saratoga, Vergennes heard rumors that the British were making peace overtures to Franklin. Vergennes then offered a full alliance to the United States.[179] On February 6, 1778, Franklin, Arthur Lee, and Silas Deane, Commissioners for the

175 U.S. Department of State, Office of the Historian, "Milestones 1776-1783," http://www.history.state.gov/milestones/1776-1783/FrenchAlliance (accessed February 3, 2012).

176 Rogers, 3.

177 Ibid., 3.

178 U.S. Department of State, Office of the Historian, "Milestones 1776-1783," http://www.history.state.gov/milestones/1776-1783/FrenchAlliance (accessed February 3, 2012).

179 Ibid., 2.

United States, signed a Treaty of Alliance and a Treaty of Amity and Commerce with France. The Treaty of Alliance had a clause that allowed Spain to join the Alliance, which they did on June 21, 1779.[180]

The first combined operation between the French and the Colonial armies took place in Rhode Island in August of 1778. Jean-Baptiste Charles Henri Hector, comte d'Estaing, left Paris in March to take command of the French Toulon squadron and prepare to sail to America.[181] He left Toulon in April and arrived off Delaware Bay where he transported the French Ambassador Conrad Alexandre Gerard de Rayneval to Philadelphia in the frigate *Chimere*.[182]

D'Estaing then sailed to New York but was prevented from closing in on the British ships because of the shallow water off Sandy Hook. The drafts of the French warships were more than those of the smaller British ships. After trying unsuccessfully to find a way into New York with the deep draft ships, Washington and d'Estaing mounted a joint operation to attack the British in Newport. Washington sent Gilbert du Motier, marquis de Lafayette, with two brigades to Newport to support the Colonial operation headed by General John Sullivan.[183]

The second French force sent under the Treaty of Alliance arrived in Newport in 1780.

The population had just been subjected to almost three years of martial law by the British army. Rochambeau arrived in Newport at 1 p.m. on July 11, 1780 to find that the town was practically deserted. He felt that he had been received inhospitably because the people stayed off the streets, and those in the windows appeared sad and depressed.[184] The remainder of the French fleet arrived by 6 p.m. That evening the tensions eased and the town officials greeted the French.[185] The Newport Town Council ordered that candles be lit in the windows of houses facing the harbor on the night

---

[180] Ibid.

[181] John B. Hattendorf, *Newport, The French Navy, and American Independence* (Newport: The Redwood Press, 2005), 3.

[182] Ibid., 5. Note that Conrad's brother Joseph Matthias Gerard de Rayneval was an Undersecretary of State to the French Government under Charles Gravier, comte de Vergennes.

[183] For details on the conflict in August 1778, see Chapter 3.

[184] Allan Forbes and Paul Cadman, *France and New England* (Boston: State Street Trust Co., 1925), 108.

[185] Hattendorf, 60.

of the French fleet's arrival to welcome them to Newport, and the French fleet set off a number of signal rockets in appreciation of the gesture.[186]

Rochambeau wrote to Washington assuring him that he had sufficient funds to pay in cash for anything that was needed by the French forces.[187] Customers with money were the most important cargo that the French ships brought to Newport. They provided a big boost in morale which was much needed after the devastation of the British occupation. The French were paying for supplies with silver. Providing food and other supplies to the French started the Newport economy on the road to recovery. The arrival of the French fleet and army brought new life to the town. The following is a quote from the diary of Dr. Ezra Stiles, the former pastor of Newport's Second Congregational Church: "There is more Business transactg and money circulatg than formally [sic]…"[188]

About a third of the French military became ill from scurvy on the voyage from France.[189] By August of 1780 most of the sick recovered. That same month there was a review in Newport of the French troops and a celebration of the French King's birthday for which the ships in the harbor were decorated and cannons were fired in salutes.[190] On the last Saturday in August "His Excellency Count de Rochambeau, General of His Most Christian Majesty's Forces in this State" visited Providence and was saluted by a discharge of cannon. He returned to Newport on Sunday.[191] At the same time the residents of Newport realized that they were not going to lose all their freedoms and be starved and oppressed as they had been under the British occupation. The Newport population resumed their lives and went about making an economic recovery.

Rochambeau's initial meeting with Washington was on September 20, 1780 at Hartford, Connecticut. This was the first of the planning conferences that led to the siege of Yorktown.[192]

---

[186]   Ibid., 61.

[187]   Forbes and Cadman, 112.

[188]   Stiles' Diary, August 17, 1780, quoted in Forbes and Cadman, 106. Stiles had become president of Yale College in 1778.

[189]   Scurvy is a vitamin C deficiency disease that occurred on long sea voyages.

[190]   *The American Journal* (Providence), August 30, 1780.

[191]   Ibid.

[192]   An interesting point that puts value on a classical education: When Washington, who could not speak French, and Rochambeau, who was trying to learn English, met without translators, they could communicate in Latin.

Washington visited Newport in March of 1781 where the French contingent gave him the honors due a field marshal of France.[193] The plan that emerged was for Lafayette and General Friedrich Wilhelm Heinrich Ferdinand von Steuben to keep General Charles Earl of Cornwallis occupied in New Jersey. Washington and Rochambeau would bring their armies down from the north. General Anthony Wayne would close off any escape by Cornwallis to the west.

An English fleet was seen off the Rhode Island coast shortly after the arrival of the French. In preparation for a British counterattack, the ships in the harbor were repositioned. The French arranged their ships on either side of Goat Island so as to defend the entrance to the harbor. Forts were established on the East Passage and in Jamestown. The French and Colonial military rebuilt the line of forts that the British had dismantled (Figure 36). In Figure 36 redoubt 28 is the remains of Green End Redoubt, and number 29 is the remains of the British nine-gun battery. Number 6 is the Redoubt de St. Onge built by the French and the Colonial Militia. It can be seen today at the east end of Vernon Avenue in Middletown.

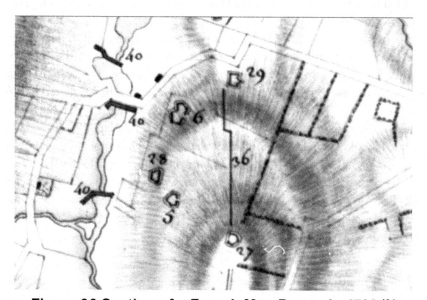

Figure 36 Section of a French Map Drawn in 1780.[194]

193 Hattendorf, 86.
194 Ref. Plan de la Ville et Environs de Newport Rade, with permission of The Clements Library, University of Michigan, Ann Arbor, Michigan.

Rochambeau left 600 troops, the Squadron, and the Rhode Island Militia to defend the town.[195] The Colonials, using small craft, ferried the French Army to Providence on June 11, 1781.[196] The entire force was transported to Providence in one day.[197] The troops from Newport met newly-landed French troops that had come down from Boston and they all marched together to Yorktown. A French fleet under Francois-Joseph Paul, marquis de GrasseTilly, comte de Grasse, blocked Chesapeake Bay to prevent the British from reinforcing Cornwallis in Yorktown. The combined forces of the Colonials and the French caused Cornwallis to surrender in October 1781. As a direct result of this loss, the American Revolution ended in 1783 with the signing of the Treaty of Paris.

France after the American Revolution

The long-term effects on France for providing assistance to the United States resulted in bankruptcy and a revolution in their government.[198] In 1789 the King called an assembly of nobles, clergy, and commoners to raise funds, but the commoners declared themselves the National Assembly and pressed for a new constitution for France. The commoners had been given a chance to take power and they were going to take it.[199]

By 1793 France had descended into chaos. The king and queen had been executed and Maximilien Robespierre had gained control of the country. Under his year-long Reign of Terror, Robespierre sent thousands of his political enemies to the guillotine before being executed by his own rivals. A new constitution was drawn up but it did not end the fighting. In the midst of the resulting chaos the French army under General Napoleon Bonaparte stepped in and stopped the riots. In November, 1799, Napoleon took power through a coup and would rule France for the following fifteen years.[200]

In 1928 there was little documentation available on the Revolutionary War forts on Aquidneck Island. The Redoubt de St. Onge was mistaken for a British fort and a stone marker (Figure 37) was placed there.[201] Analysis

---

[195] Ibid., 99.

[196] If one wants to follow Rochambeau's route from Newport one must take the Newport to Providence Ferry.

[197] Hattendorf, 99.

[198] Union County College, "French Revolution," http://www.faculty.ucc.edu/egh-damerow/french_revolution.htm (accessed March 4, 2012).

[199] French Revolution, 2.

[200] Ibid., 3.

[201] Kenneth M. Walsh, "The Story of the Analysis of Green End Fort," *Bulletin of the Newport Historical Society* 54 (Fall 1981): 113.

published in 1976 indicated that the chances of this redoubt being British were less than 1/1000000.[202] The analysis showed that the probability it was the Redoubt de St. Onge was approximately one hundred percent.

Figure 37 Stone Marker in Redoubt de St. Onge.

It is important to question history even when it is carved in stone!

Theory Related to Economic Expansion

Before going into a detailed examination of Newport's economy after the British devastated Newport, it will be beneficial to look at the theoretical possibilities for an economic recovery. Newport was a commercially organized society before the Revolution. It had private property, division of labor, and free competition.[203] In a capitalistic economic system the consumers determine the trends. What the consumers are willing to buy at a price that will allow a profit drives what the merchant management will try to provide. However, the merchandise must be within their ability to acquire and transport at an acceptable cost. The means used by the Newport

---

[202] Kenneth M. Walsh and David S. Walsh, "Memo on Location of Green End Fort," *Bulletin of the Newport Historical Society*, 49 (Winter 1976): 1.

[203] Joseph A. Schumpeter, *The Theory of Economic Development* (Cambridge: Harvard University Press, 1934), 5.

merchants were: reliable bookkeeping, accurate timely communication, and competitive methods of transporting goods. Newport had a number of entrepreneurs that were in the maritime shipping business. The profit in these businesses is the surplus over costs.[204] If an entrepreneur can develop a method of decreasing his costs or increasing his total receipts, his profit will increase.[205] The more intelligent contemporaries will examine what is being accomplished and adopt a variation that includes improved methods. An example would be the purchasing of a farm in Portsmouth above the cove between Black Point and Sandy Point to facilitate landing smuggled goods and avoiding import taxes.[206]

The entrepreneur that has innovated has created an example that his contemporaries can follow. Initially individuals will adopt the improved methods, and then whole groups will follow.[207] Eventually the supply will exceed the demand, the price for the goods will decrease, and a new equilibrium will be established at a price below the old market value.

Another type of entrepreneurial innovation is the development of a new source of material or a trade route that allows the acquiring of goods at a lower cost. The entrepreneurs of Providence obtained technology from England and started a manufacturing center. The Providence merchants took advantage of this shorter trade route to the supply, and by exploiting the steam ships and railroads were able to dominate the trade in Rhode Island.

Newport's Economy

In early 1780 Newport's economy was in terrible condition. The war was still going on and the British were still blockading. The *Newport Mercury*, published on April 5, 1780, had no ads whatsoever for consumer goods. However, by the summer Newport began to recover. In the July 22 edition of the *Newport Mercury* there were ads for timber and the opening of a new tea house.[208] On August 12 the Privateer *Rover* brought in a prize ship and sold the goods. On September 2 the first ads for sugar, rum, wines, tea, coffee, and chocolate appeared for sale at George

---

[204] Schumpeter, 128.

[205] Ibid., 129.

[206] Aaron Lopez in 1758 on Wapping Road, Portsmouth. Land Records, Portsmouth, Rhode Island.

[207] Schumpeter, 133.

[208] Based on discussions with Mary Fran Redgate, the Middletown Historical Society Archivist, May 23, 2012. The tea house may have been Whitehall, the former residence of Reverend George Berkeley.

Lawton's shop. Spermaceti candles were available from John Slocum. Jacob Isaacks was advertising consumer goods. Clearly the local economy was starting to recover. On August 21, 1781, items from France were advertised. Christopher Champlin had moved to Kingstown when the British arrived, and returned to Newport in 1780. He organized the local farmers and became one of the French army's logistic resources.[209]

On May 28, 1782, Aaron Lopez and his family started from Leicester, Massachusetts, toward Providence, Rhode Island in a number of carriages. Aaron Lopez was driving a lightweight, two-wheel gig pulled by one horse. As the party passed Scott's Pond in Smithfield, just north of Providence, Lopez let his horse go to the pond to drink.[210] The water was unexpectedly deep and all went into the pond. Lopez drowned in Scott's Pond on the way back to Newport.

On June 21, 1783, the *Newport Mercury*'s shipping news showed six sloops and one schooner inbound, and five sloops and one brigantine cleared outbound. All the ships were local except the sloop *Sally* that was inbound from New Providence Island in the Caribbean, and the brigantine *Black Prince* which was headed for Hispaniola.[211] The West Indies trade was starting up again; the import of molasses was a requirement for the rum industry. A sign of Newport's revival was the increasing production of rum which soon matched pre-war levels. More than twenty rum distillers went into production.

The economy of Newport before the Revolution was dependent on a combination of foreign and domestic trading. The pattern of that trading can be found by analyzing the shipping news published in the *Newport Mercury*. The data set in Table 6 is made up of thirty consecutive weeks, extending from May to December of 1783. In each issue the incoming and outbound ships are posted showing where they came from and their intended destination. The group of inbound ships was considered separate from the outbound ships. This allowed for a total of 60 samples.

The shipping news from the *Newport Mercury* (Table 6) indicates a pattern of trading for Newport merchants when hostilities ended after the American Revolution. The numbers of ships in domestic or foreign trade that arrive in Newport on any given week are given in terms of probability (Figure 38).

---

[209] Laurent, 14.

[210] Morris A. Gutstein, *The Story of the Jews of Newport* (New York: Bloch Publishing Co., 1936), 195.

[211] Nassau is the city on the island of New Providence, Bahamas.

Table 6 Shipping Data for Newport 1783

Month	Date		Domestic	Foreign
May	23	In Bound	5	0 Foreign
		Out Bound	9	0
	31		6	3 Hispaniola
			5	0
June	7		4	0
			9	1 Hispaniola
	13		10	2 Guadeloupe
			1	0
	21		7	0
			5	1 Hispaniola
	28		4	0
			7	1 Bermuda
July	5		5	0
			6	0
	12		5	1 Hispaniola
			5	2 Barbados, Bermuda
	19		3	3, 2 for Hispaniola, St Christopher
			1	3, 2 for Hispaniola, Halifax
	26		6	1 Hispaniola
			1	2 Halifax, Guadeloupe
August	2		3	1 Bermuda
			4	0
	16		2	2 Surinam, Halifax
			4	2 Hispaniola, Surinam
	23		4	3 St. Martin, Turks, Halifax
			4	1 Halifax
	30		3	1 Brest
			3	3 Hispaniola, 2 for Halifax
September	6		3	1 Halifax
			6	2 Hispaniola
	13		6	0
			3	4 West Indies, Augustine, 2 for Hispaniola
	20		1	2 Nova Scotia, Turks
			5	1 Hispaniola
September	27		4	1 Hispaniola
			4	1 Nova Scotia
October	4		1	2 London, New Providence
			2	2 West Indies, Nova Scotia
	11		3	1 Granada
			2	0
	25		2	0

		3	1Nova Scotia
November	1	2	2 Hispaniola, Augustine
		1	3 Nova Scotia, 2 for Hispaniola
	8	3	2 London, Guadeloupe
		3	1 Martinique
	15	1	1 Surinam
		5	1 Hispaniola
	22	2	0
		3	0
	29	1	1 Nova Scotia
		2	2 West Indies
December	6	1	1Dominica
		3	0
	13	1	3 Hispaniola
		3	1 Hispaniola
	20	1	2 Hispaniola, Gothenburg (Sweden)
		0	3 West Indies, 2 for Hispaniola
	27	1	0
		3	4 Barbados, Cork, 2 for Hispaniola

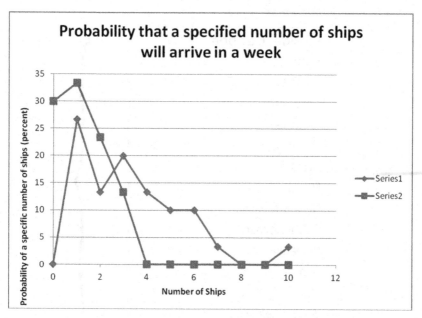

Figure 38 Probability that a Week Will Include
a Number of Shipping Events.

Series 1 is for Domestic Shipping; Series 2 is for Foreign Shipping.

The plots indicate the probability of a specific number of foreign or domestic ships entering Newport Harbor in any given week based on the 30 weeks of data in Table 7. As an example, the probability that there will be only one ship from a foreign port is 33%. The probability of six or more foreign ships is approximately zero.

Table 7 Ships in Foreign Trade to and from Newport.

Europe	**5**
Brest	1
Cork	1
Gothenburg	1
London	2
Canada	**15**
Halifax	6
Nova Scotia	9
Florida, Caribbean	**57**
Augustine	2
Barbados	2
Dominica	1
Granada	1
Guadeloupe	4
Hispaniola	33
Martinique	1
New Providence	1
St Christopher	1
St Martin	1
Surinam	4
Turks	1
West Indies	5
Bermuda	**3**
Total	**80**

A shipping event is defined as one ship either entering or leaving Newport. Domestic shipping is a ship coming from or going to a port in the United States. Foreign shipping is a ship coming from or going to a port outside the United States. Inbound ships and outbound ships were counted separately, making sixty events in total. From the data the probability of a foreign trading venture, either inbound or outbound, was 90% in any given week. The importance of this is that within three years after the arrival of the French and at the end of the Revolutionary War, international trading in Newport was in progress. Most of the trading was with the islands of the Caribbean and the coast of South America (71%). There were five trips to Europe and fifteen to Canada (25%), probably to obtain manufactured goods. The other 4% were trips to Bermuda. The typical imports from the Caribbean were molasses, sugar, and letters of credit to use in the trade with England.

In the fall of 1783 the number of merchants advertising in the *Newport Mercury* increased significantly. On September 6, 1783, the number of ads increased from one or two to seven. When the economy was excellent in 1775, the number of ads per issue was between eight and sixteen.[212] The merchants in 1783 must have believed that there were potential customers with available resources. Newport's census records indicate that the city's population was starting to grow as well. In 1782 Newport had 978 households and eight years later there were 1242, which almost equaled its prewar population. In the January 24, 1784, issue of the *Newport Mercury* there were seven ads. The shipping news indicated that there was trade with London once again. However, the trade was still mostly along the East Coast. On June 25, 1785, sloops transited from and to New York, Massachusetts, Connecticut and Nova Scotia. On May 19, 1788, a sloop cleared to go whaling.

George Champlin purchased the ship *Hydra* using profits from his dealings with the French. He used *Hydra* in the Far East and Baltic trade. This established his business as one of the strongest mercantile houses in Newport in the 1790's.[213] John Gibbs and Walter Channing reestablished their trading firms as well.[214] Gibbs and Channing merged their businesses in 1793, and by 1800 they owned seven 300 ton ships, one 600 ton ship,

---

[212] Reference Figure 13 in Chapter 2 on page 69.
[213] Laurent, 14.
[214] Ibid., 15.

three brigs, and one schooner.[215] The ships *Russel* and *The Mount Hope* made regular trips to Canton, China and the East Indies.

By 1800 the senior merchants in Newport were reaching the end of their lifespans. Of the ten top taxpayers in 1793, all but James Robinson had died before the end of the War of 1812.[216] In most cases the death of the major partner in a Newport merchant firm resulted in the dissolution of the firm. Most of the Newport firms were owned and operated by one person who had the knowledge and resources to make business decisions. These businesses were not run by committees but relied on the judgments of the senior partners/owners.

The death of George Gibbs in 1803 provides insight into the events after the loss of a major partner.[217] Gibbs was the richest taxpayer in Newport in 1801. After his death there were notices in the *Newport Mercury* indicating that the executors for his estate were: Mary Gibbs (wife), George Gibbs (son), and Walter Channing (partner).[218] All debts should be settled within three months of this notice, after which time the outstanding debts would be turned over to the attorneys to settle. In the notice on April 10, 1809, Walter Channing announced that the partnership of Gibbs and Channing, which had continued to operate after the death of George Gibbs, was dissolved as of that day. Channing would take responsibility for the claims and demands on the former partnership. Walter Channing ran the business in his name, and George Gibbs (the son) ran for Congress.[219] If there was no partner to take over the business, the executors would settle the business and sell off the remaining assets. Walter Channing was making a profit in 1807 which was the year that the Embargo Act, followed by the Non–Intercourse Act, was passed by Congress. When trade restrictions were imposed by the U.S. Government, it severely impacted the Newport merchants, including Channing who retired four years later.[220]

Simple Economics

A simple set of ideas can allow a reasonable comprehension of the 18th and early 19th century economies.[221] Before 1800 the income per person

215 George G. Channing, *Early Recollections of Newport, R.I.; From the Year 1793 to 1811* (Newport, 1868), 132.
216 *Newport Mercury* Death Notices. Robinson died in 1817.
217 *Newport Mercury*, Death Notice.
218 *Newport Mercury*, February 2,1805.
219 *Newport Mercury*, April 15,1809.
220 Channing, 156.
221 Gregory Clark, *A Farewell to Alms* (Princeton: Princeton University Press, 2007), x.

varied among individuals, but on average there was no upward trend.[222] Short-term gains in economic growth due to technological changes were absorbed by increases in population growth.[223] The average person in 1800 had a lower standard of living than his/her remote ancestors.[224] In 1800 Newport and Providence were on an equal footing, but Providence was investing in technology.

Before 1800 the long-term stability of the population was controlled by three interrelated factors. The birth rate grew and the death rate decreased with increased living standards. Living standards decreased with population growth.[225] The point where these three factors balance is the subsistence level for the local economy.[226] Subsistence does not imply a starvation level. The individual could take the resources that exceeded the survival threshold and use them as a point of leverage to obtain a return on his investment.[227] In the time before 1800 the productivity of the individual was limited to what he could produce with his own hands and his intellect. There are numerous examples throughout history of a person of superior intellect achieving a high living standard relative to the general local population in his time and location.[228]

For example, in Athens near the end of the Peloponnesian War, two bankers purchased a young slave named Pasion and trained him in the banking business. Pasion started as a porter who hauled bags of coins, then rose to become chief clerk. He did very well, made his owners rich, and eventually was freed and took over the Antisthenes and Archestratus Banking and Loan Company upon the retirement of his former owners.[229] Pasion became one of the richest men in Athens.

The technology that allowed Pasion to prosper in Athens was the same technology that was available in Newport up to 1800. Accurate books and the equivalent of letters of credit expedited commerce. Sailing ships carried goods

---

[222] Ibid., 1.

[223] Ibid.

[224] Ibid.

[225] Ibid., 21.

[226] The minimum daily requirement for calories is approximately 1500. A diet of 2 pounds of wheat per day would supply 2400 calories.

[227] A point where a person could exchange his resources for something he considered more valuable; i.e., meat from hunting for well-made arrows or a sharp stone knife. An early example is the Phoenicians who traded glassware for gold on the West coast of Africa.

[228] Lionel Casson, *The Ancient Mariners* (Princeton: Princeton University Press, 1991).

[229] Ibid., 97.

from where they were plentiful to where they were scarce and valuable. Ship speeds under sail were in the order of 5.5 knots in open water with favorable winds.[230] With this level of technology the population of Aquidneck Island could be expected to be limited in productivity by an economic principle known as the Malthusian Trap.[231] Newport's economy grew at a rate of about 7% per year during the years between 1779 and 1801. This is predicted by the Malthusian analysis. The population of Newport was greatly reduced by the British. When the British left, the economy and population expanded to approach the equilibrium economy predicted by the Malthusian limits (Figure 39). Between 1801 and 1811 the growth rate dropped to 2%. This reduced rate of growth was occurring because Newport was approaching the limit that its population, available resources, and technology could support. The negative growth rate between 1811 and 1819 was due to the impact of politics, regulations, and the actions of the War of 1812.

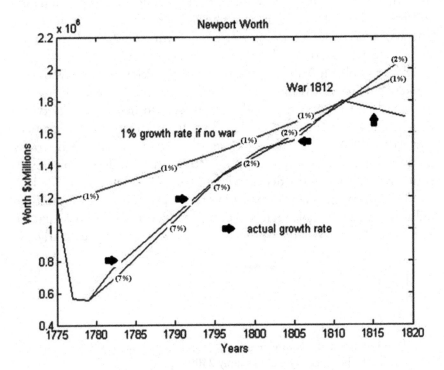

Figure 39 Growth of Newport's worth.

---

[230] Lionel Casson, 287.

[231] Clark, 1. The principle is named for Thomas Malthus, an English minister and economist.

In the time leading up to the Embargo Act of 1807, Newport was one of the most prosperous ports on the East coast. It functioned as a node on a trade network that imported goods from Europe, England and the Far East.[232] The goods came into Newport on large merchant ships and were offloaded to schooners for coastal distribution. An Indiaman of 600+tons was sent to the Far East with a cargo of 120,000 Spanish milled dollars.[233] Packet sloops ran a daily shuttle to New York.[234]

Newport's Worth

An examination of population trends (Figure 40) shows that it was increasing at about 1% per year. Since its worth was increasing faster than its population, Newport can be judged a prosperous community at the point just before the Embargo Act and the War of 1812.

The worth of Newport for state tax purposes was:

1775	1,087,658
1777	532,952 After evacuation in 1776 (51% loss)
1779	483,778 British evacuate 1779, French arrive 1780
1782	745,110 growth 15.5% per year (The Revolution ends 1783)
1796	1,341,071 growth 7.6% per year
1801	1,499,100 growth 2.25% per year
1805	1,547,800 growth 0.9% per year
1811	1,798,100 growth 2.5% per year
War of 1812	
1819	1,695,700 growth -0.71% per year (Recovering from War of 1812)

---

[232] Ibid., 156. The Embargo Act prohibited international trade.

[233] Clark, 137.

[234] Ibid., 140.

[235] See Chaper 1, page 68.

[236] The British used the property of the evacuees for firewood and building material for forts.

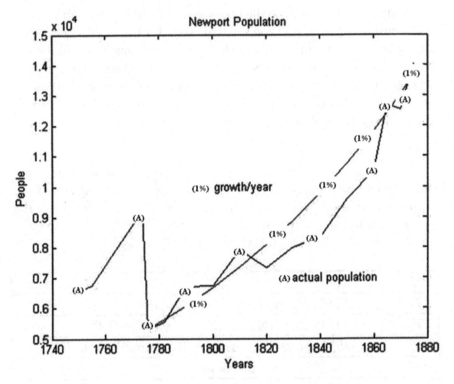

Figure 40 Newport Population Growth.

An estimate of the worth of Newport in 1775 must be determined to properly judge the extent of the city's economic recovery. There were eight tax payers (Table 8) that were in Newport in 1772 and 1775 that also paid taxes in 1785. The 1785 tax records listed the estimated value of each taxpayer's property. If the value of the taxpayer's property was the same in 1785 as in 1775, then the worth of Newport in 1775 can be estimated.

Table 8 Newport Taxpayers Used in Estimate[237]

Taxpayer	Occupation	Status 1785	Worth
John Brown	Farmer	Dead Estate taxed	$2922.00
William Champlin	Merchant	Dead Widow taxed	$2435.00
Jeremiah Clarke	Merchant	OK	$2940.00
Henry Marchant	Lawyer	Practice was decreasing in 1775	$4870.00
Simon Newton	Distiller	OK	$3430.00
Jacob R. Rivera	Merchant	Declining business[238]	$7305.00
Thomas Robinson	Merchant	OK	$3926.00
Oliver R. Warner	Merchant	OK	$3920.00

The worth of Newport for tax purposes was $1,087,658 at the height of the pre-Revolution economy. The standard deviation on this estimate is $184,231. The percentage of wealth owned by the high-end taxpayers was 77.5%. The percentage owned by the people who left Newport in 1775 just before the British Occupation was 51.7%. Thus, Newport lost more than half its worth in the evacuation.

The occupation by the British stopped the acquisition of more wealth through trade. Newport began rebuilding when the French arrived in 1780. The French army had hard currency and purchased goods and services from the people of Newport.

By 1796 the worth of Newport exceeded its pre-war total and grew after that until the War of 1812. The economic well-being of Newport had been restored. It should be noted that the trading markets, the ship construction, and the transportation methods were approximately the same as they had been in the pre-Revolution era. No major management or technology changes were required for Newport to make this recovery.

In 1801 there were twenty-three taxpayers that paid $4.50 and higher. A plot of the taxpayers (Figures 41 and 42) that paid more than $2.00 follows the expected shape.

---

[237] These values for worth came from Chapter 1, Newport Tax Records, Newport Historical Society, and the Rhode Island 1782 Census.

[238] Lost business connections when Aaron Lopez departed for Massachusetts.

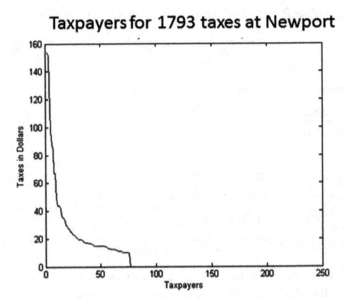

Figure 41 Taxpayers in Order.

Note that there are only 77 Newport residents that paid over $5.00 in taxes.

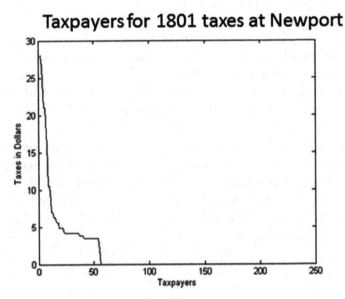

Figure 42 Taxpayers in Order. There
were 19 Taxpayers over $5.00.

The variation in the overall tax collected in various years was due to the changing needs of the government. The amount of revenue required for the year was determined and the total worth of the town was estimated. The revenue divided by the total worth determined the tax rate.

Each tax payer paid according to their worth and the tax rate.

Note that the businesses in Newport were reasonably stable between 1793 and 1801. Gibbs stayed number one, Clarke moved down, and two new merchants joined the top merchant group (Table 9).

Table 9 Taxpayer Comparison 1801 to 1793.

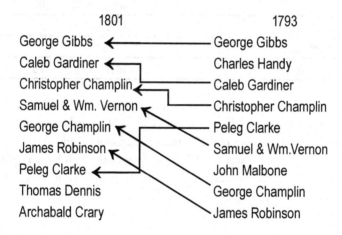

Newport Economy After 1800

A detailed list of the taxpayers in 1801 is given in Table 10. Of the taxpayers in Table 10, 10 were paying more than two English pounds in taxes (Table 11). In 1775 there were one hundred and forty eight merchants in Newport paying more than two English pounds in taxes ($9.74). Although Newport had recovered its former worth, the population of merchants doing business was significantly reduced from its pre-Revolution magnitude. The Industrial Revolution in Providence was having an impact on the magnitude of the merchant trading being done in Newport.

Table 11 List of Senior Merchants. Top 10 Taxpayers for 1793[239]

	Died	Age
'George Gibbs	1803	69
'Charles Handy	1793	64
'Caleb Gardner	1796	
'Christopher Champlin	1805	76
'Peleg Clarke	1803	70
'Samuel & Wm. Vernon	1792 (Sam), 1806 (Wm)	87
'John Malbone	1795	
'George Champlin	1809	
'James Robinson	1817	79

In the period between Newport's recovery and the War of 1812, the aging senior merchants began to die (Table 11) and were not being replaced. In 1793 there were only 77 major taxpayers (Figure 41). This is about half as many as they were in 1775 just before the British occupation. By 1801 this number was reduced still further to just 19 (Figure 42). Only James Robinson lived past the end of the War.

---

[239] *Newport Mercury* Death Notices.

Table 10 Taxpayers in 1801.

	Newport Taxes	1801	Died	Age	Age 1801
1	George Gibbs	$ 70.00	1803	69	67
2	Caleb Gardner	$ 28.00	1796		
3	Christopher Champlin	$ 26.60	1805	76	72
4	Samuel & Wm. Vernon	$ 24.50	1806	87	82
5	George Champlin	$ 21.00	1809		
6	James Robinson	$ 21.00	1817	79	63
7	Peleg Clarke	$ 17.50	1803	70	68
8	Thomas Dennis	$ 16.10	1828	77	50
9	Archabald Crary	$ 10.50	1812	71	60
10	Simeon Martin	$ 10.50	1819	65	47
11	Joseph Potter (Farmer)	$ 8.68			
12	Stephan Deblois	$ 7.00	1805	70	66
13	Jacob Smith	$ 7.00	1839	82	44
14	Henry Sherburne	$ 6.30	1824	77	54
15	Constant Tabor	$ 6.30			
16	Johathan Dennis	$ 5.95			
17	Thomas Handy	$ 5.60			
18	Robert Stevens & Son	$ 5.60	1837	50	14
19	Thomas Armstrong	$ 4.90	1814	68	55
20	David Buffum	$ 4.90	1829	85	57
21	Henry Hunter	$ 4.90	1810	85	76
22	William Langley	$ 4.90	1817	77	61
23	Joseph Sisson	$ 4.48	1823	95	73

A plot of all the taxpayers paying more than two dollars in 1801 shows a knee in the curve at 10 taxpayers. At this point the earnings and worth of the taxpayers shows a tendency to flatten (Figure 43).

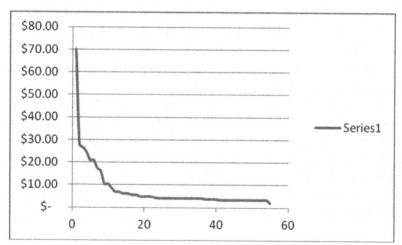

Figure 43 Newport Taxpayers Paying over $2.00 in 1801.

In the Newport merchant trading partnerships, the senior partner provided all the guidance in the high risk business of international trading. The knowledge base developed by each of these merchants in the process of developing a successful trading establishment was irreplaceable in the short-term. A short list of merchants dying as the years progressed shows the extinction of Newport's major talents that made international trade so profitable.

Top Merchant Taxpayers Alive in Year:

1792	10
1793	9
1794	8
1795	7
1800	6
1803	4
1805	3
1806	2
1809	1 WAR 1812 to 1815
1816	1
1817	0

After the Embargo Act was lifted there was a limited recovery but it did not approach the pre-Embargo Act activity.[240] The town became even less active when the few remaining "capitalists" withdrew from business pursuits in Newport.[241] There was an effort to begin a whaling business but this proved to be unprofitable. Competition from the coal-gas lighting utilities eliminated most of the market for whale oil lamps. Gas street lighting was demonstrated in Newport in 1806 by David Melvell, and in 1817 Baltimore installed gas street lights.[242]

Of the twenty-three top Newport taxpayers in 1801, nineteen stayed connected to the Newport area and their deaths were noted in the *Newport Gazette* or the Providence newspapers. Maritime trading was a business highly dependent on the senior partner for direction and financing. Newport needed these senior merchant men ready to do business when the war ended in 1815. Unfortunately for the Newport economy these men had died and had not been replaced.

---

[240] Ibid., 156.

[241] Ibid.

[242] Laurence Urdang, *The Timetables of American History* (New York: Simon & Schuster, 1996), 165, 175.

An examination of Table 10 indicates that only nine of the twenty-three merchants survived the war. Of the nine, three more died before 1820. This left five minor merchants and one major merchant, Thomas Dennis, to rebuild Newport. Captain Dennis was both a sea captain and a merchant. He sold the merchandise he acquired on his trips in his Newport store, and he ran a public auction in Newport in 1802. He captained his ship to the Caribbean and the Baltic on trading ventures. On a voyage to the Caribbean in 1805 he was captured by French pirates but managed to get back to Newport. In 1809 he advertised for sale 200 boxes of glass window panes and 50 tons of Swedish steel.[243] Evidently he was trading in the Baltic before the War of 1812. In 1814 and 1815 he acted as a broker for commercial and farm property.

There were indicators that Dennis was slowing down near the end of the War of 1812. On March 25, 1815, he advertised a 346 ton ship for sale that was just finished and had not been in the water.[244] It may have been a ship he intended to sail himself, but at sixty-four years of age he did not want to go to sea. He apparently retired in 1819. In 1820 his estate in the Point Section was up for rent, and his store followed in 1822.[245] The Captain died in 1828.

There were four taxpayers that did not have obituaries. Joseph Potter was a farmer in Newport, and other than paying taxes, had no coverage in the local newspapers. There were several Joseph Potters in Rhode Island. It may have been that he moved off the island.

Constant Tabor moved off Aquidneck Island to Providence in 1816. He died in Providence in 1825.[246] John Dennis, the brother of Thomas, was a ship captain in Newport. He was the Master of the sloop *Semiramis*, and was caught smuggling brown sugar in 1799.[247] Dennis died in Newport in 1831 at 81 years of age. He was not detected in the initial searches because his first name on the tax records is listed as Jonathan, but in the newspapers he is referred to as John. Thomas Handy was working in the legal profession in Newport in 1819 and was involved in local civic organizations.[248] He filed for bankruptcy in April of 1823 and died in 1843.[249]

---

243 *Newport Mercury* Ad, April 4, 1809.
244 Ibid., March 25, 1815.
245 Ibid., December 2, 1820.
246 *Providence Patriot*, November 2, 1825.
247 *Newport Mercury*, October 15, 1799.
248 *Newport Mercury*, July 01, 1802.
249 *Rhode Island Republican*, April 16, 1823; *Newport Mercury*, April 15, 1843.

If there were no changes in the trading environment, this loss of talented merchants and their capital would make recovery a difficult task. Faced with the adverse actions of the American government, the war with Great Britain, and the loss of the senior merchants, the remaining Newport maritime trading partnerships dissolved and sold out or shifted to fishing, whaling, or coastal trading.

To an outside observer, Rhode Island is a small region that should be considered as an economic unit. When viewed this way, Rhode Island expanded economically as Newport dominated the maritime trade. There was a pause during the Revolution when Newport was occupied, then a recovery until the War of 1812. As Newport was recovering, Providence was rapidly expanding as its industries grew and the transportation technology improved. When only economic factors are concerned, there was a steady growth of the Rhode Island economy from the end of the Revolution to the Civil War and beyond. The economic center shifted from Newport to Providence after the War of 1812.

A characteristic of a capitalistic economy is a phenomenon known as creative destruction.[250] The entrepreneurs' projects are the source of new jobs, higher wages, and economic progress. In the process of growing the new venture, they push aside the older competitors.[251] "Sooner or later most businesses will fail, sometime damaging whole communities as well as individuals."[252] In the end, the consumers gain the most. They have an improved product at a lower cost. The new entrepreneurs will be supported until an even newer, better product is marketed.

When Providence became an industrial center, the Providence merchants could effectively compete with the Newport merchants in the sale of manufactured goods previously imported from England. When the railroad was introduced into New England, the Providence merchants could offer better service than available from Newport's coastal trade.

---

[250] Thomas K. McCraw, *Prophet of Innovation Joseph Schumpeter and Creative Destruction* (Cambridge: Belknap Press, 2007), 7.

[251] Ibid.

[252] Ibid.

CHAPTER 5

Politics, Issues,
and the Impact of the War of 1812

In the time between 1801 and 1812, when the United States declared war on Great Britain, there were four key groups with four different agendas. The French under Napoleon were seeking to control all of Europe. The English were trying to stop the French. The United States wanted the British out of the Americas and the Newport merchants wanted to do business without interference. In 1803 the U.S. purchased the rights to the Louisiana Territory from Napoleon and wanted to expand westward, but the British were selling guns to the Native American tribes to the west via Canada. The Newport merchants were doing a good business by selling to both sides in the Napoleonic War. The British impressment of seamen from the merchant ships was a problem for the Newport merchants, but not a disaster.

The French

In the time before the American and French Revolutions the armies were professional organizations that were expensive to train and maintain. In military conflicts the armies on each side would try to outmaneuver the opposition. The army that could gain the advantage would inflict limited damage on the opponent who would then surrender. This meant that the losing side would be able to fight another day. Napoleon brought three major changes to this mode of warfare. First, he assembled an army of conscripts. These troops were less expensive and more numerous. The second development was the lightweight, mobile artillery with long-range capability. Third, he sought total annihilation of the opposing army. He was not satisfied with simply defeating his enemy.[253]

---

[253] Azar Gat, *War in Human Civilization* (Oxford: Oxford University Press, 2006), 502.

In 1793 Napoleon became a general after playing a successful part in defending the port of Toulon from the British. In 1796 he was appointed Commander of the French army in Italy. He achieved a decisive victory there by 1797, and he invaded Egypt in 1798. After gaining control of the Egyptian interior, the French Mediterranean fleet that had been supporting him was destroyed by Admiral Lord Horatio Nelson at the Battle of the Nile.

Napoleon returned and took over France in a military coup in November 1799. He was made Consul for Life in 1802 after signing the Peace of Amiens with England.[254] The following year he sold the rights to Louisiana to the United States, and then Great Britain declared war on France later that year. In 1804 Napoleon crowned himself Emperor and prepared to invade England. However, Lord Nelson thwarted him again at the Battle of Trafalgar in 1805. By the beginning of 1806 the *Newport Mercury* reported the news of Nelson's rout of the French. [255] At this point the merchants of Newport recognized that without a fleet the French could not come to their rescue in case of a conflict with the British.

Great Britain

The British navy was the first line of defense and the source of Britain's ability to project power in the world. Britain's main contributions to Napoleon's defeat were the blockade of French trade, control of the sea lanes which enabled them to get their supplies to the armies opposing Napoleon, and insuring that a French army could not reach British soil.[256] By 1813 the British navy had 1,017 warships of twenty guns or more. The cost of a 74-gun ship of the line in 1793 was $23,900.[257] This was about twenty-four times the cost of a Newport-built merchant ship. The French were thought to have the best hydrodynamic scientists and ship designers of the time. Many of the British ships were copies of the French designs.[258] The time required to build a ship of the line was between four and five years in wartime, and longer when there was no urgency.[259] Before the American Revolution the British navy would cut back to conserve funds. Old ships would be kept beyond their useful life to keep up the

---

[254] The *Newport Mercury* took note of Napoleon's new title on July 6, 1802.

[255] See *Newport Mercury,* January 16, 1806.

[256] Angus Konstam, *British Napoleonic Ship-of-the-Line* (Oxford: Osprey Publishing, 2001), 3.

[257] $4.87 to the British Pound.

[258] Konstam, 9.

[259] Ibid., 11.

appearance of numbers. The American Revolution caught the British navy by surprise and it took several years for the British to produce a fleet capable of defeating the combined fleets of the French, Spanish, and Dutch.[260] In 1801 the British Navy had 180 ships of the line, but many were old and in poor condition. Twenty-four new warships were under construction and would enter service over the next three years.[261] The first-rate (100 gun) ships were the pride of the British navy but it was the forty, third-rate (74 guns) warships that were the workhorses of the fleet. It was the third-rate warships that maintained the blockade of the French during the war with Napoleon.[262] Through a combination of fine leadership, seamanship, and gunnery, the British were able to establish control of the seas that would last for the next one hundred years.[263]

The British naval forces in North American waters grew from three ships of the line, seven frigates and four smaller ships in 1795 to two ships of the line, thirteen frigates and twenty- five smaller ships in 1808. In the time from 1793 to 1815 the number of British fatalities due to sickness, accidents, and noncombat shipwrecks were 97,120.[264] Deaths due to combat were only 6,540, or 6.7% of the total losses of life.[265] The British navy was an all-volunteer force. The British government did not recruit men into the navy. Impressments were the only way to provide the level of manning needed to maintain the fleet even in peacetime. A ship captain would send a junior officer and some large seamen into a port to gather "volunteers", willing or otherwise. They would do the same with any ship they encountered. In contrast to the American government, the British were committed to their navy and provided the financial support for a navy with ships second to none.[266]

---

[260] Ibid.,13.

[261] Ibid.

[262] Ibid.,14,15.

[263] Gregory Fremont-Barnes, *The Royal Navy 1793 – 1815* (Oxford: Osprey Press, 2007), 4.

[264] The British navy instituted the use of lime juice in 1802 after Captain Cook avoided scurvy in his 1779 expedition by providing lime juice to his men. "Nutrition Health Review," *The Consumer's Medical Journal 62* (1992): 5.

[265] Ibid., 32.

[266] Ibid., 76.

Britain had gained control of the French colonies in North America through the Treaty of Paris in 1763.[267] Between 1793 and 1801 the British navy fought and won a number of battles against the French and Dutch fleets. The British Royal Navy grew to 600 cruising warships, including 175 ships of the line. After defeating the French in Egypt, Nelson then crushed the Danish fleet at the Battle of Copenhagen before smashing Napoleon again at Trafalgar.

Americans (neutral merchants) were making large profits trading with continental Europe and England. The British blamed the loss of shipping trade on the American use of its neutral status to steal British commerce.[268] The American merchant marine fleet expanded from 558,000 tons in 1802 to 981,000 tons by 1811.[269] American merchants needed sailors for their ships and recruited from all countries, including Great Britain. The Americans paid $16 to $18 per month for able-bodied seamen compared to the British who paid $7 per month for a navy seaman.[270] The British claimed that at least 20,000 British subjects deserted their navy to serve in the American Merchant Marine. The American estimate was about 9,000.[271]

The British were determined to keep their ships manned. By 1797 the British navy had 119,000 sailors and suffered a loss of about 10% per year from all causes.[272] They needed to recruit by force (impressments) at about 12,000 sailors per year to keep their ships manned.[273] The British navy would take any seamen they thought were born within the Empire. It was reported to Parliament in 1812 that the navy held 3,300 seamen who claimed American citizenship.[274] As long as the merchant could sail shorthanded, the impressments of seamen off American merchant ships did not significantly impact most Newport merchants. The ship's captain hired replacements at the next port. The new hires would probably be British seamen looking for higher pay and better working conditions.

---

[267] Nova Scotia on the northern border of the United States was taken earlier in 1713. This was a provision of the Treaty of Utrecht, which ended the War of the Spanish Succession.

[268] Alan Taylor, *The Civil War of 1812* (New York: Alfred A. Knopf, 2010), 110.

[269] Ibid., 104.

[270] Ibid.

[271] Ibid.

[272] Ibid., 103.

[273] Ibid.

[274] Ibid., 105.

Since the British army was occupied in Europe with Napoleon, it had stationed less than 3,000 regular soldiers in all of Canada.[275] Consequently, British military planners were concerned about the prospects of an American invasion of Canada. The desertion from the British army in Canada to the United States was prompted by the harsh discipline and low pay in the British Army, and to the freedom and good wages offered in the United States. Common laborers in the United States made four times the pay of British army privates.[276]

Politics and Objectives of the War

In the politics of the United States, if there is to be a war, there is a need for an issue that will rally the population behind the government. That issue must galvanize the people so that they will be willing to contribute the money and the lives of sons and husbands that the government will expend in a war. In the War of 1812 the government's justification was the enslavement of white American sailors on British ships. The driving motivation, however, was the intended expansion westward into the Louisiana Territory and the concern that the British, who were trading guns and ammunition to the Indians, would make this difficult. The true objective of the 1812 war was to attack Canada and remove the British from the Americas, thereby securing the westward expansion into the land of the Louisiana Purchase.[277]

The United States Navy had been allowed to deteriorate after the Revolution as a cost savings measure. In 1805 the Navy consisted of two frigates and about sixty small ships.[278] These small vessels were of no practical use in stopping the British fleet from blockading the major United States ports such as Norfolk and New York. The British would search every ship coming and going from the United States ports and take any seaman that appeared to be British. On June 22, 1807, the *USS Chesapeake* departed Norfolk for the Mediterranean Sea. It was undermanned and in poor condition to fight an engagement.[279] When the *Chesapeake* was intercepted by the *HMS Leopard*, it would not allow

---

[275] Ibid., 112.

[276] Ibid., 107.

[277] Taylor, 128.

[278] Ibid., 111.

[279] Stephen Budiansky, *Perilous Fight* (New York: Alfred A. Knopf, 2010), 63. Loose equipment was on the deck, the gun powder was stored in the hold, and there was confusion among the crew.

the *Leopard* to board her and the *Leopard* then opened fire.[280] This was an act of war. When the *Chesapeake* struck its colors, the *HMS Leopard* sent a boarding party aboard the *Chesapeake*. They took three men from the *Chesapeake* who the boarding party claimed were British deserters, and an extra man just because they could.When the news of the *Chesapeake* reached Newport, a meeting was held on July 9, 1807, at the statehouse in Newport. A committee was appointed to draft a "Resolution expressive of the indignation felt by the Citizens of Newport, at the outrage committed on our flag by the British ship of war *Leopard*."[281] The committee returned the following resolutions:

1) The insult to our National Flag, the murder of American Citizens on board the U.S. Frigate *Chesapeake* committed by the British ought to be avenged by our country. Our national honor, interests, and our national happiness all require it.

2) Should war become necessary it is our duty to be prepared for it.

3) We highly approve the attitude of Norfolk and all the other towns that have expressed their resolutions.

4) We deplore the loss of our murdered fellow citizens.

It was resolved that the committee would transmit this resolution to the President of the United States.[282]

President Jefferson was under pressure to do something. His response was to repair the small gunboats to defend the harbors and muster a militia force to threaten Canada.[283] Jefferson did not want a war because he did not want to spend the money on an army and navy that would be required to wage a campaign against Britain.[284] The British ignored most of Jefferson's demands that were issued as a result of the *Chesapeake* incident.[285] The French and British considered the Americans both weak and whiny.[286]

At the time in the United States there were two political parties. The Republicans were the dominant party and were associated with the agricultural South. The Federalist Party was primarily centered in the

---

[280] A U. S. Navy 36 gun frigate of 1244 ton displacement, http://www.history.navy.mil.
[281] *Newport Mercury* August 11, 1807.
[282] Ibid.
[283] Taylor, 113.
[284] Ibid., 115.
[285] Ibid., 116.
[286] Ibid.

Northeast and concerned with shipping. The politicians in the Republican Party did not understand the effects of their decisions on commerce and revenues, so the unintended consequences of their actions were drastic to the economy of port cities like Newport. Presidents Madison and Jefferson thought that they could starve out the British in England and the Caribbean by not trading American food products. Therefore Congress passed the Embargo Act which prohibited American ships from trading in foreign ports.

An article published in the *Newport Mercury* in January 1808 indicated that Congress thought the embargo would be effective very quickly.[287] There was also a suggestion that there was a threat of war from Napoleon if the U.S. ports were not closed to the British. A legal posting of the Embargo Act was provided in the same newspaper.

A letter from a member of Congress to a mercantile house in Newport indicated that when the embargo was lifted, it would be replaced with a Non-Intercourse Act which would antagonize Britain and hurt the Northern states.[288] This too would prove to be a disaster for Newport commerce. The British, however, were not injured at all. They obtained food from South America and found a new market for their manufactured goods. British ships took over the maritime trade that the American ships had been engaged in before the Embargo Act went into effect. In addition, the United States Navy discharged the British-born sailors so that the Navy could employ out-of-work American seamen. The British-born sailors went back to British ships for employment. Thus the embargo was ruinous for American merchants and a windfall for the British.[289] The Canadian economy was also given a boost. American goods were moved across the northern border to Canada where Canadian shippers sold them to the former customers of the Americans. Members of the Federalist Party from the Northeast accused Jefferson and his Southern allies of trying to bankrupt them. The Canadian trade showed Britain the value of the Canadian Provinces and strengthened Britain's resolve to defend them.

Congress voted to expand the army to 35,000 soldiers, but refused to appropriate funds to expand the Navy. By making this decision, it was determined that the war against Britain would principally be a land war against Canada. The House of Representatives and the Senate voted for

[287] *Newport Mercury* January 2, 1808.
[288] Ibid., February 18, 1809.
[289] Taylor, 117.

war and President James Madison signed the Declaration of War on June 18, 1812.

Congress was optimistic that America would obtain an easy victory over Canada. However, the British military had made great improvements since the American Revolution. Lord Nelson had destroyed the French and Spanish fleets in 1805 and the Duke of Wellington was routing Napoleon's forces in Spain. Long years of fighting tended to eliminate incompetent officers and produce a battle hardened force.[290] In addition, the British had learned from the Americans and the French. Wellington had scouts dressed in uniforms that would blend in with the background and were armed with rifles that were considerably more accurate than the standard infantry smooth-bore musket.[291]

It is interesting to note that during the War of 1812 the naval forces of the United States were victorious over their British counterparts. In August of 1812 the *USS Constitution* crippled the *HMS Guerriere* off Nova Scotia. The *USS United States*, commanded by Stephen Decatur, was victorious over the *HMS Macedonian* off Madeira. In December of 1812 the *USS Constitution* destroyed the *HMS Java* off the coast of Brazil. Oliver Hazard Perry was victorious on Lake Erie on September 10, 1813. In September of 1814 the American squadron defeated the British on Lake Champlain.[292]

The last battle of the War of 1812 was the defense of New Orleans by Andrew Jackson and the pardoned pirate Jean Lafitte. The British had 6000 regular troops but approached New Orleans in a cautious manner. This gave General Jackson time to erect a defensive position that included Lafitte's gunners and cannons. In the attack the British marched toward the defensive positions under cover of fog. However, the fog soon lifted, exposing the British to deadly fire from army riflemen and Lafitte's cannon firing grapeshot. In thirty one minutes the Americans had routed the 2036-man British attacking force.[293] The remaining British forces received the message that the war was over and withdrew.[294]

---

[290] Taylor, 141.

[291] These units were immortalized in the novels of Bernard Cornwell, who published twenty novels covering the adventures of Richard Sharp from 1799 to 1820. There was also a popular television series about the exploits of these troops on the BBC America channel titled *Sharp's Rifles*.

[292] Fremont-Barnes, 90, 91.

[293] Taylor, 420. The British suffered 290 dead, 1262 wounded and 484 captured.

[294] The Treaty of Ghent ending the war had been signed on December 24, 1814.

The Blockade

In the beginning of the War of 1812 the British established a blockade of the Eastern seaboard with about twenty ships. In January of 1813 the Delaware and Chesapeake Bays were blockaded. In February the gap between these two fleets was filled. By March the blockade extended along the East coast from Narragansett Bay to North Carolina. By November it reached from Cape Cod to Florida.[295] The blockade had expanded to 135 ships by 1815 when the war ended. In the beginning of the war New England ships were carrying grain and other supplies to Wellington's troops in Spain and Portugal. These ships were licensed and protected by the British.[296] When Napoleon was defeated in May of 1814 the British army's supply problem ended and the blockade was extended to the whole Eastern coast, including all of New England.[297] In the war against commercial shipping the United States Navy took 165 British ships. The British Navy took 1400 merchant ships and privateers.[298] The value of American exports and imports dropped from $114 million in 1811 to $20 million in 1815. Customs revenue dropped from $13 million to $6 million even though the tax rate was doubled in this period.[299]

Newport's Economy

Newport's economy depended on an international trading network. Newport produced items of value such as fine furniture, rum, farm products, fish, livestock, and sailing ships. Although much of the rum produced was consumed locally, most of the other goods were for the coastal or international trade. There was a close coupling between population and the economy of an area. For a family to prosper in the Newport environs there had to be at least one working family member that provided an income. People would not move into a locale unless they had good reason to believe that there would be jobs available.

Before the Industrial Revolution the number of families that a location could support depended on the available natural resources and the technology necessary to exploit that environment. In the case of Newport the harbor was the main natural resource. The sailing ships and skilled merchants developed a system of trading that included an

---

[295] Carl Benn, *The War of 1812* (Oxford: Osprey Publishing, 2002), 58.
[296] Ibid., 55.
[297] Ibid.
[298] Ibid.
[299] Ibid., 57.

international wholesale trade in raw materials for manufactured goods. The manufactured goods would then be traded with the Colonies and the Caribbean islands for raw materials. As this trade built up, it provided an expanding job market for all types of people, from distillers to lawyers to ship carpenters for both the shipyards and ships at sea.

In 1780, when the British departed and the French arrived with cash, the population began to return (Figure 44). It took about ten years for Newport to recover to the pre-Revolution level. In this time span there was no significant change in the technology employed in the Newport economy. Intelligent investors can recognize how to increase productivity through the proper implementation of existing technology and the organization of people to produce wealth. This was evident in pre-Revolution Newport where the organizational skills of Aaron Lopez made his implementation of the trading technology of his time very productive. As a result, he became the wealthiest man in Newport. The same can be said for George Gibbs and Walter Channing, who were successful in building Newport's post-Revolution economy using the same technology. The technology and the harbor facilities were at or near their peak in 1775 and again in 1801. In the years following the recovery in 1801, Newport did not change in its method or its technology.

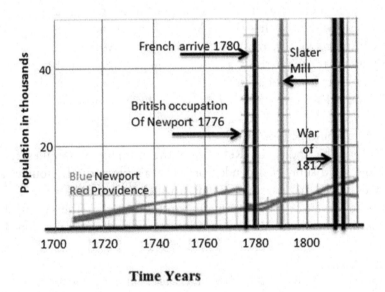

Time Years

Figure 44 Population Trends.

There were difficulties in the early 1800s. The war between England and France was in progress. The French and the English as well as their privateers were preying on American shipping. However, the losses were offset because the war was driving prices up. Newport merchants were trading with the Baltic countries and China. The risk of losing a ship was offset by buying insurance or forming a large partnership to spread the risk.

Newport's condition was best described in the memoirs of George Channing, a prominent businessman in the city:

"Until the enactment of the embargo, under President Madison, no place of the size of Newport, on the seaboard, was more distinguished for commercial activity than 'little Rody.' After the removal of the Embargo, there was a slight re-action, but nothing to indicate the previous prosperity."[300]

The few remaining large business owners retired. Once the British had control of the seas after 1805, the Newport merchants would have recognized the British ability to shut down Newport's international trade. The time of uncertainty between 1800 and 1815 made it very difficult for the merchants to calculate the market conditions accurately.[301] The possibility of losing a ship and cargo to blockading ships or privateers was a major concern. Insurance was available during wartime but it was expensive.

Insurance

In the maritime trade, various forms of insurance were available to merchants. From 1720 to 1825 maritime insurance was handled by two corporations[302] and a large number of private underwriters operating out of coffee houses such as Lloyd's.[303] In peacetime the merchant could insure his ship and cargo against loss for between 2.5% and 5% of its value. Because in peacetime the probability of loss would be low, many shippers did not buy insurance. However, the shippers who did insure their cargo made the insurance business very profitable.[304] In 1801 the British ship *Lord Nelson*, bound for Antigua, was valued at £4000 and insured for loss at 11.55%, even though the mean probability of loss was only 5%. During wartime, the insurance rates were as high as 20% to 40%, depending on

---

[300] Channing, 156.

[301] Peter J. Coleman, *The Transformation of Rhode Island, 1790 – 1860* (Providence: Brown University Press, 1963), 49.

[302] Royal Exchange Assurance Company and The London Assurance Company

[303] Maciej Kotowski, *Hull Clubs and British Maritime Insurance*, http://www.ocf. berkeley.edu/ (accessed February 16, 2012), 4.

[304] Faye M. Kert, "The Fortunes of War," *The Northern Mariner 8* (October 1998): 11.

the route.[305] The insurance companies were still making a good profit. For the period between 1810 and 1835, Dr. Maciej Kotowski[306] calculated the average insurance rate at 7.24%, with a standard deviation of 3.31%.[307]

Technology

The Industrial Revolution, with its economic opportunities, began in Rhode Island when Slater Mill was built near Providence in 1793. Robert Fulton invented the *Nautilus*, a four-man submarine, in 1798. John C. Stevens built the first screw-driven steamboat in 1802. James Watt's steam engine was available in the U.S. in 1803. Fulton's steamboat made a speed of 4.7 knots going up the Hudson River.[308] The *Phoenix*, using low pressure steam technology, was the first ocean-going steamboat in 1809.[309] Even though the Industrial Revolution was in full swing, none of this technology was imported into Newport in a timely fashion.

At the end of the War of 1812, the Anglo-American commercial treaty ended discriminatory duties on U.S. and British ships. However, with no infusion of new technology into the Newport economy, the growth rate was limited even after the War of 1812 was over.[310] To add to Newport's troubles, a major hurricane hit it in September of 1815.[311] The storm surge was eight feet above normal high tide, which did considerable damage to Newport Harbor and the docks and warehouses. In addition, the Portsmouth to Tiverton Bridge, which provided a land link from Boston to Newport, was washed away. There were six fathoms of water where the tollhouse had been standing.[312]

Economic Impact of the War of 1812

The cost of the War to the United States was 1877 lives and $13 million. Great Britain lost 33 vessels per month for a loss of $40 million.[313] The accumulated war debt of the United States was $105 million, while the British debt was $1.893 billion.[314] The Canadian maritime trade

---

[305] Ibid.
[306] Dr. Kotowski is a member of the Department of Economics, UC Berkeley.
[307] Kotowski, 27.
[308] A knot is one nautical mile per hour.
[309] Urdang, 156-166.
[310] 1815 Treaty of Ghent.
[311] It was known as "The Great Gale of 1815".
[312] *Providence Gazette*, September 30, 1815.
[313] Kert, 1-2.
[314] Ibid., 2. $4.87 = £1

tripled during the war, then dropped to just double its pre-war levels. The Canadian merchants took over a large part of the U.S. Caribbean trade.

The blockade was effective in suppressing American merchant ships. In 1813 only five of the forty-four American ships docked in Boston were able to clear the port. After the war ended the shipping business improved quickly. In March of 1815, 144 ships cleared Boston and 118 of them were headed for foreign ports.[315]

The shipping activity in Newport and Providence for this same timeframe indicated that:

	Newport	Providence	
	Domestic	Domestic	Foreign
March 11	5	8	0
March 18	2	0	0
March 25	8	11	

Most of the Newport ship traffic appears to have been coastal commerce.[316] Providence had several ships going to the Southern coastal states, probably for cotton.[317] Two ships cleared Providence for foreign ports. By March of 1815 the Port of Providence was doing more shipping business than Newport. However, most of the foreign trade in New England was being conducted through Boston.

Status After the War of 1812

Newport's position as a major maritime trading center did not recover after the hurricane of 1815. A whaling business was started in Newport but it ran into difficulties because the emerging coal gas technology produced a lower cost alternative to oil lamps and candles. Newport's commerce had become stagnant.[318]

---

[315]   Kert, 7.

[316]   *Newport Mercury, Providence Gazette*, Shipping News for March 1815.

[317]   *Newport Mercury* March 11, 1815.

[318]   Taylor, 156.

CHAPTER 6

Rhode Island's Economy
from the War of 1812 to the Civil War

Pre-Industrial Newport

In the time before the Industrial Revolution the economics of the environment required that on the average there had to be a balance between births and deaths in the human population.[319] The number of surviving children per woman in Europe between 1300 and 1800 was 2.04.[320] In early societies the bulk of consumption was in food, shelter and clothing.[321] In a society where the resources are fixed, an increase in the birth to death ratio will decrease the standard of living for the population.[322] Leading up to the 1800's, all the technological advances were so slow that they only resulted in a slow increase in population and minimum income gains. The example in Chapter 3 illustrates how an infusion of high productivity technology can increase the value of labor and wealth. After 1800 there is a limited increase in technology and a slow ramp upward in the Newport population.

In the time just before the War of 1812 the merchants of Newport recognized that the international trade was going to be depressed by the U.S. Government and the impending war. They sold their buisnesses and retired or went elsewhere. The maritime trade, which had been the backbone of the Newport economy, was depressed and did not recover as it had after the Revolution (Figure 45).

The distillery business continued. John and Samuel Whitehorne reorganized their business in 1805.[323] Samuel Whitehorne was a warden of

---

[319] Gregory Clark, *A Farewell to Alms* (Princeton: Princeton University Press, 2007), 19.
[320] Ibid., 21.
[321] Ibid., 21.
[322] Malthusian equilibrium, Ibid., 30.
[323] *Newport Mercury March 16, 1805.*

Trinity Church, acted as administrator of estates, and sold real estate.[324] An ad in 1830 indicates that he and his brother John were retailing molasses, rum, and Russian duck.[325] His house on Thames Street was for sale in 1835 but he couldn't sell it. In November of 1836 he was elected president of the Merchants Bank. The business was importing Russian hemp and iron in 1836. It is likely that Whitehorne was also in the slave trade to support the distillery requirements for molasses.[326] Shipping losses caused him to declare bankruptcy in 1843.

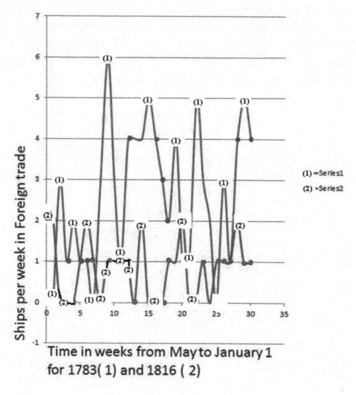

Figure 45 Comparison of Foreign Shipping after the Revoultion vs. The War of 1812.

---

[324] *Newport Mercury* June 1821.

[325] Duck was a sail cloth; in this case it had been imported from Russia.

[326] Newport Restoration Foundation, http://www.newportrestoration.org/visit/whithorne/history_architecture (accessed June 29, 2012).

The Growth of Providence

The growth in the Providence population was not due to upstate human reproductive prowess but the active recruitment of immigrants from French Canada, Ireland and other locations to supply the rapidly expanding factory system with workers. Providence and Newport had the same population in 1800 (Figure 46). Newport had recovered from the impact of the Occupation and was operating a maritime trade economy. Providence was beginning a manufacturing economy with the establishment of Slater Mill. The War of 1812 suppressed Newport's economy but the manufacturing economy of Providence was less affected. Newport's major merchants were shut down by the Embargo Act, and they also anticipated the difficulties that a war with Britain would cause the international trade. They sold their businesses and retired while Providence expanded in both the manufacturing and maritime trade.

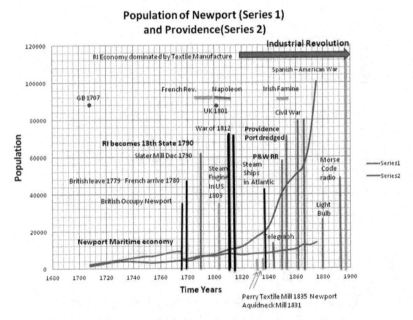

Figure 46 Newport, Providence and the Industrial Revolution.

Newport Technology

In 1790 there were well-established shipbuilding, rope making, and distilling industries in Newport. There was also a handicraft iron industry that produced bolts and harpoons.[327] However, there was no industrialization introduced into the Newport economy until 1831 when two cotton mills were constructed on Thames Street. In 1831 Aquidneck Mill was built, and four years later (1835) Perry Mill was built (Figures 47 and 48). Two other mills, the Williams Wollen Mill (1836-1860) and the Coddington Mill (1837-1869) were lost in fires.

Newport was shifting to a manufacturing economy but was at a disadvantage. Being on an island was an advantage to Newport in the 1700's when all the transportation was by water and the livestock was protected from mainland predators. It became a disadvantage in the 1800's. By then, Newport was isolated from mainland resources and transportation, in particular the railroad.

Shipbuilding in Newport peaked from 1830 to 1839, and then fell off because the shipyards were building sailing ships instead of shifting to the new steam technology (Table 12).

Table 12 Newport Ship Construction 1790-1859[328]

1790 to 1799	2176 tons
1800 to 1809	2071
1810 to 1819	824
1820 to 1829	2568
1830 to 1839	6487
1840 to 1849	2923
1850 to 1859	2498

---

[327] These merchant/sea trading industries had to diversify in the 1800's. See Peter J Coleman, *Transformation of Rhode Island 1790 – 1860* (Westport, Ct.: Greenwood Press, 1985), 33.

[328] Ibid.

Figure 47 Perry Mill.

Figure 48 Aquidneck Mill.

While Newport was trying to rebuild its economy, Providence and the surrounding areas were exploiting the technology from the Industrial Revolution to develop new technologies and products. Land transportation systems, including roads and railroads, were built to move in raw materials and ship finished products to markets. The area around Providence became one of the most industrialized in the United States.

After the Army Corps of Engineers dredged the Port of Providence to accommodate large cargo ships, Providence became the primary port in Rhode Island.[329] Steamship operations between Providence, Newport, and New York began in 1821.

Newport revived after the War of 1812 but its growth was limited by several factors:

1) Most of the capital and talent did not return after it was driven off by the Embargo Act and the British blockade.

2) With the exception of the slave and molasses trades, the foreign trade was small scale compared to Providence.[330]

3) Newport had direct access to only Middletown and Portsmouth. Mainland markets were under the control of Providence merchants.

4) The location impeded the development of turnpikes and railroads. Rail and road access might have made Newport a major shipping port.[331]

Along with the British and French interference with Newport's trade, the Embargo Act and the War of 1812 forced Rhode Island investors to shift their funds from sea ventures to manufacturing.[332] The northern part of the state had water for power and washing textiles. There was a large labor pool and no regulations to inhibit industrialization in 1800.[333] After 1815, power looms and cotton cleaning machinery became available in the cotton cloth manufacturing process.[334] In 1836 Newport had mills producing both cotton and woolen cloth.[335]

---

[329] Ibid., 66.

[330] The slave trade was banned in 1807 but still carried on by some merchants outside the U.S.

Samuel Whitehorne was suspected of being in the Triangular Trade in the 1830's to support his distillery.

[331] Ibid., 67, 68.

[332] Ibid., 71.

[333] Ibid., 73.

[334] Ibid., 80.

[335] Ibid., 135.

Fabric mills	1809	1812	1815	1832	1840	1850
Warwick	6	9	11	13	29	9
Newport	0	0	0	1	4	3[336]

In 1850 Newport had two base metal firms producing $13,000 worth of products per year. Most of the Newport area enterprises were small firms employing from two to ten people. There were twenty-four of these small businesses along South Thames Street in 1857. The coal mine in Portsmouth employed about forty people.[337] The Aquidneck Mill employed about 100 people. This mill stopped production and changed owners in 1857 due to the world-wide depression. It was later renovated and went back into operation. After a number of owners, the Richmond Manufacturing Company produced cloth and employed 175 people. In 1884 another downturn ended the production of cloth. The mill changed hands and products, and by 1900 it was owned by the Newport and Fall River Street Railway Company.[338] The Williams Woolen Mill employed about fifty people when it burned down in 1860. The Coddington Mill in Newport employed 220 workers in 1860.[339] The Perry Mill produced cloth and employed about 125 people. After 1888 the mill stopped producing cloth and went through a number of diverse uses.[340]

Providence Area Development

Providence was in the middle of the Industrial Revolution. In the 1850s there were 25 firms in the city of Providence that were producing $1,425,900 worth of products per year.[341] The industrial capital that had been invested in Providence was $2,548,518. The industrial capital in Newport, $416,100 in 1850, was less than one fifth that of Providence. The capital available in the banking establishments was considerably greater in Providence than in Newport.

---

[336] There was a fire that destroyed one of the mills.

[337] Ibid., 158.

[338] Zipf, 17.

[339] Ibid., 133.

[340] Ibid., 18.

[341] Ibid., 149.

Banking capital in millions of dollars ($M)[342]

Year	1800	1810	1820	1830	1840	1850	1860
Providence	322	822	1,472	3,516	6,867	8,466	15,208
Newport	100	350	545	545	730	680	855

Providence became the hub of both the railroad and road transportation networks.[343] By 1837 railroads went through Providence and connected Boston and New York with coastal Conneticut.[344] The main post road from Boston to New York went through Providence, while the mail route through Newport was a secondary loop which involved three ferries (Figure 49).

Newport restarted whaling voyages in 1816, had two more voyages in 1820, and regularly sent out whaling ships until 1856. By that time coal gas had made inroads into the lighting oil market.[345] Whaling did not recover after the economic depression of 1857.[346]

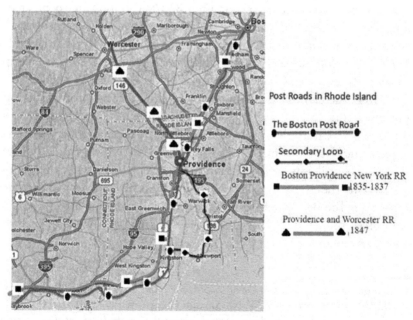

Figure 49 Post Road System

---

[342] Ibid., 185.

[343] Zipf, 159, Providence and Worcester Railroad.

[344] Frank Heppner, *Railroads of Rhode Island* (Charleston: The History Press, 2012), 72.

[345] Gas lights in Providence in 1847.

[346] Zipf, 67.

International Financial Crisis

The Panic of 1857 was the first worldwide financial crisis. It started in England, where the Palmerston administration was printing paper money with no backing in gold or silver. This action violated the Peel Banking Act which required gold and silver reserves to back up the paper money in circulation. When this practice became known, it created a panic in England and depressed the English and European economies.

There was prosperity in the United States in the early 1850s and a number of investors had extended themselves with loans to buy land and railroad stock or made loans directly to railroads. Western America had been selling goods to British and European markets.[347] When those markets became depressed, the American economy became depressed and did not recover until after the American Civil War.[348]

Tourist Industry

In the late 1700's and early 1800's summer visitors would rent rooms or houses for the season. In the ten years after 1820 Newport became popular as a summer vacation destination. There were approximately 500 visiters per week.[349] The social life was informal at first but became more formal and crowded by 1850.[350] Technology helped Newport's tourist industry. In the 1830s steam ships and railroads connected Charleston, Savanna, New York and Newport.[351]

In 1847 the Fall River Line was providing luxurious accommodations from New York to Newport by ship, and between Newport and Boston via railroad.[352] Up until the Civil War the summer population was a mix of upper middleclass from both the South and the North. In many cases the heads of families were also buisness associates. The summer population grew and in the 1830s hotels were built to accommodate the summer vacationers. The Bellevue Hotel was opened on Catherine Street in 1825. Two hotels, the Atlantic House and the Ocean House, were opened on Bellevue Avenue.[353]

---

[347] George Brown Tindall and David E. Shi, eds., *America: A Narrative History*, 5th ed., Vol. 1 (New York: W. W. Norton and Company, 1999), 707-708.

[348] John M. Murrin, et al., eds., *Liberty Equality Power: A History of the American People*, 2nd ed., vol. 1 (Fort Worth: Harcourt Brace, 1999), 488.

[349] Eliza Cape Harrison and Rosemary F. Carroll, *Newport's Summer Colony 1830-1860* (Newport: Newport History, Fall 2005).

[350] Ibid., 3.

[351] Ibid.

[352] Ibid., 43.

[353] Jefferys, 43.

In the mid-1800s Newport began to attract very wealthy summer residents from New York and elsewhere. Bellevue Avenue was at that time a rough dirt road. In 1850 land could be purchased for $300 per acre. Land speculators purchased the land around Bellevue Avenue and on the Point section of Newport for approximately $300 to $400 per acre, and were selling it for $2613 to $5226 per acre in 1853.[354]

Kingscote was built in 1841 for George Noble Jones. It was the first of the Bellevue Avenue Summer Cotages.[355] Malbone Hall was built by Jonathan Prescott Hall on the site of the original Malbone house on Ocean Drive in 1849. Chateau-sur-Mer was built by a successful China trade merchant, William Shepard Wetmore, in 1852 on Bellevue Avenue.

Summary of Newport Business

A summary of Newport business (Figure 50) provides an overview of the transition from maritime shipping to Tourism and Navy as main components of the Newport economy.

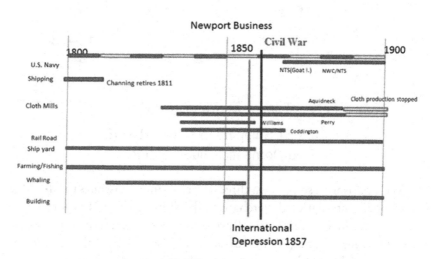

Figure 50 Newport Business 1800 to 1900.

The two cotton mills stopped producing cloth (Figure 50), but the property was sold and transitioned through a number of uses.

The shipping industry after the War of 1812 was depressed.

---

354 City Documents of George H. Calvert, Mayor of Newport (Coggeshall and Pratt, 1854) available at the Newport Historical Society.

355 Jane Mulvagh, *Newport Houses* (New York: Rizzoli International Publications, 1989), 66.

The average traffic in domestic ships entering or leaving Newport was 4.88 ships per day with a standard deviation of 2.21 ships (Figure 51). The average for foreign shipping dropped to less than one per day (.94 with a Standard Deviation of .958).[356]

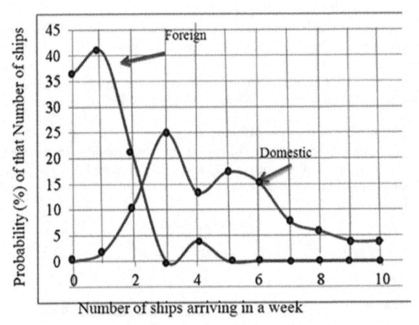

Figure 51 Shipping in Newport 1816:
Red Domestic, Blue Foreign.

A comparison of shipping at three different times illustrates the decrease in Newport's international merchant trade. Ship traffic in Newport was at its maximum in 1744. After the Revolution the trade revived but did not reach the same volume (Figure 52). After the War of 1812 the amount of shipping in and out of Newport was greatly reduced. A large percentage of this trade was made up of foreign ships coming to trade with the Newport population.

---

[356] *Newport Mercury*, Shipping News for the years under consideration.

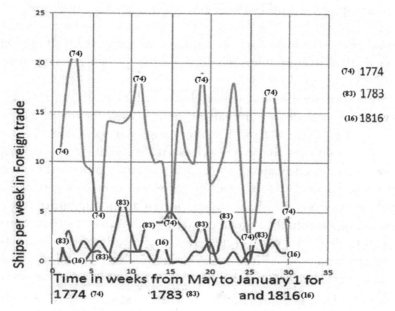

Figure 52 A Comparison of Shipping Volume for 1774 (Peak Volume) with 1783 (Post-Revolution) and 1816 (Post-War of 1812).[357]

Freedom and a Capitalistic System

In a relatively free running capitalistic economy there is a large group of people (customers) that have done productive work and as a result have something valuable (money) that can be exchanged for goods that they would like. There is a second, smaller group of people that recognize the needs and wants of the customers and have accumulated the resources to establish a business which can provide a needed product at a cost below what the customers will pay, thereby making a profit. A third group, looking at the profits being made by the second group, work out a method of providing the customers with the same or better goods at a lower price. They take over the second group's customers who are loyal only to themselves. The second group changes to be more competative or goes out of buisness. The first group is happy as they have more money now and their standard of living has increased. The members of the second group that still want to work take jobs with the

---

[357] Note that the values are integers (ships); however to indicate each point would make the graph too crowded

third group or some other viable enterprise. They also might retire and not do work for hire. The losers in this process are the investors in the second group that lost assets when the second group failed. If they were properly diversified, the loss would be a small percentage of their total assets and they could recover.

This scenario illustrates what happened to maritime trading in Newport. In nature, an animal species can exist for long periods of time until an event occurs that alters some part of the environment that is critical to the life of the species. At this point the species adapts or becomes extinct. Capitalism is an evolutionary process that cannot remain stationary.[358] If the trading environment of Newport and the whole state of Rhode Island are considered as the capitalistic system, then changes within the system may result in overall gains while causing economic losses in a small sector. This is termed Creative Destruction by Joseph Schumpter, Professor of Economics at Harvard.[359] The key to Newport's decline in maritime trade was a change in the trading environment to which the Newport merchants could not adapt. Newport had four distinct trading patterns. The first was with England for manufactured goods. The second was a coastal trade that exchanged raw material for imported manufactured goods. The third was a Caribbean trade of livestock and manufactured goods for molasses and letters of credit from England. The fourth was the Triangular Trade where rum was traded to West Africa for slaves, which in turn were traded to the Caribbean for English letters of credit and molasses. The molasses was brought back to Newport and traded with the other colonies or made into rum. The two key features of this trading environment were that the manufactured goods were produced at a distance (England) from the resale market (Continental America), and that the market for African slaves in the southen United States and the Caribbean remained viable.

The occupation of Newport by the British from 1776 to 1779 stopped trade, chased away a number of prominent merchants, and did major damage to the town's infrastructure, but it did not change the trading environment. Therefore it was not the cause of a permanent decline in Newport's international trade. The analysis shows that Newport recovered and was back in international trading by 1801.

---

[358] Joseph A Schumpeter, *Capitalism, Socialism, and Democracy 3ed.* (New York: Harper & Brothers, 1950), 82.

[359] Schumpter, 83.

Schumpeter pointed out that the changes in a capitalistic system come from within the system. The primary drivers for change are: new consumer goods, new methods of production or transportation, new markets, and new organizations that improve productivity.[360] Slater Mill was the start of Newport's problems. As the Industrial Revolution developed in Northern Rhode Island, the center for manufactured goods shifted from England to Providence. The Providence merchants were aggressively and successfully competing with the Newport merchants. Newport's merchants were still making profits up to the War of 1812. In the time before the War it became apparent to the new business investors that Newport was a bad choice for long-term investment, when compared to the Providence area. The entrepreneurs that had been in Newport were moving elsewhere. The aged, established merchants were not being replaced.

Not all the technology produced adverse effects for Newport. The advent of steamships and railroads improved Newport's tourist buisness.

---

[360] Ibid.

Epilogue

Post Civil War

During the Civil War the Providence woolen industry achieved significant profits producing woolen uniforms for the Union Army. In 1875 the population of Providence was slightly more than seven times that of Newport. Newport made a greater percentage of its money from farms and fisheries (Table 13) than Providence; however, both made most of their money from manufacturing.[361]

Table 13 Income from Products (1876).

Location	Population	Farm/Forest	Fisheries	Manufactures	Total
Newport	14,028	$34,275	$43,246	$1,614,245	$1,691,766
		(2%)	(2.55%)	(95.4%)	
Providence	100,675	$92,464	$191,123	$52,782,875	$53,066,462
		(0.17%)	(0.36%)	(99.4%)	

Tourist Industry

The tourist industry which started in Newport before the Civil War continued, but the character of the population changed. Before the War the summer population was a mix of Southern and Northern business families. After the Civil War the population was wealthier and the Newport summer society was more structured.[362]

The Newport Casino was built in 1881 as both a private and public club.[363] Wakehurst was built in 1884 by J.J. Van Alen.[364] Ochre Court, now

---

[361] Rhode Island Census Board, *Report on the Census of Rhode Island* (Providence: State of Rhode Island, 1877).
[362] Harrison and Carroll, 11.
[363] Ibid., 92.
[364] Ibid., 218.

part of Salve Regina University, was built in 1891.[365] Marble House was built in 1892 by William K. Vanderbilt at a cost of $11,000,000. [366] The Breakers, built between 1893 and 1895 by Cornelius Vanderbilt, provided an additional example of the Newport Summer Cottage.

Newport was in a building boom. While the money spent on these summer houses did not show on the economic data, it provided jobs in the building trades for Newport residents and tax revenue for the city of Newport. As it is now, the tourists with money and the support staffs that were paid to maintain these summer residences were valued customers for the Newport business establishments. The U.S. Naval Academy moved to Newport during the Civil War and moved back to Annapolis at the end of the war. Goat Island was established as a development center for torpedoes in 1869.[367] The Naval Training Station was established in 1883, and the Naval War College in 1884.

Railroads reached Newport in 1863 and electric trolley service was initiated in1889.[368]

A summary of Newport businesses (Chapter 6, Figure 50) provides an overview of the transition from maritime shipping to Tourism and Navy as main components of the Newport economy. The two cotton mills stopped producing cloth (Figure 48), but the properties were sold and transitioned through a number of uses.

---

[365] Ibid., 120. It was donated to Salve Regina College in 1947.
[366] Ibid., 148.
[367] Jefferys, 57.
[368] Heppner, 116.

CHAPTER 7

Analysis, Summary, and Conclusions

In this section the economy of Newport will be characterized and analyzed. In deference to the historic topic of this work, only math techniques developed before 1830 will be used as the tools for analysis. For all those who object to modern mathematics in the analysis of history, it should be remembered that Isaac Newton developed calculus and published his *Philosophy Naturalis Principia Mathematica* in 1687. Gottfried Leibniz was publishing papers on differential calculus as early as 1684. It is Leibniz's calculus notations that are in use today. *Bayes' Theorem*, which is the basis for this modeling and analysis, was developed by the Reverend Thomas Bayes (1701 to 1761). His work on Probability Theory was published posthumously. Bayes also defended Newton's calculus against criticism by Reverend George Berkeley, formerly of Ireland and Middletown, Rhode Island.

Bayes' Theorem was refined and the results published by Pierre-Simon Laplace (1749-1827). Laplace published *Essai philosophique sur les probabilites* in 1814. It is Laplace's rendition of Bayes' work that is used in this analysis. It has only been in the last ten years that the power of modern desktop computers has made Bayesian Analysis of large data sets practical for the general population.

Newport Capitalism

Newport's economic system was an unconstrained capitalistic system. Joseph Schumpeter described capitalism in detail.[369] The leaders of the capitalistic society achieved their position by being successful in business.[370] Rising and falling within the framework of the business community was directly related to making and losing money. The business game is similar

---

[369] Joseph A. Schumpeter, *Capitalism, Socialism and Democracy 3ed* (New York: Harper & Brothers, 1950), 72.

[370] Ibid., 73.

to poker. Spectacular prizes are obtained by a small number of winners.[371] A large number of businessmen make a modest return or fail but work very hard because they all want the big win.[372] A person will succeed in business based on his talent and luck. This is an important factor in examining a capitalistic society.[373]

Background for Analysis

From its founding in 1639 until 1775, Newport built an economy based on coastal, Caribbean and international trade. The estimated worth of Newport in 1774 was $1,087,658.[374]

The tonnage handled by the port was estimated based on the number of ships entering and leaving the port and the nominal tonnage for each ship and its class. In 1763 the port of Newport handled 51,210 tons of cargo. By 1774 Newport's volume had increased by thirty times to 1,125,290 tons of cargo.[375] Up until this point the merchants of Newport had a free hand in their operations. The British government was circumvented with deceptions, threats, bribery, and force. Aaron Lopez had established a facility in 1758 on Wapping Road in Portsmouth to support his smuggling operations. Business for the merchants of Newport was very good.

Economics and Technology

It is worth discussing a simple example of how technology impacts an economy. We will start with a group of 100 farmers with no technology available to them. They dig up useful plants and move them closer to the village and replant them so that they can be more easily harvested. Each farmer generates two units of farm produce per year. One unit he needs to maintain his family; the second he can invest. The group of farmers now can invest 100 units in luxuries or technology.

If one of the farmers saves his surplus and invests in a horse and steel plow, his productivity increases so that he can produce twenty units per year. It is costing him two units to support the horse, a new barn, and his wife's new wardrobe, but now he has seventeen units to invest. He is a smart investor so he buys his neighbor's farm, another horse and plow,

---

371 Schumpeter, 73.
372 Ibid., 74.
373 Ibid.
374 See Page 87.
375 Victor St. Laurent II, "Newport: Revival and Decline 1783-1876" (MA. Thesis, University of Rhode Island, 1969)

and hires his neighbor to farm it for three units. This is the start of an economic empire.

Soon the output of the group of 100 is producing 1700 units instead of 100. The introduction of technology is making everyone better off because they have on average twice as much income as they had had before. The leaders are much more affluent because they recognized the gains in productivity from implementing the technology.

In 1776 Adam Smith showed the interaction of price with profit, economic growth with wages, and supply and demand's impact on employment.[376] This free enterprise system was self-sustaining and self-controlling. Newport was able to operate as a free running, capitalistic entity before the Revolution because the Colonial government neutralized the power of the British customs service. Between 1780 and 1801 Newport merchants went back to international trade, hampered only by the war in Europe. After 1807 the U.S. government and a number of foreign governments limited Newport's trading options.

Rhode Island Technology

With the establishment of Slater Mill in the Providence area, technology moved from a curious set of experiments to methods that could change the world at unprecedented rates.[377] Technology needs two types of people for it to be successfully introduced into an economy. The first person is the inventor who sees a need and produces a methodology or device that will be useful to a number of people. The second person is an entrepreneur that funds and expands the technology throughout the benefiting industry. In many cases, as the first entrepreneur is spreading the technology, a second entrepreneur obtains the technology and starts competing with the first entrepreneur. Also in many cases the second entrepreneur will introduce improvements into the technology that will allow him to successfully compete with the first. Lawrence Miller described this rise and fall of businesses as they changed management styles.[378]

The commercial partnerships in Newport operated in their traditional fashion with no change in the technology from the 1760s to 1807. In the time before the Revolution, even though the same technology was used by all, Aaron Lopez did better than most because he worked harder, paid more

---

[376] James Burke and Robert Ornstein, *The Axemaker's Gift* (New York: Penguin, 1997), 172.

[377] Ibid., 177.

[378] Miller, 2.

attention to detail, and had a factor in the Caribbean that was much better than most at organizing that end of the business. In a free market, the customers choose the winners and losers. The merchant that can provide the best products at a reasonable cost will sell his products and flourish. If the market becomes limited, the poorly performing merchants will go out of business. By limited, it is meant that all or most of the customers can be satisfied by the more efficient merchant. The less efficient merchant has insufficient customers to make a profit.

Economics on a Large Scale

From 1700 to the early 1800s, with the exception of the British Occupation, Newport was engaged in world-wide commerce. In the colonial era there was trade with England, Africa, the Caribbean and the north coast of South America. By the early 1800s Newport was trading with Canton, China and the Baltic countries, and was sending whaling expeditions as far south as the Falkland Islands.

There are three key components that interacted in the Newport economy. The first was a society of merchants and craftsmen that sometimes cooperated on joint ventures and other times operated with their own teams of people on commercial ventures. This type of organization was flexible and very responsive to market changes. It strived to maximize profits by providing goods and services in a timely manner that fit the market requirements. The second was a group of large companies and governments that were bound by tradition, where advancement of individuals was more dependent on internal politics than on performance. This group's response to changing circumstances was slow and controlled more by custom than by an assessment of the situation. The third group in the economy was the aggregate of the consumers of all these products. The consumers responded to good service and lower prices. If a merchant was first to market, the consumers would be willing to pay a premium for early available products. As the market developed and more ships arrived with similar goods, the lowest price became important for sales.

English economists had two outlooks on the situation. Thomas Malthus published an analysis of food supply versus population growth.[379] Based on population data that he obtained from Benjamin Franklin, the population of a settlement would double every twenty-five years while the food supply increased at a linear rate. At some point the population would reach equilibrium with the food supply and the population would

---

[379] Buchholz, 47. See pages 129.

then stabilize. Some of the stabilizing mechanisms were starvation, infant mortality, plague, and early death in adults.[380]

This was the behavior of a closed system. In an open system, as the environment became worse, part of the population would migrate elsewhere and there would be a return to equilibrium.

David Ricardo offered a different economic perspective. Ricardo's education was limited compared to Malthus's who had graduated from Cambridge University with honors. Ricardo had a firm grasp of economics, however, and became very rich and famous, even testifying as an expert before Parliament.[381] Ricardo's analysis was based on an open system where goods could be traded freely. When each country produces the products that it is most efficient at making, there are financial gains to be made in a trading venture. These gains come, Ricardo observed, because each country specializes in producing the goods for which its comparative cost is lower.[382] Commodities derive their exchangeable value from two sources: their scarcity and the quantity of labor required to obtain them.[383]

Under a system of perfectly free commerce, each country naturally devotes its capital and labor to such employments as are most beneficial to them. It is this principle which determined that wine should be made in France and Portugal, that corn should be grown in America and Poland, and that hardware and other goods should be manufactured in England.[384]

Within a country, profits are approximately on the same level. If the profits from investments in Providence should exceed those made in Newport, investors would speedily move from Newport to Providence.[385] This is apparently what happened in Newport when the Embargo Act shut down trade and the Federal government prepared to go to war with England. The large merchant houses of Newport were literally dying out. Nine of the top ten highest taxpayers died before the end of the War of 1812. Since international trade was not going to be a profitable enterprise, the capitalists took their money elsewhere.

---

[380] Ibid., 49.

[381] Ibid., 52. If evaluated in contemporary terms, his estate would be worth $100,000,000.

[382] David Ricardo, *On the Principles of Political Economy and Taxation* (London: John Murray, 1821), Library of Economics and Liberty, http://www.econlib.org/library/Ricardo/ricP.html (accessed April 18, 2012).

[383] Ibid.

[384] Ibid., 31.

[385] Ibid.

Newport

In the years after the Revolution, there were two sets of businessmen in Rhode Island. One set was in Newport, primarily engaged in the maritime trade. This group operated a distribution network that linked England and its manufactured goods with coastal America and the Caribbean for raw materials. There was also a trade loop with Africa where rum and livestock were exchanged for gold and slaves, and then to the Caribbean where the slaves were traded for sugar, molasses, and letters of credit. Then the ships went back to Newport where the sugar was sold to the retail merchants, the molasses was sold to the rum distillers, and the letters of credit were used in the trade with England.

Newport's finances in 1774 were dependent on a maritime trading economy. There were two distinct branches. The first was an international trading pattern that included England and other European countries, the Caribbean Islands, and the Triangular Trade. The second branch was the coastal trade that included Connecticut, New York and the East Coast colonies. Each time a ship would come in, the profit from the venture would find its way into the Newport economy. The salary and bonuses earned by the Captain and Mate from trading would be used to buy food, clothes, shelter, and luxuries by their family members between voyages. The same was true for the crew's salaries. The merchant's profits also supported their bookkeepers, clerks, apprentices, and warehousemen between trips, as well as a part-time group of laborers to handle loading and unloading of the ships. In good trading times this group of laborers would move from ship to ship to load and unload them as they arrived in Newport.

The butcher, the baker, and the candlestick maker, as well as a host of other specialized businesses, supported the Newport population. In 1774 all of these businesses depended on the profitability of the international trade. The occupation of Aquidneck Island by the British and their German mercenaries from 1776 to 1779 shut down trade and caused significant damage to Newport. However, the French, who arrived in 1780 with plenty of money, did much to revive the city.

Christopher Champlin moved back to Newport in 1780 and started the town on the recovery process. Gibbs and Channing also moved back and the economy of Newport was rebuilding. By 1796 Newport was worth more than it had been just before the Revolution. By 1801 Newport's economic growth rate began to slow. However, trade had developed with the Baltic countries and China, and the merchants seemed to be working around the problems of the war between Britain and France. Newport continued to have a positive growth rate up until 1807.[386]

Newport did not get railroad service until 1864. By this time Newport had begun to engage in manufacturing and was also becoming a favored vacation place for the rich and famous.

At this point the urban legend will be put to rest.[387] It is a common belief among historians discussing the Newport maritime economy to blame the occupation of Newport from 1776 to 1779 for the demise of Newport's maritime trade. It simply is not so. We see that with the help of the French infusion of cash and with Newport maritime traders coming back after the British departure that Newport's maritime trade was rebuilt and was working quite well up until the early 1800s.

The next step in the analysis is to discover what did put an end to Newport's maritime economy. To explore this further we need to examine what was going on in the northern part of the state.

Providence

The businessmen in the northern part of the state had a resource that Newport did not, namely useful rivers that could provide water power. In 1793 Providence businessmen started looking at technology as a way to a richer future. Slater Mill was built on the Blackstone River at Pawtucket Village. By 1900 Benjamin and Robert Knight had built the largest textile empire in the world and Providence had become the leading producer of woolen goods in the United States. There were factories producing machine tools, metal files, silverware, steam engines, and rubber.[388]

Providence needed methods of logistic support for these industries. The technologies related to transporting of goods were rapidly becoming available. Before railroads there were canals such as the Blackstone which extended from Worcester, Massachusetts to Providence. Steamboats went from Providence to New York on a daily basis. By 1820 Providence's cotton industry had surpassed maritime trade as Rhode Island's economic base. In 1826 the feasibility of steam locomotives was demonstrated by George Stevens of New Jersey, and five years later a locomotive of American design replaced horses on the B&O railroad.[389] The Providence and Worcester

---

[386] See Figure 46.

[387] 'urban legend' is a term coined by Professor Brunvand of the University of Utah.

[388] See Appendix A.

[389] History of Railroads and Maps (memory.loc.gov/ammem/gmdhtml/rrhtml/ rrintro.html) (accessed on March 19, 2012).

Railroad began service in 1844. Gas lights were introduced in Providence in 1847, and six years later the Port of Providence was dredged to 35 feet to allow large ships to enter.[390]

The merchants of Providence could obtain trade goods from the manufacturing facilities in Providence and the northern part of Rhode Island. This put them in a position to compete effectively with the Newport merchants who had to get their manufactured goods from England. The Newport merchants still had the advantage of an established trade and customers that they had been servicing for a time. They may have been able to compete with the Providence merchants for a period of time. However, the federal government of the United States caused a great deal of difficulty for the Newport merchants. The U.S. Government made a number of blunders that proved costly to the New England states starting in 1807. The first was the Embargo Act in 1807 which stopped international trade. The Canadian and British merchants picked up the customers that the Newport merchants could no longer service. At this point most Newport merchants, faced with the adverse actions of the Federal government and an impending war, dissolved their businesses.

The U.S. Government mistakenly thought that it would be easy to push the British out of Canada, so it declared war on Britain in 1812 and tried to take Canada. The British, who had control of the oceans after the destruction of the French and Spanish fleets at Trafalgar, established a blockade off the East Coast, and maritime trade as a primary business in Newport ended. The end of the maritime trade business could have been anticipated based on what is known of business trends today. It was probably foreseen by the major businessmen in Newport who sold their businesses and retired, and the capitalists that took their money and invested elsewhere.

Technology and Management

There is a manager's dilemma in every successful commercial operation. This was explored in detail by Clayton Christensen in his national bestseller *The Innovator's Dilemma*.[391] The problem, according to Christensen, is when to produce and introduce innovative technology into a process that is working very well as it currently stands. Company managers work for the shareholders, or for themselves if they own the

---

[390] See Appendix A.

[391] Clayton M. Christensen, *The Innovator's Dilemma* (New York: Harper Collins, 2006).

company. The manager must decide whether to use his investment capital to expand his existing business by buying another sailing ship or invest in a steam powered ship that may take several years to prove profitable. If the company is well established and making money, there is a tendency for the management to avoid technology risks in favor of proven methods. This usually puts the older commercial organizations on the road to bankruptcy.

New companies with younger, less experienced managers find a technology that will provide a competitive edge, develop and expand it, and take away the older company's customer base. This was not quite the case with Newport. Newport had one major enterprise: acting as a trading hub for foreign and coastal trade. The only product that was manufactured in Newport and exported in quantity was rum. In the twenty years following the Revolution, Newport was rebuilt into a maritime trading center using the same technology and methods as had been used before the American Revolution. Meanwhile, during this time Providence was experimenting with manufacturing.

Economics of the International Merchant

There were five major factors that impacted the profitability of the international merchant:

1) Loss of a ship due to natural causes such as weather and rough seas.
2) Bad timing;
   a) Arriving at a port behind a number of ships so that the market was already saturated with merchandise similar to his, and the prices were low.
   b) Arriving at a port behind a number of ships where the port merchants no longer had outgoing cargo to sell, or the cargo that was available was expensive.
3) Economic depression in the customer's location.
4) Loss of ship and/or cargo to blockading warships or privateers/ pirates.
5) Government regulations that inhibited trade in profitable venues.

Stochastic Analysis

A computer based stochastic analysis was undertaken to assess the reason that the major merchants of Newport decided to go out of business or retire between 1801 and 1811. All the merchants operated in the same fashion. The first step was to assemble a cargo of some value that they thought could be sold at a considerable profit at a preplanned destination. The merchants acquired a ship at some cost, hired a crew, and sent their cargo to be sold at the destination. The merchant's factor at the destination arranged for a cargo for the return trip. The return cargo was worth considerably more than the outbound cargo. After paying the shipping cost, the difference in value of the cargoes was the profit.

The sensitivity of the merchants' profit to events on a voyage can be estimated through the use of a computer model. A relatively unconstrained capitalistic process is a mixture of skill and chance.[392] Chance is represented by random variables. The skill of the merchant is represented by the threshold that must be reached to produce an outcome. The following computer program, written in MATLAB script, draws on Bayes' Theorem. It models the risks that a Newport merchant faced. In MATLAB script the '%' indicates a comment.

The following MATLAB computer models are not very detailed but they are a reasonable representation of the system that the merchant used to do business.[393]

Computer Model

```
% NptModel
Clear
MajMerchant = zeros(2,120);
% Matrix of 2 major merchant variables for 10 years (120 months);
Merchant = zeros(5,120);
% Matrix, major merchant under 5 loss conditions for 10 years (120 months);
% Crew and ship cost
Capt = 53; % dollars/month;
FstMate = 53; % dollars/month;
SeaMan = 43; % dollars/month
Ship = 2000/120 ; % cost of ship that lasts 10 years, dollars per month
TimeTrip = 3; % three month trip
Trip_Cost = (Capt+ FstMate+3*SeaMan+Ship)*TimeTrip;
Cargo = zeros(3,1); % initial value, intermediate value, final value;
```

[392] Joseph A. Schumpeter, *Capitalism, Socialism, and Democracy 3ed.* (New York: Harper & Brothers, 1950), 73.

[393] Barry L. Nelson, *Stochastic Modeling Analysis & Simulation* (Mineola, NY: Dover Publications, 1995), 23.

```
Months = 120;
Cargo(1,1) = 5000; % Value of cargo going out
Cargo(2,1) = 5000; % Value of cargo 1st stop
Cargo(3,1) = 50000; % Value of cargo returned
investment = Cargo(1,1)+Ship; % merchant's investment in trip
profit = Cargo(3,1)-Cargo(1,1)-Trip_Cost; % Profit for each 3 month trip

ShipLoss = zeros(1,120);
Loss = [3, 2, 1, 0, -1]; % Matrix of loss thresholds
%PSL = zeros (1,Months);

k = 1; % Counting variable, passes through loss loop
m = 1; % Counting variable for length of trip
while(k<6); % LOSS LOOP

n=1;
while(n<121) % Ten years of trips at given loss
            % Time loop for 10 years = 120 months

        if(m>=TimeTrip) % if the trip is completed

            ShipLoss(1,n) = (randn(1)); % A normaly distributed variable
            used in a loss of ship event
        The
        MajMerchant(1,n)= profit; % Record profit for trip

        if(ShipLoss(1,n)>Loss(k)) % If ship is lost
            MajMerchant(1,n)=-investment; % Record loss if ship is lost
        end;
        m=0; % Reset m, length of trip in months
        end; % end of trip loop

        if(n>1) % Calculate cumulative profit or loss
        MajMerchant(2,n) = MajMerchant(2,n-1)+ MajMerchant(1,n);
        Merchant(k,n) = MajMerchant(2,n);
        end;
        m=m+1; % increment m (months/trip)
        n=n+1; % increment n count of months
end
```

```
k=k+1; % Increment Loss variable
end
time = 1:Months; %Time variable for plotting
plot(time,Merchant(1,time),'k');
hold;
plot(time,Merchant(2,time),'r');
plot(time,Merchant(3,time),'b');
plot(time,Merchant(4,time),'g');
plot(time,Merchant(5,time),'.');
        title('Merchant Profit sensitivity');
xlabel('Time Months');
ylabel('Cumulative Profit');
hold off;
```

variables used in the initial values for the program represent an approximation of the values of ship and cargo. The probability of loss thresholds are: +3 Std. Dev. P_loss = 0.13%[394]

+2 Std. Dev.	2.28%
+1 Std. Dev.	15.87%
0 Std. Dev.	50.00%
-1 Std. Dev.	84.00%

Typical P_Loss rate for ships traveling from England to the Caribbean was about 5%. A profit of ten to twenty times the investment could be made in high risk venues such as carrying grain to Europe during the start of the Napoleonic War.

The computer model can be used to examine the probable impact of increased profit and risk on the decision process of the Newport merchants. The results were calculated for ten years of trading using a ship that carried a cargo worth $5000 outbound on forty trips at three months per round trip.[395] A cumulative profit for a loss-free environment would be $1.8 million. The very low loss environment (Std. Dev. = 3) is slightly less than that.

---

[394] SD is Standard Deviation on a Normal probability distribution; P_Loss is the probability that the ship is lost.
[395] 40 trips at 3 months each is 120 months, or 10 years.

The high-gain market with a profit gain of 10 (Figure 53) illustrates the resilience of such a market to ship loss. Even with a severe loss standard deviation of -1 there is still a profit.

In a high-gain market where the profit is only five times the initial investment, the high ship loss case results in bankruptcies. If the loss is only 50% (SD = 0), there is a significant profit (Figure 54). When the profit decreases to a factor of two in a moderate market, the merchant cannot tolerate a 50% loss in shipping (Figure 55).

VERY HIGH GAIN (X10) MARKET

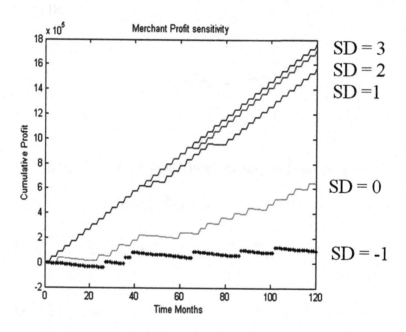

Figure 53 Cumulative Profit Over 10 Year Period.

In a low gain market, the shipping loss has to be less than about 30% for the enterprise to be profitable (Figure 56).

HIGH GAIN (X5) MARKET

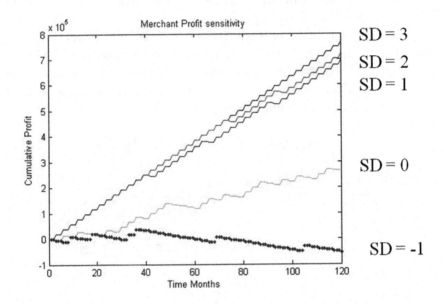

Figure 54 Cumulative Profit Over 10 Year Period.

MODERATE GAIN (X2) Market

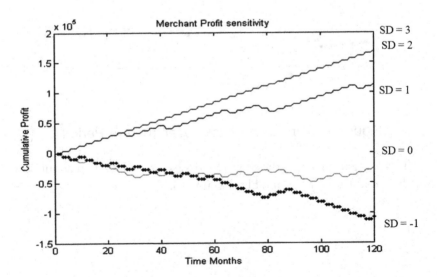

Figure 55 Cumulative Profit or Loss Over 10 Year Period.

LOW GAIN (X1.5) MARKET

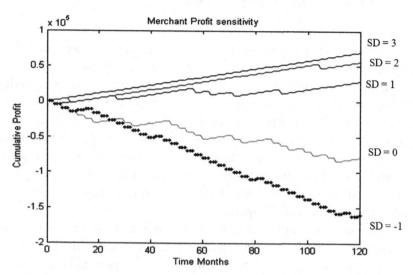

Figure 56 Cumulative Profit or Loss Over 10 Year Period.

The major merchants of Newport were considering their future in the time from 1801 to 1811. The price of flour in Europe was ten times what it was in Newport. Because the U.S. was neutral in the Napoleonic war, the merchants were making good profits.[396] With the high prices, the merchants could tolerate a 50% loss to privateers and blockade ships and still make a profit. The same is true if the profit dropped to a gain of five in value.[397] However, if the profit dropped to two or less, the merchants would be out of business.[398] Up until 1807 the merchants were operating at a profit even in the adverse war environment. However, when the U.S. Government passed the Embargo Act in 1807, it completely shut down the port of Newport to foreign trade.

Newport was further depressed in 1815 when a hurricane wrecked the harbor and washed away the Portsmouth-Tiverton Bridge. With the high-end merchants gone, it was difficult to raise funds to repair the bridge.[399] If there had been no other changes, Newport might have

---

[396] Figure 51.
[397] Figure 52.
[398] Figure 53, Figure 54.
[399] *Providence Gazette*, September 30, 1815 and Newport Mercury, September 30, 1815.

recovered. However, the Industrial Revolution in Rhode Island, centered in Providence, brought important changes.

Business Lifecycle

The life cycle of a business starts with an entrepreneur recognizing an opportunity.[400] This person or an associate builds the business. An example would be Aaron Lopez who learned the coastal trade and then expanded into international trade. As long as the environment that made the business viable remained unchanged, the business could expand and reach some natural limit. As the limit is approached, the business practices become both more refined and more rigid.[401] As the enterprise reaches a point where there can be no progress without major change, it may be doing well but be brittle in the sense that a change in the business environment may undermine its ability to compete.[402]

Newport was isolated, had no water power, and had to receive all of its major shipments by sea. This became a disadvantage as the Providence area developed manufacturing on a large scale. Newport had a deep water port and could accommodate large merchant ships, but this became much less important when the Providence harbor was dredged so that it, too, could accommodate large ships. Northern Rhode Island became one of the largest cloth producing areas of the world. The manufactured products could be shipped directly from the Port of Providence.

The advent of another technology related to transportation allowed the Providence merchants to compete directly for Newport's coastal trade. Initially shipping from Providence depended on sailing ships and canals. During the early 1800s steam ships became available and railroads connected Providence with New York and Boston.

The railroad allowed a land-based option for distributing Providence's manufactured goods. Since the railroad ran from Boston to Providence, then along the Connecticut coast, the coastal towns of Connecticut and Massachusetts could ship their products to New York and Boston by railroad.[403] These new transportation technologies caused Newport to lose its importance in both the coastal and international maritime trade.

---

[400] Miller 1989, 2.
[401] Ibid., 111. Miller describes this as the "bureaucratic" stage of a business.
[402] Clayton M. Christensen, 21.
[403] Jefferys, 43.

In the end, it was the Federal government that created the catastrophic circumstances that put an end to Newport's maritime trading economy. The Embargo Act and the War of 1812 ended the viability of the international maritime trade in the period from 1807 to 1815. This time there would be no French bailout; Nelson had destroyed the French fleet at Trafalgar. After the war Newport could not recover as it did after the Revolution because of competition from the Providence industrial center and aggressive Providence merchants. There was still fishing and coastal trading after 1820, but the prominent international merchants of Newport had died or retired. Providence was now the center of Rhode Island economics and manufacturing innovation. It made the items that Newport had been importing from England.

The railroad, with its higher speeds and reliability, was another disruptive technology. Benjamin Hazard, attorney and legislator from Newport, opposed a railroad through South County as it would provide competition for Newport's coastal trade.[404] The railroad was pushed from both the New York and Boston ends and expanded from New York along the Connecticut coast to Providence, and from Boston down to Providence. When the railroad was completed, it provided a less expensive and more reliable option to Newport's coastal trade.

Summary and Conclusions

From the time that Newport was established, the island farms were very productive because mainland predators that gained access to the island were quickly eliminated. This surplus was used to establish a trading relationship with Britain for manufactured goods, and with the Caribbean islands for molasses and sugar. This enterprise was expanded in the 1700s to include coastal trade and expanded trade with England. Rum production in Newport became a major industry.

Although most of the rum production was consumed in the Colonies, about twenty five to thirty percent was used in the Triangular trade. In the Triangular Trade, rum and livestock were shipped to the African Gold Coast and traded for slaves and gold. The slaves were transported to the Caribbean and traded for sugar, molasses and letters of credit from British merchants.

Britain had established Navigation Laws which were meant to direct trade in a fashion beneficial to British merchant profits. These laws were ignored by the colonial merchants whenever it was convenient. Aaron Lopez

---

[404] Heppner, 60.

established a smuggling facility in Portsmouth, Rhode Island in 1758 on Wapping Road just south of Braman Lane. It must have been profitable because he expanded his holdings in 1770. In Newport, smuggling was the general practice and was protected by the local government.

George II died in his water closet in 1760 and was succeeded by his grandson George III.

George III made a number of strategic errors. First, he settled the war with France such that they could rebuild their military and let them keep some profitable possessions in the North Atlantic and Caribbean. Second, he tried to get the American Colonies to pay the British war debt when he had no way to enforce the collection short of war. Predictably the Colonies rebelled and the British used force. Benjamin Franklin obtained both covert and, in the end, overt aid from the French, and the British lost.

The British had occupied Newport for almost three years, shut the port down, and caused significant damage to homes and facilities. It is assumed that this put Newport in a decline from which it could not recover. The facts show this is not true. The hard evidence shows that Newport recovered by 1801. Its facilities were repaired and international trading was doing well.

The reason Newport could recover was that the transportation technology had not changed. There were valuable goods in foreign ports that could be obtained in exchange for U.S. commodities and sold at a profit in the United States. Newport ships were trading with China, the Baltic countries and, as ships of a neutral nation, with both sides of the Napoleonic War.

The end of the Newport merchant international trading business came from a number of cascading events. The first was the Louisiana Purchase from France in 1803. This motivated the U.S. President and Congress, which was under the control of the Southern land holders, to desire westward expansion. The British were selling guns and ammunition to the Indians via Canada.

The politicos wanted the British out of the Americas.

The second event was the industrialization of Providence and northern Rhode Island starting with Slater Mill. The smart investors that had been in Newport were moving north. There was a span of thirty years from the time the French came to Newport until the beginning of the 1812 war. The major merchants of Newport were old and there was no new blood to replace them. Admiral Nelson had destroyed the French navy; there would be no French rescue in a war with England.

Third, the U.S. Government shut down the U.S. ports to foreign trade starting in 1807 with the Embargo Act. This ill-advised action shifted English trade to Brazil, and the American food producers shipped their goods via Canada. Canadian shipping tripled during the war. The majority of Newport's major merchants sold out, retired, or died before the end of the 1812 war.

Fourth, transportation technology was advancing rapidly. Steam ships and railroads linked New York, Charleston, Savanna, Providence and Boston. Newport's sailing ships could not compete.

Newport and Technology

Manufacturing spread to Newport when steam engines became available. Steam powered mills started on the Newport waterfront because the coal that powered them had to be transported by boat. But in the downturns in the economy these plants were shut down.

The Newport climate, which was mild in winter and comfortable in summer, attracted a tourist and summer vacation trade which was exploited. From 1880 to the beginning of World War I, Newport became known as the "Queen of Resorts".[405] Yachting became a summer sport. The New York Yacht Club established a branch in Newport. The climate of Newport also made it a good location for the Navy. The Naval Torpedo Station and the Navy schools, including the Navy War College, were established in Newport. These activities formed the backbone of economic activity into the 20th century.

Newport did not recover its position as an international trading center. The improvement in the transportation technology did make Newport more accessible to tourists and they came at a rate of 500 visitors per day in the time before the Civil War. After the War of 1812, Newport shifted to a manufacturing and tourist economy.

Even if the Embargo Act and the War of 1812 had not taken place, Newport's position in the maritime trade would have been untenable in the face of aggressive competition from the Providence merchants and manufacturers.

---

[405] Stensrud, 343.

Appendix A

Long Tables and Time Line
Data Tables of Economic Trends

Table A-1

Newport taxes adjusted to United States Silver dollars in 1801. Taxes collected before 1800 were in British Pounds. One British Pound equaled $4.87 United States Silver Dollars.

Note: Bold: Taxpayer left Newport before 1779
     Underline: Taxpayer in Newport between 1777 and 1779
     The amounts are not adjusted for inflation.

Newport Taxes in U.S. Dollars		Newport Taxpayer					
	1	1772	1775	1785	1789	1793	1801
A_____	2						
John Almy	3	0.00	0.57	0.00	0.00	15.69	0.00
John Anthony	4	0.00	11.21	0.00	0.00	0.00	0.00
Joseph Anthony	5	0.00	22.43	0.00	0.00	0.00	0.00
Peleg Anthony	6	0.00	52.72	0.00	0.00	12.77	0.00
William Atherton	7	0.00	0.00	16.47	0.00	0.00	0.00
Thomas Armstrong	8	0.00	0.00	0.00	0.00	0.00	4.90
Robert Auchmulty	9	0.00	0.00	0.00	0.00	18.74	3.85
Stephen Ayrault	10	0.00	34.76	0.00	6.41	48.67	0.00
B_____	11					0.00	
Babcock Farm	12	0.00	0.00	0.00	0.00	17.15	0.00
Nathan Bebee	13	0.00	4.48	28.23	0.00	11.19	0.00
John Baker	14	0.00	0.00	0.00	3.28	0.00	0.00

Seth Barton	15	0.00	0.00	0.00	0.00	0.00	4.20
William Bateman	16	0.00	0.00	0.00	0.00	0.00	3.50
John Bell	17	24.82	17.95	0.00	0.00	0.00	0.00
Job Bennet	18	19.71	13.46	0.00	0.00	0.00	0.00
Nathaniel Bird	19	21.41	0.00	0.00	0.00	0.00	0.00
John Bofs	20	0.00	0.00	16.47	0.00	0.00	3.50
John Bours	21	24.82	11.21	0.00	0.00	13.14	3.50
Henry Bowers	22	0.00	15.11	0.00	0.00	0.00	0.00
Robert Brattle	23	0.00	2.80	0.00	0.00	22.47	0.00
Benjamin Brenton	24	23.85	16.26	0.00	0.00	0.00	0.00
Jahleel Brenton	25	23.85	16.26	0.00	0.00	0.00	0.00
Joseph Briggs	26	0.00	0.00	0.00	0.00	9.73	0.00
Mellard Briggs (Capt)	27	0.00	0.00	0.00	0.00	14.11	0.00
Willard Briggs	28	0.00	0.00	0.00	0.00	0.00	3.50
Francis Brinley	29	16.55	11.21	0.00	0.00	0.00	0.00
George Brown	30	0.73	0.57	0.00	0.00	0.00	0.00
John Brown	31	23.12	0.00	14.11	0.00	0.00	0.00
Peleg Brown	32	0.00	0.00	0.00	0.00	0.00	4.20
George Buckmaster	33	0.00	0.00	0.00	0.00	12.41	0.00
David Buffum	34	0.00	0.00	0.00	0.00	0.00	4.90
Ebinizer Burrill	35	0.00	0.00	0.00	0.00	0.00	4.20
William Burroughs	36	0.00	0.00	0.00	0.00	17.03	0.00
C_____	37					0.00	
Cahoone & Yeates	38	33.09	22.43	0.00	0.00	14.60	0.00
James Carpenter	39	13.14	11.01	0.00	0.00	0.00	0.00
Samuel Carr	40	13.14	5.15	0.00	0.00	0.00	0.00
James Center	41	0.00	0.00	0.00	0.00	11.19	0.00
Walter Chaloner	42	9.73	5.60	0.00	0.00	0.00	0.00
George Champlin	43	9.73	5.60	11.76	0.00	67.16	21.00
William Champlin	44	0.00	15.61	0.00	0.00	0.00	0.00
Christopher Champlin	45	29.69	39.28	0.00	0.00	129.45	26.60
Christopher Champlin	46	0.00	0.00	0.00	0.00	0.00	3.50
Chace	47	0.00	0.00	84.68	0.00	0.00	0.00
William Channing	48	0.00	0.00	0.00	0.00	26.77	0.00
David Chesebrough	49	24.58	11.21	0.00	0.00	0.00	0.00
Benjamin Church	50	18.01	12.33	0.00	0.00	14.92	0.00

Peleg Clarke	51	0.00	10.10	0.00	0.00	97.33	17.50
James Clarke	52	28.71	11.21	0.00	0.00	0.00	0.00
Jeremiah Clarke	53	11.44	11.21	14.11	0.00	0.00	0.00
Joseph Clarke	54	0.49	0.57	0.00	0.00	14.60	0.00
Nathanial Clarke	55	0.00	5.60	10.58	0.00	0.00	0.00
Thomas Clarke	56	0.00	0.00	0.00	0.00	0.00	3.78
Ethon Clarke	57	0.00	0.00	0.00	0.00	20.52	4.20
Elisha Coggeshall	58	29.69	20.18	0.00	0.00	19.47	0.00
Nathaniel Coggeshall	59	9.73	16.81	0.00	0.00	0.00	0.00
James Coggeshall	60	24.82	16.81	0.00	0.00	16.06	0.00
John Coggeshall	61	0.00	0.00	0.00	0.00	9.98	0.00
Nath Coggeshall Jr	62	16.55	6.71	0.00	0.00	0.00	0.00
Edward Cole	63	49.40	0.00	0.00	0.00	0.00	0.00
Samuel Collins	64	16.55	37.01	0.00	0.00	0.00	0.00
John Collins	65	56.21	11.21	0.00	0.00	41.37	0.00
John Cooke	66	0.00	0.00	0.00	0.00	24.86	0.00
Peter Cooke	67	20.44	11.21	0.00	0.00	0.00	0.00
Silas Cooke	68	29.69	0.0	0.00	0.00	0.00	0.00
Edward Cote	69	0.00	28.02	0.00	0.00	0.00	0.00
Thomas Cottrell	70	0.00	0.00	0.00	0.00	12.45	0.00
Matthew Cozzens	71	9.98	16.81	0.00	0.00	0.00	0.00
Thomas Cranston	72	27.98	16.81	0.00	0.00	0.00	0.00
Archabald Crary	73	0.00	0.00	0.00	0.00	0.00	10.50
Fredrick Crary	74	0.00	0.00	0.00	0.00	0.00	3.50
D_____	75					0.00	
Silas Dean	76	0.00	0.00	0.00	0.00	0.00	3.50
Stephen Deblois	77	0.00	0.00	0.00	0.00	0.00	7.00
Johnathan Dennis	78	0.00	0.00	0.00	0.00	0.00	5.95
Thomas Dennis	79	0.00	0.00	0.00	0.00	0.00	16.10
John Dupuy	80	9.73	8.96	0.00	0.00	0.00	0.00
Samuel Dyre	81	66.17	39.26	56.45	0.00	0.00	0.00
E_____	82					0.00	
Caleb Earl	83	16.55	11.21	0.00	0.00	0.00	0.00
Jonathan Easton	84	24.82	16.81	0.00	0.00	0.00	4.20
Nicholas Easton	85	46.23	31.39	0.00	0.00	0.00	4.20
Benjamin Ellery	86	0.00	11.21	0.00	0.00	0.00	0.00

F_____	87					0.00	
John Falcon	88	0.00	0.00	0.00	0.00	0.00	4.20
John Faxon	89	0.00	0.00	0.00	0.00	18.25	0.00
Ebenezer Flagg	90	9.73	28.02	0.00	0.00	0.00	0.00
Samuel Fowler	91	41.12	10.10	0.00	0.00	43.80	0.00
Samuel Freebody	92	13.14	7.85	0.00	0.00	13.06	4.20
Thomas Freebody	93	9.73	7.85	0.00	0.00	12.41	0.00
John Fry	94	11.44	16.81	0.00	0.00	0.00	0.00
John Fryers	95	34.55	33.66	0.00	0.00	0.00	0.00
G_____	96					0.00	
Caleb Gardner	97	34.55	22.43	0.00	0.00	151.59	28.00
William Gardner(Capt)	98	0.00	0.00	0.00	0.00	14.96	4.20
George Gibbs	99	41.12	11.21	0.00	0.00	167.90	70.00
Samuel Goldthwait	100	9.98	11.21	0.00	0.00	0.00	0.00
Thomas Green	101	16.55	22.43	0.00	0.00	22.39	0.00
William Gyles	102	23.12	22.43	0.00	0.00	0.00	0.00
H_____	103					0.00	
John Hadwen	104	29.69	22.43	0.00	0.00	14.60	0.00
John Halliburton	105	16.55	11.21	0.00	0.00	0.00	0.00
Joseph Hammond Jr	106	13.14	0.00	0.00	0.00	0.00	0.00
William Hammond	107	0.00	0.00	0.00	0.00	14.60	0.00
Charles Handy	108	39.66	22.43	0.00	0.00	153.58	0.00
John Handy	109	0.00	0.00	0.00	10.95	0.00	0.00
Thomas Handy	110	0.00	0.00	0.00	0.00	0.00	5.60
Samuel and Moses Hart	111	16.55	11.21	0.00	0.00	0.00	0.00
Widow Harrison	112	0.00	0.00	0.00	0.00	14.92	0.00
Isaac Hart	113	0.00	11.21	0.00	0.00	0.00	0.00
Saml Hart est	114	24.82	16.81	0.00	0.00	0.00	0.00
George Hazard	115	22.39	0.00	0.00	0.00	27.42	0.00
Godfrey Hazard	116	0.00	0.00	0.00	0.00	0.00	4.20
Nathanial Hazard	117	0.00	0.00	0.00	0.00	0.00	3.50
Thomas Hazard	118	0.00	0.00	0.00	0.00	11.68	0.00
Benjamin Hicks	119	0.00	0.00	0.00	0.00	10.22	0.00
Samuel Holmes est	120	27.25	0.00	0.00	0.00	0.00	0.00
James Honeyman	121	51.10	35.89	0.00	0.00	0.00	0.00
Giles Hosier	122	13.14	0.00	0.00	0.00	0.00	0.00

Henry Hunter	123	24.82	17.95	0.00	0.00	35.45	4.90
William Hunter	124	27.98	20.18	0.00	0.00	11.19	0.00
David Huntington	125	0.00	0.00	0.00	0.00	19.47	0.00
I_____	126					0.00	
George Irish	127	39.66	22.43	0.00	0.00	0.00	0.00
J_____	128					0.00	
Joseph Jacob	129	23.12	8.39	0.00	0.00	0.00	0.00
Samuel Johnson	130	34.55	22.43	0.00	0.00	0.00	0.00
K_____	131					0.00	
James Keith	132	16.55	11.21	0.00	0.00	0.00	0.00
L_____	133					0.00	
William Langley	134	0.00	0.00	0.00	0.00	21.17	4.90
Charles La Salle	135	0.00	0.00	0.00	0.00	14.60	0.00
Aaron Lakers	136	0.00	0.00	0.00	0.00	9.98	0.00
George Lawton	137	0.00	11.21	0.00	0.00	0.00	0.00
Isaac Lawton	138	18.01	12.33	0.00	0.00	0.00	0.00
John Lawton	139	23.85	16.26	0.00	0.00	0.00	0.00
Robert Lawton	140	13.14	10.08	0.00	0.00	0.00	0.00
Samual Lawton	141	0.00	0.00	0.00	0.00	0.00	3.50
Hyam and Simeon Levy	142	9.98	22.39	0.00	0.00	0.00	0.00
Moses Levy	143	41.12	33.64	0.00	0.00	0.00	0.00
Robert Lillibridge Jr	144	16.55	11.21	0.00	0.00	0.00	0.00
Solomon Littlefield	145	9.98	2.25	0.00	0.00	0.00	0.00
Aaron Lopez	146	182.96	158.12	0.00	3.65	0.00	0.00
Danial Lyman	147	0.00	11.21	0.00	0.00	10.10	3.50
Josias Lyndon	148	24.82	0.00	0.00	0.00	0.00	0.00
M_____	149					0.00	
Evan Malbone	150	56.21	39.80	0.00	0.00	0.00	0.00
Francis Malbone	151	56.21	39.80	0.00	0.00	0.00	0.00
John Malbone	152	0.00	0.00	0.00	0.00	83.81	0.00
Kathy Malborn	153	0.00	0.00	0.00	0.00	14.32	0.00
Henry Marchant	154	32.85	28.02	23.52	0.00	43.80	0.00
Jonathan Marsh	155	11.44	7.85	0.00	0.00	0.00	0.00
Simeon Martin	156	0.00	31.39	0.00	0.00	32.95	10.50
Benjamin Mason	157	41.12	33.64	0.00	0.00	0.00	0.00
John Mawdsley	158	39.42	33.64	0.00	0.00	0.00	0.00

John Miller	159	0.00	10.10	0.00	0.00	0.00	0.00
David Moore	160	23.12	16.81	0.00	0.00	0.00	0.00
Edward Mumford	161	0.00	0.00	0.00	0.00	14.92	0.00
Paul Mumford	162	16.55	13.46	0.00	0.00	9.98	0.00
John Mumford	163	3.41	16.26	0.00	0.00	0.00	0.00
Peter Mumford	164	14.84	17.95	0.00	0.00	0.00	0.00
N_____	165					0.00	
August Newman	166	0.00	0.00	12.90	0.00	0.00	0.00
Simon Newton	167	11.92	13.46	16.47	0.00	0.00	0.00
Beny Nicholas (Ferry man)	168	0.00	0.00	10.58	0.00	0.00	0.00
O_____	169					0.00	
John Oldfield	170	0.00	0.00	10.58	0.00	0.00	0.00
Jonathan Otis	171	29.69	3.37	0.00	0.00	0.00	0.00
H. John Overing	172	24.82	20.18	0.00	0.00	35.69	0.00
P_____	173					0.00	
Simon Pease	174	56.21	44.85	0.00	0.00	0.00	0.00
Jacob Polock est	175	51.10	0.00	0.00	0.00	0.00	0.00
Ichabod Potter	176	16.55	0.00	0.00	0.00	0.00	0.00
Joseph Potter (Farmer)	177	0.00	0.00	0.00	0.00	0.00	8.68
R_____	178					0.00	
William Read	179	16.55	0.00	0.00	0.00	0.00	0.00
Jonas L. Redwood	180	16.55	8.96	0.00	0.00	0.00	0.00
Abraham Redwood Jr	181	16.55	16.81	0.00	0.00	0.00	0.00
Wm. Redwood Jr	182	16.55	8.96	0.00	0.00	0.00	0.00
Abraham Redwood	183	27.98	16.81	0.00	0.00	0.00	0.00
Ebenezer Richardson	184	27.98	24.66	0.00	0.00	0.00	0.00
Thomas Richardson	185	34.55	26.91	0.00	0.00	0.00	0.00
Abraham Rivera	186	0.00	0.00	0.00	0.00	14.60	0.00
Jacob R. Rivera	187	66.17	44.85	35.28	0.00	0.00	2.10
James Robinson	188	11.44	7.85	0.00	5.47	67.16	21.00
John Robinson	189	0.00	0.00	0.00	0.00	0.00	4.20
Thomas Robinson	190	34.55	11.21	18.82	0.00	10.06	0.00
William Robinson (Capt)	191	16.55	11.21	0.00	0.00	0.00	3.50
William Rogers	192	27.25	22.43	0.00	0.00	0.00	0.00
George Rome	193	82.49	67.28	0.00	0.00	0.00	0.00

S_____	194					0.00	
John Scott	195	49.40	6.71	0.00	0.00	35.00	3.85
Joseph Scott	196	16.55	13.44	0.00	0.00	0.00	0.00
George Scott Doc	197	16.55	18.49	0.00	0.00	12.41	0.00
Moses Seixas	198	6.57	0.00	0.00	0.00	17.03	0.00
Isaac Sentes Doc	199	0.00	0.00	0.00	0.00	16.42	0.00
Elisha Sheffield	200	80.50	50.47	0.00	0.00	0.00	3.50
Sheffield	201	11.92	0.00	0.00	0.00	24.82	0.00
Edward Sisson	202	0.00	0.00	0.00	0.00	0.00	3.50
Joseph Sisson	203	0.00	0.00	0.00	0.00	0.00	4.48
Gideon Sisson	204	33.09	28.02	0.00	0.00	0.00	0.00
Henry Sherburne	205	0.49	0.00	0.00	0.00	11.82	6.30
John Slocum	206	36.26	25.79	0.00	0.00	16.51	3.85
Jacob Smith	207	0.00	0.00	0.00	0.00	0.00	7.00
John Stanton	208	0.00	0.00	0.00	0.00	11.70	0.00
Thomas Stelle	209	33.09	28.02	0.00	0.00	0.00	0.00
Robert Stevens & Son	210	16.55	15.69	0.00	0.00	0.00	5.60
Robert Stoddard	211	36.26	24.66	0.00	0.00	0.00	0.00
T_____	212					0.00	
Constant Tabor	213	0.00	0.00	0.00	0.00	29.20	6.30
James Tanner	214	16.55	6.71	0.00	0.00	0.00	0.00
John Tanner	215	25.79	16.81	0.00	0.00	0.00	0.00
Nickolas Taylor	216	0.00	15.69	0.00	0.00	11.19	0.00
Thomas T Taylor	217	9.98	2.25	0.00	0.00	0.00	0.00
James Taylor	218	11.44	2.25	0.00	0.00	0.00	0.00
Henry Tew (Capt)	219	0.00	0.00	0.00	0.24	0.00	0.00
Jonathan Thurston	220	24.82	3.37	0.00	0.00	0.00	0.00
John Thurston	221	11.44	11.21	0.00	0.00	17.52	0.00
William Tilley	222	4.26	0.00	0.00	0.00	0.00	0.00
Joseph Tillinghast	223	13.14	6.71	0.00	0.00	0.00	0.00
John Tillinghast	224	59.37	33.64	0.00	0.00	0.00	0.00
John Townsend	225	9.98	6.71	0.00	0.00	19.47	0.00
William Tweedy	226	16.55	13.44	0.00	0.00	0.00	0.00
John Tweedy	227	19.71	8.96	0.00	0.00	0.00	0.00
V_____	228					0.00	
Samuel & Wm. Vernon	229	49.40	40.35	0.00	0.00	88.07	24.50

Samuel Vernon	230	0.00	0.00	0.00	0.00	43.52	3.50
Samuel Vernon Jr	231	0.00	2.25	0.00	0.00	0.00	4.20
W_____	232					0.00	
Godfrey Wainwood	233	9.73	0.00	0.00	0.00	0.00	0.00
Philip Wanton	234	11.92	5.60	0.00	0.00	0.00	0.00
Gideon Wanton	235	18.01	7.50	0.00	0.00	0.00	0.00
John G. Wanton	236	18.01	8.96	0.00	0.00	0.00	0.00
Joseph G. Wanton	237	12.63	8.96	0.00	0.00	0.00	0.00
Joseph & Wm. Wanton	238	90.52	67.28	0.00	0.00	0.00	0.00
Edward Wanton	239	41.12	8.96	0.00	0.00	0.00	0.00
Elias Warner	240	0.00	0.00	0.00	0.00	23.36	0.00
Oliver R. Warner	241	19.71	15.69	18.82	0.00	0.00	0.00
John Warren	242	24.58	5.11	0.00	0.00	0.00	0.00
Charles Wickham	243	45.99	13.44	0.00	0.00	29.89	0.00
Thomas Wickham Jr	244	11.44	4.50	0.00	0.00	16.42	0.00
Charles A. Wigneron	245	18.74	0.57	0.00	0.00	0.00	0.00
Anthony Wilbour	246	0.00	0.00	0.00	0.00	0.00	4.20
Philip Wilkinson	247	9.73	5.60	0.00	0.00	0.00	0.00
Benjamin Wright	248	11.44	9.31	0.00	0.00	0.00	0.00
Lemuel Wyatt	249	11.44	5.60	0.00	0.00	0.00	0.00

Table A-2 Shipping Data 1762-1763.

Ship	Master	To/From	In/Out	yy/mm/dd
Sloop New York Packet Boat	Henry Collard	New York	in	620511
Sloop Industry	John Earl	New-York	in	620511
Stoop Orange	John Cox	Virginia	in	620511
Schooner Elizabeth	Nathaniel Sloo	N. Carolina	in	620511
Sloop Abigail	William Brewer	Philadelphia	in	620511
Sloop Greenwich	Holden Rice	S. Carolina	in	620511
Sloop Rhoda	Christ. Shelden	S. Carolina	in	620511
Schooner Greyhound	John Law	Dominico	in	620511
Pettiauger Little Sally	Bridges	N. Carolina	in	620525
Sloop Betsey	Parker	N. Carolina	in	620525
	Vial	N. Carolina	in	620525

Sloop Betsey	Cozzens	New-York	in	620525
Schooner Olive Branch	Valentine	Virginia	in	620525
Sloop Silence	Stone	Boston	in	620525
Sloop Rising-Sun	Bucklin	New-York	out	620525
	Miller	Philadelphia	out	620525
Sloop Abigail	Brewer	Philadelphia	out	620525
Brig Hope	Cowdry	Philadelphia	out	620525
Sloop Elizabeth	Gardner	Philadelphia	out	620525
	Dyre	Philadelphia	out	620525
Sloop Ranger	Wyatt	Philadelphia	out	620525
Stoop Orange	Cox	Virginia	out	620525
Schooner Elizabeth	Sloo	N. Carolina	out	620525
	Hosier	Newfoundland	out	620525
Sloop Harlequin	Wilcocks	Maryland	out	620525
	Thuritori	Georgia	out	620525
Sloop Lively	Palmer	Egg-Harbor	out	620525
Sloop New York Passage Boat	Henry Collard	New-York	in	620727
Sloop. Providence Packet	William Chace	New-York	in	620727
Sloop Neptune	James Drew	Pifcataway	in	620727
Sloop Mary	William Liam/net.	Halifax	in	620727
Sloop Molly	Jonathan Sallboy	Falmouth	in	620727
Brig. Two. Sisters	Samuel James	Jamaica	in	620727
Sloop Edmund	James Seawell	Jamaica	in	620727
Sloop Mary	Levi Shearman	Jamaica	in	620727
Sloop Mary	John Lee	Jamaica	in	620727
Sloop Peggy	Gregory Cozzens	Jamaica	in	620727
Sloop Friendship	John Flag	Jamaica	in	620727
Sloop Victory	John' Nush	New-Providence	in	620727
Sloop Diana	Thomas Remmington	Barbados	out	620727
Sloop Black Prince.	James Bourk	Guadaloupe	out	620727
Sloop Newport	George Janyerin	Piscataway.	out	620727
Sloop Elizabeth	Silvester Gardner	Philadelphia	out	620727
Sloop Hannah	Elmer Hathaway	Philadelphia	out	620727
Schooner Peacock	Wm :Grinnell	Philadelphia	out	620727
Sloop Susannah	Andrew Langworthy	Boston	out	620727

Sloop Cedar Swamp	Abraham Van Emburgh	New York	out	620727
Sloop Molly;	Jonathan Salsbury	Nova-Scotia	out	620727
Schooner Betty	Thomas Munro	Philadelphia	in	620824
Sloop Rainbow	Jarnes Allen	Philadelphia	in	620824
Sloop Kingbird	Constant Viall	Philadelphia	in	620824
Sloop Industry	Robert Lawton	Philadelphia	in	620824
Sloop Newport Pssage-Boat	John Blagg	New York	in	620824
Schooner Nancy	John Skinner	New York	in	620824
Sloop Charming Polly	Unknown	New York	in	620824
Sloop Dolphin	Jushua De St. Croix	New York	in	620824
Sloop Cornelia	Robert Castle	Martinico	in	620824
Brig Dolphin	Thomas Rodman	Martinico	in	620824
Sloop Batchelor	Ychn Codtiinsta	Martinico	in	620824
Brig Hope	Nathaniel .Potter	St. Christophers	in	620824
Brig Grayhound	John Coultas	St. Christophers	in	620824
Schooner Runner	John .Hoyle	Jamaica	out	620824
Sloop Cornelia	Robert Castlei	Philadelphia	out	620824
Slccp Kingbird	Constant: Viali	Philadelphia	out	620824
Sloop Silence	Nathaniel Stone.	Boston	out	620824
Sloop Charming Polly	Moses Waterman	New-York	in	620831
Sloop Dolphin	Joiltua Dc St. Croix	New York	in	620831
Sloop Industry	Robert Lawton	Philadelphia	in	620831
Sloop Defiance	Thomas Sturgis	Boston	in	620831
Schooner Three Brothers	James Mitchell	Virginia	in	620831
Sloop Elitabeth	William Bewsheer	Maryland	in	620831
Brig Greyhound	John Coultass	St. Chrristophers	in	620831
Sloop Bachellor	John Coddington	Martinico	in	620831
Sloop Abigail	William Brewer	Philadelphia	out	620831
Sloop Rebecca	William Budden	Philadelphia	out	620831
Sloop Fliendthip	Chistopher Ellery	Philadelphia	out	620831
Sloop Sally	Zebedee Irenell	Philadelphia	out	620831
Sloop Dolphin	Joihua De St Croix	New-York	out	620831
Sloop Two Partners	John Dunuell	New-York	out	620831
Schooner Successs	John Carpenter	Connecticut	out	620831
Sloop Chance	Moses Waterman	Jamaica	out	620831
Brig Wainscott	James Brown	Jamaica	out	620831

Scooner Peacock	Grinnell	Philadelphia	in	620914
Sloop Kingbird	Vial	Philadelphia	in	620914
Sloop Susannah	Langworthy	Boston	in	620914
Sloop Elizabeth	Dtinfcomb	Maryland	in	620914
Brigantine Nancy	Ste:Con	Maryland	in	620914
Schooiler Dolphin	Garria	New. York	in	620914
Brigantine Betsey	Moore	Madeira	in	620914
Sloop Mary	Hollowel	Nova-Scotia	out	620914
Schooner Speedwell	Goaffrey	Casco-Bay	out	620914
Sloop Sword Fish	Jenkins	Casco-Bay	out	620914
Sloop Beaver	Parke	Casco-Bay	out	620914
Sloop Providence Pacquet	Chace	New-York	out	620914
Sloop Rabbit	Vole	Virginia	out	620914
Brig Leopard	Nation	Maryland	out	620914
Brig Hope	Cowdry	Philadelphia	out	620914
Sloop Induftry	Earl	Philadelphia	out	620914
Sloop Nancy	Bears	Philadelphia	out	620914
Sloop Defiance	Sturges	Boston	out	620914
Sloop Apollo	Morris	Africa	out	620914
Sloop Enterprize	Tillinghast	Jamaica	out	620914
Schooner Two Friends	Carr	NewProvidence	out	620914
Brig Joseph and Samuel	Brown	Amsterdam	out	620914
Sconner Grayhound	Allen	North Carolina	in	620921
Sloop Mary	Wightman	Virginia	in	620921
Sloop Elizabeth	Gardner	Philadelphia	in	620921
Sloop Prosperous Polly	Unknown	New-York	in	620921
Brig Two Sisters	Everson	St. Kitts	in	620921
Sloop Speedwell	Mahew	Nevis & St.Martins	in	620921
Sloop Friendihip	Pottcr	Nova-Scotia	out	620921
Schooner Boreas	Munro	Nova-Scotia	out	620921
Sloop Diamond	Cornet	Halifax	out	620921
Sloop Shad	Frolics	New-York	out	620921
Schooner Greyhound	Allen	North. Carolina	out	620921
Schooner Albemarle	Clarke	New-London	out	620921
Sloop Dolphin	Grinman	Philadelphia	out	620921

Sloop Elizabeth	Duabomb	Maryland	out	620921
Brig Renard	Dordin	Africa	out	620921
Sloop Rhoda	Sheldon	Halifax	in	620926
Sloop Savannah	Martin	New-London	in	620926
Sloop True Briton	Davis	New-Haven	in	620926
Sloop Polly	Multhurp	New-Haven	in	620926
Sloop Moore Yatch	Ycmmons	Philadelphia	in	620926
Sloop Hannah	Hathaway	Philadelphia	in	620926
Sloop Dolphin	Duncan	St. Georges	in	620926
Sloop Voluntier	Carpenter	South-Carolina	in	620926
Sloop Theisher	Goddard	Philadelphia	out	620926
Sloop Ranger	Nichols	Philadelphia	out	620926
Sloop Dolphin	James	South-Carolina	out	620926
Sloop Kingbird	Brown	South-Carolina	out	620926
Sloop Dolphin	De St. Croix	New-York	out	620926
Sloop Patience	Willcocks	Viginia	out	620926
Sloop Molly	Chace	Viginia	out	620926
Sloop Rhoda	Sheldon	Barbados	out	620926
Sloop Wheel of Fortune	Bardin	Gaudaloupe	out	620926
Sloop Moore Yatch	Yemmons	Jamaica	out	620926
Sloop Silence	Stone	Boston	in	621005
Sloop Polly	Wimp	New-Haven	in	621005
Sloop Hannah	Hathway	Philadephia	in	621005
Sloop Sally	Grinell	Philadephia	in	621005
Sloop Abigail	Brewer	Philadephia	in	621005
Sloop Nancy	Bears	Philadephia	in	621005
Sloop Newport Pacquet	Unknown	New York	in	621005
Sloop Vidory	Kinnicut	Gudaloupe	in	621005
Ship Ranger	Nichols	Philadelphia	out	621005
Sloop Susannah	Lagworthy	Philadelphia	out	621005
Sloop Don Carlos	Benny	New York	out	621005
Sloop Polly	Mulirup	New Haven	out	621005
Sloop True	Briton	New Haven	out	621005
Brig Three Brothers	Skillin	Boston	out	621005
Sloop Susannah	Martin	New-London	out	621005
Brig Freelove	Dexter	Barbados	out	621005

Sloop Nancy	Bears	Philadelphia	in	621012
Sloop Industry	Earl	Philadelphia	in	621012
Brig Hope	Cowdry	Philadelphia	in	621012
Sloop Dplphin	De St Croix	New York	in	621012
Sloop Sally	Forster	New London	in	621012
Schooner Diana	Crowell	New York	in	621012
Sloop Ranger	Wyatt	Philadelphia	out	621012
Sloop Defiance	Nichols	New Haven	out	621012
Sloop Susannah	Pease	Viginia	out	621012
Sloop Silence	Stone	Boston	out	621012
Sloop Sally	Carpenter	Madeira	out	621012
Sloop Edmund	Sewall	Africa	out	621012
Sloop Patucket	Hopkins	Gaudaloupe	out	621012
Sloop Kinnicut	Jackson	Barbados	out	621012
Sloop Nancy	Wright	Havannah	out	621012
Schooner Charming Sally	Potter	Nova Scotia	in	621019
Sloop Polly	Taggart	South-Carolina	out	621019
Sloop Roby	Durtec	South-Carolina	out	621019
Schooner Nancy	Shearman	Philadelphia	out	621019
Sloop Elizabeth	Gardner	Philadelphia	out	621019
Sloop Fancy	Gould	Philadelphia	out	621019
Schooner Betty	Thornton	Maryland	out	621019
Sloop Dolphin	De St. Croix	New-York	out	621019
Sloop Katy	Sarredars	New-York	out	621019
Sloop Polly	Hill	Amboy	out	621019
Sloop Fortune	Fairbanks	New-Haven	out	621019
Sloop Mary	Wightman	Virginia	out	621019
Schooner Charming Sally	Potter	Nova-Scotia	out	621019
Sloop Peggy	Gardner	Jamaica	out	621019
Sloop Eunice	Negus	Barbados	out	621019
Schooner Venus	Tarbox	Falmouth	in	621026
Sloop Beaver	Parker	Falmouth	in	621026
Sloop Defiance	Sturgis	Boston	in	621026
Sloop Nelly	Peck	New-York	in	621026
Schooner Lyon	Waft	Fishing Voyage	in	621026
Sloop Friendsbip	Ellery	Piscatapua	in	621026

Sloop William	Coggefhall	Nantucket	in	621026
Sloop Betsey	Parker	Conneaieut	in	621026
Sloop Ranger	Nichol:	Philadelphia	in	621026
Schooner Chester	Thomas	Maryland	in	621026
Brig Charming Abigail	Wanton	Caudalouph	in	621026
Sloop Abigail	Anthony	Philadelphia	out	621026
Sloop Revenge	Dogget	Casio-Bay	out	621026
Pettiaieger Little Sally	Bridges	Virginia	out	621026
Sloop Sally	.Durfee	Philadelphia	out	621026
Sloop Sally	Chace	Philadelphia	out	621026
Schooacr Diana	Crowell	Boston	out	621026
Sloop Industry	Earl	Philadelphia	out	621026
Brig Hart	Clark	Jamaica	out	621026
Brig Providence	Thompsin	LONDON	out	621026
Sloop Don Carlos	Benny	New York	in	621102
Sloop Susannah	Langworthy	New York	in	621102
Sloop Thresher	Goddard	Philadelphia	in	621102
Sloop Dolphin	Greenman	Philadelphia	in	621102
Sloop Amherst	Ventris.	New-Haven	in	621102
Sloop Lydia	Davis	Boston	in	621102
Sloop Rabbit	Vofe	Virginia	in	621102
Sloop Three Friends	Carpenter	Africa	in	621102
Brig Rebecca	Thurflon	Georgia	in	621102
Schooner Two Friends	Carr	New .Providence	in	621102
Schooner Venus	Tarbox	Casco-Bay	out	621102
Sloop William	Coggelhall	Nantucket	out	621102
Sloop Rainbow	Lawrence	Philadelphia	out	621102
Sloop Volenture	Carpenter	Philadelphia	out	621102
Sloop Betsey	Parker	New-London.	out	621102
Sloop Dolphin	Gibbs	Amboy	out	621102
Brig Northern Lass	Fairbanks	New-York	out	621102
Sloop Prince George	Peck	Africa	out	621102
Sloop Susannah	Langworthy	New-York	in	621113
Sloop Friendfhip	Griffin	New-York	in	621113
Sloop Providence Packet	Chace	New-York	in	621113
Sloop Fortune	Faiibanks	New-York	in	621113

Sloop Dolphin	Greenman.	Philadelphia	in	621113
Sloop Dolphin	James	South Carolina	in	621113
Sloop Free-Bounty	Holier	Boston	in	621113
Sloop Elizabeth	Hatch	Falmouth	in	621113
Schooner Ranger	Remmington	New-Haven	out	621113
Sloop Amherst	Ventris	New-Haven	out	621113
Sloop Mayflower	Ingraham	Philadelphia	out	621113
:loop Mary	Weaver	Philadelphia	out	621113
Brig Nancy	Stetson	Philadelphia	out	621113
Sloop Trial	Sherman	Philadelphia	out	621113
Sloop Defiance	Sturgis	Boston	out	621113
Brig Windmill	Champlin	Sonth-Carolina	out	621113
Sloop Charming Molly	Arnold	Sonth-Carolina	out	621113
Sloop Greyhound	Barlow	Sonth-Carolina	out	621113
Schooner Sally	Northam	South-Carolina	out	621113
Sloop Speedwell	Waterman	South-Carolina	out	621113
Sloop Susannah.	Chaninan	Maryland	out	621113
Schooner Chester	Thomas	Maryland	out	621113
Sloop Dolphin	St Croix	New York	in	621122
Schooner Albemarle	Clarkl	Philadelphia	in	621122
Sloop Abigail	Anthonyl	Philadelphia	in	621122
Sloop Industry	Earl	Philadelphia	in	621122
Sloop Greyhound	Strange	South-Carolina	in	621122
Sloop Sally	Swain	Salem	in	621122
Sloop Silence	Stone	Boston	in	621122
Sloop Dolphin	Martindale	Maryland	out	621122
Sloop Hannah	Godfrey	South-Carolina	out	621122
Brig Success	Stoddard	South-Carolina	out	621122
Sloop Dolphin	Eldridge	New-York	out	621122
Schooner Relief	Hubbs	Philadelphia	out	621122
Brig Two Sisters	Start	Philadelphia	out	621122
Sloop Adventure	Whiting	North-Carelina	out	621122
Sloop Lydia	Davis	North-Carelina	out	621122
Sloop Greenwich	Hill	New-Haven	out	621122
Sloop Victory	Kinnicut	Jamaica	out	621122
Sloop Batchellor	Lance	Jamaica	out	621122

Sloop Providence	Briftow	Jamaica	out	621122
Sloop Mary	Lee	Jamaica	out	621122
Brig Greyhound	Gardner	Martinico	out	621122
Sloop Rising-Sun	Bucklin	Havannah	out	621122
Sloop Neptune	Malbone	Virginia	in	621129
Sloop Sally	Bucklin	Virginia	in	621129
Sloop Polly	Hill	Amboy	in	621129
Sloop Defiance	Havens	North-Carolina	out	621129
Sloop Friendship	Viall	North-Carolina	out	621129
Sloop Sally	Toogood	North-Carolina	out	621129
Sloop Sally	Goddard	Maryland	out	621129
Sloop Adventure	Blethin	Maryland	out	621129
Sloop Sally	Mulford	Cape-May	out	621129
Schooner John	Buckley	Boston	out	621129
Brig Hope	Cowdry	Philadelphia	out	621129
Sloop Thresher	Goddard	Philadelphia	out	621129
Sloop Four Brothers	Killam	Philadelphia	out	621129
Sloop Dolphin	St. Croix	New-York	out	621129
Schooner New-York Packet	Collard	New-York	out	621129
Brig Betsey	Carey	Jamaica	out	621129
Sloop Speedwell	Bowcrs	Jamaica	out	621129
Sloop Sword-Fish	Rodman	Havannah	out	621129
Sloop Newport	Janverin	Piscataway	in	621206
Sloop Fancy	Gould	Philadelphia	in	621206
Sloop Elizabeth	Gardner	New-York	in	621206
Sloop Ranger	Hathaway	Boston	in	621206
Sloop Fanny	Tillinghaa	Amsterdam	in	621206
Brig. Portland	Bowers	South-Carolina	out	621206
Sloop Dolphin	James	South-Carolina	out	621206
Sloop Fancy	Simmons	North-Carolina	out	621206
Sloop George	Arnold	North-Carolina	out	621206
Sloop Fame	Allen	North-Carolina	out	621206
Sloop Indultry	Earl	Philadelphia	out	621206
Sloop Abigail	Anthony	Philadelphia	out	621206
Sloop Friendthip	Griffis	New-York	out	621206
Sloop Don Carlos	Benny	New-York	out	621206

Sloop Silence	Stone	Boston	out	621206
Sloop Neptune	Dillingham	Maryland	out	621206
Sloop Swallow	Hazard	Maryland	out	621206
Sloop Sally	Eckstine	Maryland	out	621206
Sloop Friendship	Ellery	Maryland	out	621206
Sloop Three Brothers	Claghorne	Maryland	out	621206
Schooner Two Brothers	Muchemort	New Haven	out	621206
Sloop Sally	Grinnell	Virginia	out	621206
Ship William	Morris	Guadeloupe	out	621206
Sloop Mary	Turner	Jamaica	out	621206
Sloop Harlequin	Smith	Jamaica	out	621206
Sloop Marygold	Johnston	Barbados	out	621206
Sloop Mary	Daggett	Lisbon	out	621206
Sloop Bachelor	Church	Boston	in	621213
Schooner Royal Phillip	Nickerfon	Cape-May	in	621213
Sloop Africa	Hammond	Virginia	in	621213
Sloop Polly	Taggart	South-Carolina	in	621213
Sloop. William	Tillinghast	North-Carolina	in	621213
Sloop Tryal	Spearman	Philadelphia	in	621213
Sloop Hanover	Pitts	New-York	in	621213
Schooner Abigail	Church	Maryland	out	621213
Sloop Three Sifters	Clark	Maryland	out	621213
Sloop Hopewell	Pease	Maryland	out	621213
Sloop Hopewell	Williams	Maryland	out	621213
Schooner Seaflower	Harlow.	North-Carolina.	out	621213
Sloop Ranger	Hathaway.	North-Carolina.	out	621213
Sloop Beaver	Clarke.	North-Carolina.	out	621213
Sloop Polly	Hill.	North-Carolina.	out	621213
Sloop Industry	Hammond.	North-Carolina.	out	621213
Sloop Dove	Sisson.	North-Carolina.	out	621213
Sloop Seaflower	Unknown.	North-Carolina.	out	621213
Sloop Ranger	Nichols.	North-Carolina.	out	621213
Sloop Newport	Janverin	Virginia	out	621213
Schooner Nancy	Lewis	Philadelphia	out	621213
Sloop Patient Endeavour	Reed	South-Carolina	out	621213
Brig Sally	Woodberry	South-Carolina	out	621213

Brig Betsey	Moore	Madeira	out	621213
Brig Freelove and Nancy	Burdick	Jamaica	out	621213
Sloop Pitt	Tanner	Jamaica	out	621213
Sloop Industry	Remmington	Barbados	out	621213
Sloop Little Betsey	Duncan	New-Providence	out	621213
Sloop Susannah	Owen	Antigua	out	621213
Sloop Hanover	Pitts	New York	in	621220
Sloop Roby	Durfee	South-Carolina	in	621220
Sloop Sally	Upton	North. Carolina	in	621220
Sloop Volunteer	Carpenter	Philadelphia	in	621220
Schooner Friendship	Ball	Boston	in	621220
Sloop Hopewell	Williams	Maryland	out	621220
Sloop Ranger	Ruffen	Maryland	out	621220
Schooner Olive Branch	Valentine	Maryland	out	621220
Sloop Sally	Hathaway	Maryland	out	621220
Sloop Ranger	Nichols	North-Carolina	out	621220
Sloop Mary	Hatch	North-Carolina	out	621220
Sloop Lively	Palmer	North-Carolina	out	621220
Sloop Abigail	Strange	North-Carolina	out	621220
Sloop Industry	Ladd	North-Carolina	out	621220
Sloop Wren	Palmer	Egg-Harbour	out	621220
Sloop Neptune	Malbone	Virginia	out	621220
Sloop Africa	Hammond	Virginia	out	621220
Snow Britannia	Wendell	Boston	out	621220
Sloop Volunteer	Carpenter	South-Carolina	out	621220
Sloop Britannia	Crow	Philadelphia	out	621220
Sloop Scaflower	Gardner	Nantucket	out	621220
Sloop Susannah.	Lanzworthy.	New-York	out	621220
Sloop Neptune	Drew	Jamaica	out	621220
Sloop Hannah	Sheldon	Barbados	out	621220
Snow Adventure	Fargersbn	Africa	out	621220
Sloop Freebounty	Fairbanks	New-Providence	out	621220
Sloop Kingbird	Brown	South Carolina	in	621227
Sloop Mary	Weaver	New-York	in	621227
Schooner Harlequin	Niles	New-York	in	621227
Brig Sea-Horse	Clark	New-Providence	in	621227

Sloop Molly	Chace	Maryland	in	621227
Brig Hope	Cowdry	Philadelphia	in	621227
Schooner Actaeon	Larcher	South-Carolina	out	621227
Sloop Mary;	Weaver	South-Carolina	out	621227
Sloop Kingbird	Allan	North-Carolina	out	621227
Sloop Speedwell	Ingell	Maryland	out	621227
Sloop Revenge	Dogget	Virginia	out	621227
Sloop George	Battar	Virginia	out	621227
Sloop Martha	Reed	Virginia	out	621227
Schooner Speedwell	Hall	Virginia	out	621227
Sloop Providence Parquet	Douglass	New-York	out	621227
Sloop Dolphin	Swasey	Barbados	out	621227
Sloop Polly	Gortoni	Barbados	out	621227
Snow Diana	Mastin	Barbados	out	621227
Sloop Nancy	Jones	Havannah	out	621227
Sloop Dolphin	Duncan	Jamaica	out	621227
Ship Polly	Tosh	Jamaica	out	621227
Sloop Betsey	Boutin	Jamaica	out	621227
Brig Hope	Cowdry	Philadelphia	in	630103
Sloop Patience	Will!cocks	Philadelphia	in	630103
Sloop Industry	Earl	Philadelphia	in	630103
Sloop Abigail	Anthony	Philadelphia	in	630103
Schooner Four Friends	Sears	Nova-Scotia	in	630103
Sloop Providence Parquet	Douglass	New-York	in	630103
Sloop Don Carlos	Benny	New-York	in	630103
Sloop Hanover	Pitt	New-York	out	630103
Schooner New-York Passage Boat	Collard	New-York	out	630103
Sloop Molly	Hammond	North-Carolina	out	630103
Sloop Seaflower	Hathaway	North-Carolina	out	630103
Schooner Charming Polly	Potter.	North-Carolina	out	630103
Sloop Roby	Durfee	South. Carolina	out	630103
Brig Prince of Wales	Watson	South. Carolina	out	630103
Brig Defiance	Duncan	South. Carolina	out	630103
Sloop Correspond	Durfee	Maryland	out	630103
Sloop Endeavour	Nicholl	Maryland	out	630103

Sloop Hope	Johnson	Jamaica	out	630103
Sloop Widow	Rogers	Africa	out	630103
Sloop Four Brothers	Killam	Philadelphia	in	630110
Sloop Thresher	Weaver	Philadelphia	in	630110
Brig Nancy	Stutson	Philadelphia	in	630110
Sloop Dolphin	St Croix	New York	in	630110
Sloop Four Brothers	Potter	Maryland	out	630110
Schooner Three Brothers	Marshall	Virginia	out	630110
Sloop Grayhound	Cornell	North Carolina	out	630110
Sloop Morning Star	Ward	Antigua	out	630110
Sloop Friendship	Griffis	New York	in	630117
Sloop Susannah	Langworthy	New York	in	630117
Sloop Wolf	Wanton	Grandterre	in	630117
Sloop Dolphin	Eldred	Maryland	out	630117
Sloop Diamond	Aken	Virginia	out	630117
Sloop Providence Pacquet	Douglass	New York	in	630131
Sloop Hanover	Pitts	New York	in	630131
Sloop Charming Molly	Arnold	South Carolina	in	630131
Sloop Dolphin	St Croix	New York	out	630131
Schooner Ranger	Rogers	South Carolina	out	630131
Schooner Two Friends	Mumord	New Providence	out	630131
Sloop Polly	Taggart	Jamaica	out	630131
Sloop Three Friends	Carpenter	Africa	out	630131
Schooner Besey Ann	Alleyne	Boston	in	630207
Sloop Susannah	Chapman	Maryland	in	630207
Schooner New York Passage Boat	Collard	New York	out	630207
Sloop Molly	Chase	South Carolina	out	630207
Sloop Dollar Kegg	Bent	North Carolina	out	630207
Sloop Molly	Price	Jamaica	out	630207
Sloop Dolphin	Whiston	Jamaica	out	630207
Brig Dolphin	Easton	Jamaica	out	630207
Sloop BathSheba	Church	St Croix	out	630207
Sloop Sally	Grinnell	Virginia	in	630214
Sloop Dolphin	James	South Carolina	in	630214
Schooner Actaeon	Larcher	South Carolina	in	630214

Schooner Betty	Thornton	Maryland	in	630214
Sloop Rainbow	Allen	Philadelphia	in	630214
Sloop Abigail	Anthony	Philadelphia	in	630214
Sloop Greyhound	Strange	North Carolina	out	630214
Sloop Nelly	Peck	North Carolina	out	630214
Schooner Friendship	Nutting	Virginia	out	630214
Brig Diamond	Wickham	Africa	out	630214
Sloop George	Whipple	Barbadoes	out	630214
Schooner Eagle	Rodman	Jamaica	out	630214
Sloop Robe	Sailsbury	Jamaica	out	630214
Sloop Phebe	Oldridge	Jamaica	out	630214
Sloop Industry	Greenman	Antigua	out	630214
Sloop Endeavour	Andrews	Antigua	out	630214
Brig Sea Horse	Clarke	New Providence	out	630214
Sloop Two Partners	Dunwell	Maryland	in	630221
Sloop Neptune	Malbone	Virginia	in	630221
Sloop Greyhound	Barlow	Boston	out	630221
Schooner Betsey-Ann	Amory	Boston	out	630221
Sloop Two Partners	Dunwell	New-York	out	630221
Sloop New-York Passage-Boat	Taylor	New-York	out	630221
Sloop Fancy	Easton	North-Carolina	out	630221
Sloop Hannah	White	New-Haven	out	630221
Sloop Sally	Aborn	New-Haven	out	630221
Sloop Speedwell	Rogers	New-Haven	out	630221
Brig Rebecca	Clark	South Carolina	out	630221
Brig Diana	Sweet	Hamburgh	out	630221
Sloop Polly	Grinnell	Barbados	out	630221
Sloop Rabbit	Vole	Surrinam	out	630221
Sloop Defiance	Thompson	Falmouth	in	630228
Sloop Volunteer	Carpenter	South Carolina	in	630228
Sloop Dolphin	James	North Carolina	out	630228
Sloop Prosperous Polly	Carpenter	St. Christophers	out	630228
Schooner Albemarle	Durfee	Gibraltar	out	630228
Sloop Neptune	Malbone	Gibraltar	out	630228
Sloop Industry	Earle	Granada	out	630228

Schooner Free-Mason	Rogers	Martinico	out	630228
Schooner Kitty	Carr	Africa	out	630228
Sloop Revenge	Dogget	Antigua	out	630228
Ship King George	Howe	Jamaica	out	630228
Sloop Defiance	Thompson	Falmouth	in	630307
Sloop Volunteer	Carpenter	South-Carolina	in	630307
Sloop Africa	Hammond	Virginia	in	630307
Sloop Correspond	Durfee	Virginia	in	630307
Sloop Sally	Luther	Virginia	in	630307
Sloop Polly	Thachcr	New-Haven	in	630307
Sloop Dolphin	St. Croix	New-York	in	630307
Schooner Abigail	Church	Maryland	in	630307
Sloop Defiance	Thompson	Casco-Bay	out	630307
Sloop Friendship	Viall	New-Haven	out	630307
Brig Juno	Martin	BRISTOL	out	630307
Schooner Three Brothers	Marshall	Virginia	in	630314
Sloop Roby	Durfee	Georgia	in	630314
Sloop Rising-Sun	Taylor	South-Carolina	in	630314
Sloop Britannia	Crow	Philadelphia	in	630314
Sloop Sword-Fish	Rodman	Havannah	in	630314
Sloop Hanover	Wanton	New-York	out	630314
Snow Prince William	Wanton	Barbados	out	630314
Sloop Free-Mafon	Le Favour	Jamaica	out	630314
Sloop Fair Lady	Coddington	Havannah	out	630314
Sloop Charming Molly	Arnold	Granada	out	630314
Sloop Martha	Reed	Viginia	in	630321
Sloop Three Sally's	Clark	Virginia	in	630321
Sloop Fancy	Simmonds	North-Carolina	in	630321
Sloop Sally	Gooding	Maryland	in	630321
Sloop Yellow-Bird	Clark	Teneriffe	in	630321
Sloop Dove	Crosswell	New-Providence	in	630321
Sloop Susannah	Langworthy	New York	out	630321
Sloop Dolphin	St. Croix	New York	out	630321
Schooner Greyhound	Stoddard	Maryland	out	630321
Sloop Polly	Thacher	New-Haven	out	630321
Schooner Aetwon	Bowers	South-Carolina	out	630321

Sloop Three Sally's	Bourroughs	Gibraltar	out	630321
Pettianger Little Sally	Bridges	Virginia	in	630328
Sloop Little Betsey.	Duncan	Ncw-Providence	in	630328
Sloop Providerce Pacquet	Douglas	New-York.	out	630328
Sloop Mary	Weaver	New-London	out	630328
Ship Royal Charlotte	Lingey	Maryland	out	630328
Sloop Abigale	Anthony	Philadelphia	out	630328
Sloop Wolfe	Christey	West- Indies	out	630328
Sloop Success	Coddington	New Providence	out	630328
Brig Hope	Chapman	Antigua	out	630328
Sloop Grayhound	Strange	North Carolina	in	630404
Sloop Ranger	Nichols	North Carolina	in	630404
Sloop Wrin	Palmer	North Carolina	in	630404
Sloop Lydia	Davis	North Carolina	in	630404
Sloop Defiance	Havens	North Carolina	in	630404
Sloop George	Butler	Virginia	in	630404
Sloop Four Brother'	Potter	Virginia	in	630404
Sloop Hopmvell	Williams	Virginia	in	630404
Shop Molly	Chace	South Carolina	in	630404
Sloop Charming Polly	Saxton	Long- Island	in	630404
Schooner Betsey Ann	Amory	Boston	in	630404
Sloop Neptune	Dillingham	Maryland	in	630404
Sloop Sally	Upton	Georgia	out	630404
Sloop Sally	Godding	Georgia	out	630404
Shop Susannah	Martin	New-London	out	630404
Sloop Neptune	Dillingham	Whaling Voyage	out	630404
Schooner Speedwell	Hamilton	Boston	out	630404
Sloop Charming Polly	Saxton	Long Island	out	630404
Sloop Thresher	Goddard	Philadelphia	out	630404
Brig Swan	Stelle	North-Carolina &. Cadiz	out	630404
Sloop Patience	Willcocks	Barbados	out	630404
Brig Windmill	Champlin	Barbados	out	630404
Sloop Sally	Grinnell	Turks Island	out	630404
Sloop Freebounty	Hoffer	Turks Island	out	630404
Brig Elizabeth	Godfrey	Amsterdam	out	630404

Sloop Seaflower	Shearman	North Carolina	in	630411
Brig Prince of Wales	Watson	South Carolina	in	630411
Sloop Swan	Congdon	North Carolina	out	630411
Sloop Spry	Bunker	Whaling Voyage	out	630411
Sloop Seaflower	Shearman	Whaling Voyage	out	630411
Sloop Mary	Wightman	Virginia	out	630411
Sloop Trial	Shearman	Turks Island	out	630411
Sloop Roby	Durfee	New Castle	out	630411
Sloop Fanny	Tillinghast	Martinico	out	630411
Ship Britannia	Warner	Hondorus Bay	out	630411
Brig Nancy	Austin	Fyall	out	630411
Schooner Rachel	Sleght	Amboy	in	630418
Scooner Speedwell	Hudson	Boston	in	630418
Sloop Susannah	Langworthy	New York	in	630418
Sloop Newport Pacquet	Taylor	New York	in	630418
Schooner Swallow	Ivis	New Haven	in	630418
Sloop Dove	Sisson.	North Carolina	in	630418
Sloop Industry	Ladd	North Carolina	in	630418
Sloop Ranger	Wyatt	Philadelphia	out	630418
Sloop Britannia	Smith	Philadelphia	out	630418
Sloop Harlequin	Wilcocks	Philadelphia	out	630418
Schooner Three Brothers	Marshall	Falmoth	out	630418
Sloop Fancy	Simmonds	Maryland	out	630418
Sloop Swordfish	Rodman	Havannah	out	630418
Brig Molly	Allen	Leward Islands	out	630418
Brig Prince of Wales	Watson	Madeira	out	630418
Pettiauger Little Sally	Bridges	Virginia	in	630418
Schooner Speedwell	Hudson	Boston	in	630418
Sloop Susannah	Langworthy	New-York	in	630418
Sloop Newport Pacquet	Taylor	New-York	in	630418
Schooner Swallow	Ivis	New-Haven	in	630418
Sloop Dove	Sisson	North-Carolina	in	630418
Sloop Induftry	Ladd	North-Carolina	in	630418
Sloop Ranger	Wyatt	Philadelphia	in	630418
Slcop Britannia	Smith	Philadelphia	out	630418
Sloop Harliquin	Wilcocks	Philadelphia	out	630418

Schooner Three Brothers	Marshall	Falmouth	out	630418
Sloop Fancy	Sinunonds	Maryland	out	630418
Sloop Swodrfish	Rodman	Havannah	out	630418
Brig Molly	Allen	Leward Islands	out	630418
Brig Prince of Wales	Watfon	Madeira	out	630418
Sloop Greyhound	Strange	North-Carolina	out	630418
Sloop Dollar-Kegg	Bent	North-Carolina	in	630424
Sloop Mary	Hatch	North-Carolina	in	630424
Sloop Elizabeth	Newton	North-Carolina	in	630424
Schooner Charming Sally	Potter	North-Carolina	in	630424
Sloop Abigail	Anthony	Philadelphia	in	630424
Sloop Swallow	Hazard	Maryland	in	630424
Sloop Adventure	Blethin	Maryland	in	630424
Schooner Speedwell	Hull	Maryland	in	630424
Sloop Providence Pacquet	Douglass	New-York	in	630424
Sloop Hanover	Wanton	New-York	in	630424
Sloop Peggy	Calvert	Virginia	in	630424
Sloop Wheel .Fortune	Bardin	Guadalupe	in	630424
Schooner Ranger	Rogers	New-Providence	in	630424
Sloop Charming Sally	Carpenter	Fyall	in	630424
Sloop Dolphin	Shove	New London	out	630424
Sloop Dolphin	St. Croix	New-York	out	630424
Sloop Newport Pacquet	Unknown	New York	out	630424
Sloop Ranger	Nicholls	Boston	out	630424
Sloop Ranger	Soule	North-Carolina	out	630424
Sloop Greenwich	Low	Dominique	out	630424
Sloop Diamond	Carpenter	Martinico	out	630424
Brig Charming Sally	Wanton	Barbados	out	630424
Sloop Rising-Sun	Bucklin	Hull	out	630424
Sloop Sally and Polly	Pielee	New-York	in	630502
Sloop Speedwell	Ingell	Maryland	in	630502
Sloop Three Brothers	Claghorn	Virginia	in	630502
Schooner Friendship	Nutting	Virginia	in	630502
Sloop Friendship	Larcher	Boston	in	630502
Sloop Fidelity	Appleton	New-London	in	630502
Sloop Friendship	Ellery	North-Carolina	in	630502

Sloop Endeavour	Elliott	Barbados	in	630502
Brig Ospray	Stanton	Teneriffe	in	630502
Ship Friendship	Gardner	Guadeloupe	in	630502
Sloop Molly	Chace	Georgia	out	630502
Schooner Swallow	Lockwood	New-London	out	630502
Sloop Britannia	Fobey	Boston	out	630502
Sloop Rachel	Sleght	Amboy	out	630502
Sloop Peggy	Calvert	Virginia	out	630502
Sloop Don Carlos	Clark	New-York	out	630502
Sloop William	Tillinghast	Isequcbo	out	630502
Schooner Speedwell	Morey	Bristol	out	630502
Sloop Yellow-Bird	Clark	Leward-Islands	out	630502
Sloop Humbird	Minthorn	Granada	out	630502
Sloop Industry	Sheldon	Antigua	out	630502
Sloop Newport Pacquet	Hlicks	Africa	out	630502
Ship Confirmation	Hyers	London	out	630502
Sloop King-Bird	Allen	North-Carolina	in	630509
Sloop Fancy	Easton	North-Carolina	in	630509
Sloop Thresher.	Goddard	Philadelphia	in	630509
Sloop Polly	Wady	Amboy	in	630509
Sloop Patucket	Hopkins	Grandterre	in	630509
Sloop Defience	Sturgis	Boston	in	630509
Sloop Industry	Green	Antigua and St. Martins	in	630509
Sloop Diana	Remington	North-Carolina	out	630509
Sloop King-Bird	Allen	North-Carolina	out	630509
Sloop Mary	Hatch	North-Carolina	out	630509
Sloop Hopewell	Waterman	North-Carolina	out	630509
Sloop Harliquin	Barney	New-York	out	630509
Sloop Susannah	Langworthy	New-York	out	630509
Sloop Mary	Crow	New-York	out	630509
Sloop Providence Pacqnet	Douglas	New-York	out	630509
Sloop Sally and Polly	Pielee	New-York	out	630509
Sloop Friendship	Munro	Piscataqua	out	630509
Sloop Abigail	Anthony	Philadelphia	out	630509
Sloop Four Brothers	Potter	Boston	out	630509

Sloop Fidelity	Appleton	New-London	out	630509
Sloop Susannah	Martin	New-London	out	630509
Sloop Charming Sally	Stanton	New-London	out	630509
Sloop Fortune	Fairbanks	Connecticut	out	630509
Sloop Lydia	Allen	South Carolina	out	630509
Sloop Voluntier	Carpenter	South Carolina	out	630509
Sloop Defiance	Cooko	Maryland	out	630509
Sloop Susannah	Hicks	Maryland	out	630509
Sloop Dolphin	Fields	New-Haven	out	630509
Sloop Africa	Hammond	Martinis	out	630509
Brig Defiance	Duncan	South Carolina	in	630516
Sloop SeaFlower	Hathaway	South Carolina	in	630516
Sloop Patience Endeavour	Reed	South Carolina	in	630516
Schooner Peggy	Rackclift	Maryland	in	630516
Sloop Unity	Bunker	Philadelphia	in	630516
Sloop Harliquin	Willcocks	Philadelphia	in	630516
Sloop Silence	Stone	Boston	in	630516
Schooner Sally	Northam	Musquito Shore	in	630516
Brig Betsey	Moore	Maderia	in	630516
Sloop Sally	Grinnell	Turks Island	in	630516
Scooner Relief	White	Newfoundland	out	630516
Sloop Defiance	Sturgis	Boston	out	630516
Sloop Nancy	Wright	Jamaica	out	630516
Sloop Susannah	Easton	Jamaica	out	630516
Sloop Friendship	Felix	Barbados	out	630516
Sloop Ranger	Wyatt	Philadelphia	in	630523
Sloop Abigail	Anthony	Philadelphia	in	630523
Schooner Dolphin	Mayhew	North-Carolina	in	630523
Sloop Endeavour	Nichols	North-Carolina	in	630523
Sloop Dolphin	Swansey	Saltortugas	in	630523
Brig Freelove and Nancy	Burdiek	Musquito-Shore	in	630523
Schooner Charming Sally	Potter	Nova-Scotia	out	630523
Schooner Betty	Westcott	Nova-Scotia	out	630523
Brig Freelove and Nancy	Burdick	Philadelphia	out	630523
Sloop Defiance	Rice	Connecticut	out	630523
Schooner Olive Branch	Perry	Nova-Scotia	out	630523

Brig Defiance	Duncan	Hull	out	630523
Sloop Dove	Crofwell	Africa	out	630523
Brig Two Sisters	Holway	Jamaica	out	630523
Sloop Providence Pacquet	Douglass	New York	in	630530
Sloop Sally	Upton	Georgia	in	630530
Sloop Britannia	Smith	Philadelphia	in	630530
Sloop Four Brothers	Potter	Boston	in	630530
Brig Hart	Clarke	Jamaica	in	630530
Sloop Peggy	Gardner	Jamaica	in	630530
Sloop Elizabeth	Easton	Philadelphia	out	630530
Sloop Thresher	Goddard	Philadelphia	out	630530
Sloop Silence	Stone	Boston	out	630530
Sloop Salisbury	Carpenter	Boston	out	630530
Sloop Four Brothers	Potter	Boston	out	630530
Sloop Unity	Bent	North-Carolina	out	630530
Sloop Don Carlos	Clark	New-York	out	630530
Schooner Three Sisters	Sheffield	St. Christophers	out	630530
Sloop Britannia	Owen	Barbados	out	630530

Table A-3 Merchants Advertising in 1775.

	Merchants	Ads
1	Benjamin Almy	5
2	Job Almy	3
3	Peleg Barker	11
4	Joseph Belcher	2
5	John Bell	9
6	Clarke Brown	12
7	Caleb Carpenter	1
8	John Channing	1
9	Christopher Champlin	23
10	Jabez Champlin	4
11	Nat & Jerimier Clarke	1
12	Shearman Clarke	12
13	Job Cornell	3
14	Stephen Debloise	3

15	Arthur Dennis	1
16	Charles Dunbar	1
17	Danial Dunham	1
18	Joseph Durfee	18
19	William Finch	8
20	Josiah Flagg	1
21	George Gibbs	3
22	Samual Goldthwait	3
23	Thomas Green	4
24	William Grinnell	14
25	John Halliburton	1
26	Israel Horsefield	8
27	Peter Langley	3
28	George & Robert Lawton	22
29	Thomas Grey Lueby	3
30	Gould Marsh	3
31	Robinson,ChamplinandMinturn	4
32	Reak&Okey	2
33	Brenton Perkins	8
34	Ezekiel Price	7
35	Daniel Rogers	3
36	Jonathan Rogers	18
37	Gideon Siffon	5
38	Tosh Sisson	3
39	Richard Low&Peter Smith	3
40	John Stevens	2
41	Thomas Tew	3
42	Nicholas Tillinghast	2
43	Thomas Tripp	2
44	Francis Vandale	1
45	Samual&William Vernon	1
46	Gideon Wanton	3
47	John Wanton	8
48	Philip Wanton	1
49	John Warren	5
50	Samuel Wickham	2

Table A- 4
Merchants_Advertising_During_the_Occupation

	1777	1778	1779	Total
James Arthur	0	3	0	3
John Askew (Priveteer)	0	1	0	1
Stephan Ayrault	0	0	5	5
James Blackie	0	3	0	3
Bourk&Lawton	0	1	0	1
Alexander Bryson	0	16	0	16
Lewis Buliod	0	8	1	9
James Center	2	0	0	2
Christopher Champlin	0	0	0	0
Nat Chandler	0	3	0	3
William Clowet	0	0	1	1
Coddington	0	1	0	1
Silas Cooke	0	3	0	3
B.C. Cutler	0	2	0	2
Stephen Deblois	1	1	0	2
Charles Dunbar	0	3	0	3
Caleb Gardner	3	0	0	3
Samual Goldsbury	0	11	1	12
Samual Goldthwait	0	8	7	15
George Gracie	0	1	0	1
John Grayart	0	2	0	2
Joh Grozart	0	3	0	3
John Haliburton	0	1	0	1
George Hall	0	5	0	5
Isaac Hart	2	1	0	3
Nathan Hart	1	13	3	17
Moses&Samual Hart	0	8	1	9
James Hastie	0	3	5	8
James Henderson	0	0	2	2
Israel Hoursfield	1	0	0	1
John Howe	2	19	8	29
Jacob Isaacks	1	5	0	6

Alexander Johnstone	0	1	0	1
Bernard Kane	0	0	1	1
David Knox	0	0	3	3
Anthony Lechmere	1	4	0	5
John Malbone	3	0	0	3
James McCallum	0	2	0	2
Thomas McKie	0	5	0	5
James Moffatt	1	2	0	3
John Morrison	0	0	0	0
Edward Mumford	0	0	3	3
Thomas Pagan	0	1	0	1
Elizabeth Peckham	0	4	0	4
Moses Pitcher	0	1	0	1
Myer Polock	1	1	0	2
Thomas Powis	0	9	3	12
Philip Robinson	0	13	3	16
William T Robinson	0	5	0	5
William Ryson	0	2	0	2
Joshua St Croix	0	3	3	6
Miller & Sheaffe	0	0	1	1
John Simpson	0	0	3	3
Robert Spence	0	1	12	13
Robert Templeton	0	1	0	1
Charles Walker	0	1	0	1
William Wanton	0	2	0	2
John Watson	0	4	0	4
Thonas Wickham	0	1	0	1
James Wignell	0	0	1	1

Historic Events Time Line[406]

The following is a timeline of events that influenced the history at Newport:

In 1663- Rhode Island Chartered by Charles II as the first sectarian state.

---

[406] This time line was compiled from numerous Historic time lines available on the WEB and augmented with information from the Bibleograply.

In 1696 - The Royal African Trade Company of England lost its monopoly on the slave trade.

In 1696 - The Navigation Act: All colonial trade must be in English-built ships.

In 1701 - Act of Settlement: Parliament appoints Anne to the English throne.

In 1706 - Anne naturalized George II a British citizen.

In 1706 - George II becomes Prince of Wales.

In 1707 - Parliaments of England and Scotland unite to form Great Britain.

In 1710 - South Sea Investment Company was formed.

In 1720 - South Sea Investment Company's stock collapsed.

In 1727 - George II becomes king.

In 1733 - The Molasses Act: Imposed heavy duties on molasses, rum and sugar imported from non-British islands in the Caribbean.

In 1740 - War of Austrian Succession.

ln 1743 - Victory in Europe, Battle of Dettingen.

In 1750 - The Iron Act: Banned the construction of iron mills and steel furnaces in the Colonies.

In 1751- The Currency Act: Banned the paper money of the New England colonies.

In 1751 - Prince of Wales dies and George III becomes Prince of Wales.

In 1755 - Sixty families of Portuguese Jews arrive in Newport from Lisbon, including Aaron Lopez.

In 1756 - Start of Seven-Year-War between Britain and France; William Pitt, Secretary of State, runs the war.

In 1758 - Aaron Lopez buys a farm in Portsmouth RI for smuggling via the Sakonnet River

In 1760 - George II dies in his water closet at age 77 and George III becomes king.

In 1762 - Lord Bute was made Duke of Newcastle.

In 1763 - The port of Newport handled 51,210 tons of cargo; Touro Synagogue founded.

In 1763 - Peace of Paris ends Seven-Year-War on terms favorable for French recovery.

Pitt had doubled Briton's national debt with the war expenses. Parliament wanted the Colonies to pay the debt.

In 1764 - The Sugar Act: Was passed as a revenue-raising measure.

In 1765 - The Stamp Act: Was a direct tax on all printed material.

In 1765 - The Quartering Act: Required Colonists to house British troops.

In 1766 – The Stamp Act was repealed and the Declaratory Act was passed stating that Parliament had supremacy over the Colonies.

In 1767 – The Townshend Act placed duties on Colonial importation of glass, lead, paints, paper, and tea.

In 1769 - James Watt patented the steam engine; Richard Arkwright invented the spinning frame.

In 1770 – The Boston Massacre occurred.

In 1771 – Newport was the leading shipbuilder (179 topsail vessels were built between 1769 and 1771).

In 1773 – The Tea Act took place. Boston Tea Party.

In 1774 - First Continental Congress formed to handle protests.

In 1774 – The Coercive (Intolerable) Act, the Boston Port Act, and the Administration of Justice Act were passed. The port of Newport handled 1,125,290 tons of cargo.

In 1775 – Battles took place between Colonial and British troops at Lexington and Concord. Newport was threatened by British man-of-war. Approximately 2,000 people left Newport, including a number of wealthy merchants (Aaron Lopez, Joseph Anthony). British won early battles.

In 1776 – Adam Smith publishes "Wealth of Nations". The British occupy Newport. On December 7 there were 7 British ships of the line, 4 frigates, and 70 transports which landed 6,000 troops, about 3,000 British and 3,000 Hessian.

In 1777 – George Washington won the battle at Saratoga with supplies obtained from the French by Benjamin Franklin and smuggled to Washington.

In 1778 – The U.S. and French sign a treaty of alliance. Also, the Siege of Newport which was the first multinational event of the revolution. Colonials and French vs. British and Hessians.

In 1779 – The English withdraw from Newport. About 900 houses and some warehouses were destroyed. Loyalists departed with the British troops.

In 1780 – 8,000 French troops were in Newport. Christopher Champlin returned to Newport. He traded with the French and started a shipping company.

In 1781 – Cornwallis surrendered.

In 1782 – Newport population was 5,532 people.

In 1783 – The Treaty of Paris ended the American Revolution. John Gibbs and Walter Channing established businesses in Newport. Newport was recovering. More than twenty rum distillers began production.

In 1783 - First hot air balloon flight. Transportation technology is changing.

In 1783 - Levi Pease established first long distance stage coach line on Upper Post Road in central Massachusetts.

In 1784 - Edmund Cartwright invented the steam-powered loom.

In 1789 - The Bastille fell in France.

In 1793 - Reign of terror begins in France. Decimal system was introduced in France.

In 1793 - Samuel Slater built Slater Mill on the Blackstone River at Pawtucket village. This was the start of American Industrial Revolution.

In 1799 - Napoleon gained power in France.

In 1801 - Ireland and England merge into the United Kingdom.

In 1803 - Louisiana Purchase from France.

In 1803 - James Watt's steam engine in U.S.

In 1805 - Nelson won at Trafalgar.

In 1807 - Slave trade abolished in British Empire.

In 1807 - Congress passed Embargo Act which prohibited foreign trade.

In 1807 - Fulton steamboat launched (4.7 knots going up river).

In 1809 - Congress passed Non-Intercourse Act.

In 1810 – George, Prince of Wales, became Prince Regent George IV.

In 1812 to 1815 – U.S. versus Britain in War of 1812.

In 1815 - Wellington won at Waterloo.

In 1815 - The Great Gale in Newport.

In 1820 - Cotton manufacture replaced trade as economic base.

In 1824 - Fort Adams started.

In 1842 - Dorr's Rebellion.

In 1843 - New State Constitution.

In 1844 - Providence and Worcester Railroad operational.

In the 1840's - Newport started its venue as a vacation spot for the rich.

In 1845 - Old Colony Railroad with service to Newport via Fall River Line Ship.

In 1846 to 1848 - Mexican – American war.

In 1847 - Providence & Worcester Railroad, gas lights in Providence.

In 1847 - Fall River Line: Boston by train to Fall River and New York via Newport.

In 1849 - California Gold Rush.

In 1850 – Land on Bellevue Ave (a dirt road) was purchased for $300/acre and resold for over $5000/acre a few years later.

In 1853 - Port of Providence dredged to allow large ships.

In 1853 - Commodore Perry sailed to Edo Bay, opening Japan to trade.

In 1858 - U.S. – China trade Treaty.

In 1859 - John Brown raided Harpers Ferry and was executed for murder/treason.

In 1860 - Lincoln elected.

In 1861 to 1865 - U.S. Civil War.

In 1862 - *Monitor* versus *Merrimack*, iron warship sea battle.

In 1863 - French troops took Mexico City.

In 1864 - Railroad service to Newport started; Old Colony and Newport R.R.

In 1864 - Lincoln reelected.

1n 1867 - U.S. bought Alaska from Russia.

In 1868 - Grant elected president.

In the 1870's - Summer cottages were built on Bellevue Avenue by Astor, Vanderbilt, and Wetmore.

In 1876 - General Custer's last stand.

In 1877 - Rhode Island School of Design founded.

In 1884 - Naval War College opened.

In 1888 - Woonsocket was created by consolidating mill villages of Woonsocket, Clinton, Social, Globe, Vernon, and Hamlet.

In 1897 - Pembroke College opened as a department of Brown University.

In 1898 - Spanish- American War; USS *Main* was blown up in Havana Harbor; U.S. got Puerto Rico, Guam, and the Philippines.

In 1898 - U.S. annexes Hawaii.

By 1900 Benjamin and Robert Knight of RI had established the largest cotton textile empire in the world.

By 1900 the woolen industry, which started to expand in the 1860s, was flourishing.

Providence ranked first in the nation in the production of woolen goods.

Base metal production was prominent. Brown and Sharpe was the largest producer of machine tools in the nation.

Providence had the largest steam engine factory in the country.

William Nicholson was the world's largest producer of metal files.

The American Screw Company produced more metal screws than any company in the world at that time.

Gorham Manufacturing Company was the country's largest producer of silverware.

The rubber industry was founded (United States Rubber Company).

In 1903 - The Wright Brothers first flight.

Appendix B

MATLAB Script M Files

Income Distribution

```
Mer = zeros(1000,1);
n = 1;
m = 1;
Ax = [0, 1000, 0, 1];
% randn has 0 mean, sd = 1;
PB = .1; %Profit Bias is 10% of 1 SD
while(n<1001)
        while(m<1001)
            Mer(m) = (randn)+ PB + Mer(m);
            m=m+1;
        end
        m=1;
        n=n+1;
end
M = 1:1000;

% Sort **************************************************
st = 1;
n=1;
while(st > .5) %Sort Taxpayers, high payers first
        st = 0;
        while n<1000
            if (Mer(n,1)<Mer(n+1,1));
            D = Mer(n,1);
            Mer(n,:)= Mer(n+1,1);
            Mer(n+1,1) = D;
```

```
        st=1;
    end
    n=n+1;
end
n=1;
end
NMer(1:1000) = Mer(1:1000)/Mer(1);
plot(M,NMer);
axis(Ax);
title('Wealth Distribution for 1000 merchants');
xlabel('Merchants');
ylabel('Wealth');
```

Modified While Loop
```
while(n<1001)
        while(m<1001)
            if(m<100)
                PB = .1 +.3*((m^2)/10000);
            else
                PB=.1;
            end
            Mer(m) = (randn)+ PB + Mer(m);
            m=m+1;
        end
        m=1;
        n=n+1;
end
M = 1:1000;
```

% STPM Simulation of Newport Merchants
```
clc;
hold off;
n=1;
m=1;
k=2;
TPM = zeros(300,8);
People = 0;
% The table in Appendix A of tax information was saved as a text file and
when % going from Word to text, the file formatting is lost. The result is
a % column vector (Named John) containing the taxpayer first name and
```

the taxes % for each year. The following MATLAB converts this into a matrix.

```
Cit = zeros(1884,2);
Cit(:,1) = isnan(John);
Cit(:,2) = John;
while(n<1885)
        if(Cit(n,1)>.5)
            Cit(n,1) = m;
            TPM(m,1)=m;
            m=m+1;
            k=1;
        end
        if(Cit(n,1)<.5)
            TMP(m,k) = Cit(n,2);
            k=k+1;
        end
        n=n+1;
end
Mer = TMP;
% This MATLAB takes the 1772 tax data from the MATRIX and sorts
it by %magnitude.
% Sort ***********************************************
st = 1;
n=1;
while(st > .5) %Sort Taxpayers, high payers first
        st = 0;
        while n<255
            if (Mer(n,2)<Mer(n+1,2));
D = Mer(n,2);
                Mer(n,2)= Mer(n+1,2);
                Mer(n+1,2) = D;
                st=1;

            end
            n=n+1;
        end
        n=1;
end
plot(Mer(1:141,2))
xlabel('Taxpayers in 1772');
```

ylabel('Tax $ at 4.87 dollars to the pound')
hold on;% This plots the value of taxes from highest to lowest and holds
the %plot for more curves
pause;

% This section of the MATLAB is a computer model of Newport commerce.
% Three parameters were adjusted to match the tax curve. They are: Profit
bias, merchant capability, and reinvestment.

% Income distribution

```
MerM = zeros(1000,1);
n = 1;
m = 1;
%Ax = [0, 150, -.2, 1];
% randn has 0 mean, sd = 1;
PB = .3; %Profit Bias is 10% of 1 SD
TF =1;
while(n<1001)
        while(m<1001)
            PB=.03; %Profit bias slightly better than even odds
            if(m<80)
                PB = .25-.25*((m^2)/(80^2));%a percentage of the merchants are
                %smarter than the majority


            end
            MerM(m) = (randn)+ PB +(MerM(m));
            m=m+1;
        end
        m=1;
        n=n+1;
end
M = 1:1000;

% Sort ************************************************
st = 1;
n=1;
while(st > .5) %Sort Taxpayers, high payers first
        st = 0;
```

```
        while n<1000
            if (MerM(n,1)<MerM(n+1,1));
                D = MerM(n,1);
                MerM(n,:)= MerM(n+1,1);
MerM(n+1,1) = D;
                st=1;


            end
            n=n+1;
        end
        n=1;
end
n=1;
% This Trade Ratio represents the ability of the high end merchants to
%reinvest so that they can trade at a faster rate i.e. More ships at one
%time.
TR = zeros(30,1);
while(n<20)
            TR(n,1) = 2/n;
            MerM(n) = MerM(n)*TR(n,1)+MerM(n);
            n=n+1;
end
ScaleAdj = .17;
NMer(1:1000) =ScaleAdj *MerM(1:1000);

plot(M(1:150),NMer(1:150),'x r');
title('Trading model vs. Taxpayer curve 1772')
text(50,50,'Solid Blue is Tax Data');
text(100,40,'Red X is Model Data');
```

Computer Model

```
% NptModel
Clear
MajMerchant = zeros(2,120);
% Matrix of 2 major merchant variables for 10 years (120 months);
Merchant = zeros(5,120);
% Matrix, major merchant under 5 loss conditions for 10 years (120
months);
% Crew and ship cost
Capt = 53; % dollars/month;
```

```
FstMate = 53; % dollars/month;
SeaMan = 43; % dollars/month
Ship = 2000/120 ; % cost of ship that lasts 10 years, dollars per month
TimeTrip = 3; % three month trip
Trip_Cost = (Capt+ FstMate+3*SeaMan+Ship)*TimeTrip;
Cargo = zeros(3,1); % initial value, intermediate value, final value;
Months = 120;
Cargo(1,1) = 5000; % Value of cargo going out
Cargo(2,1) = 5000; % Value of cargo 1st stop
Cargo(3,1) = 50000; % Value of cargo returned
investment = Cargo(1,1)+Ship; % merch% NptModel
Clear
MajMerchant = zeros(2,120);
% Matrix of 2 major merchant variables for 10 years (120 months);
Merchant = zeros(5,120);
% Matrix, major merchant under 5 loss conditions for 10 years (120
months);
% Crew and ship cost
Capt = 53; % dollars/month;
FstMate = 53; % dollars/month;
SeaMan = 43; % dollars/month
Ship = 2000/120 ; % cost of ship that lasts 10 years, dollars per month
TimeTrip = 3; % three month trip
Trip_Cost = (Capt+ FstMate+3*SeaMan+Ship)*TimeTrip;
Cargo = zeros(3,1); % initial value, intermediate value, final value;
Months = 120;
Cargo(1,1) = 5000; % Value of cargo going out
Cargo(2,1) = 5000; % Value of cargo 1st stop
Cargo(3,1) = 50000; % Value of cargo returned
investment = Cargo(1,1)+Ship; % merch
            MajMerchant(1,n)= profit; % Record profit for trip

        if(ShipLoss(1,n)>Loss(k)) % If ship is lost
            MajMerchant(1,n)=-investment; % Record loss if ship is lost
        end;
        m=0; % Reset m, length of trip in months
        end; % end of trip loop

        if(n>1) % Calculate cumulative profit or loss
        MajMerchant(2,n) = MajMerchant(2,n-1)+ MajMerchant(1,n);
```

```
        Merchant(k,n) = MajMerchant(2,n);
        end;
        m=m+1; % increment m (months/trip)
        n=n+1; % increment n count of months
end

k=k+1; % Increment Loss variable
end
time = 1:Months; %Time variable for plotting
plot(time,Merchant(1,time),'k');
hold;
plot(time,Merchant(2,time),'r');
plot(time,Merchant(3,time),'b');
plot(time,Merchant(4,time),'g');
plot(time,Merchant(5,time),'.');
    title('Merchant Profit sensitivity');
    xlabel('Time Months');
    ylabel('Cumulative Profit');
    hold off;
```

Bibliography

Primary Sources

Anderson, Fred. "The Real First World War and the Making of America." *American Heritage* 56, no. 6: 75. M AS Ultra School Edition, EBSCO host (accessed January 8, 2013). (November/December 2005),

Channing, George. *Early Recollection of Newport, RI from 1793 to 1811.* Newport: A.J.Ward; Charles E. Hammett, Jr., 1868.

Cullum, George W., Col., Corps of Engineers, U.S. Army, (Ret.). *Historical Sketch of the Fortification Defenses of Narragansett Bay Since the Founding in 1638 of the Colony of R.I.* Washington, D.C., 1884.

Fage, Edware Lew'nt of Artillery. *Plan of the works which form the Exterior Lines of Defence, for the town of Newport in Rhode Island also of the Batteries and Approaches made by the Rebels on Honeyman's Hill during their attack in August 1778, Drawn by Lew'nt Hage at Newport in Nov., 1778.* Photostat held at the Newport Historical Society.

Forbes, Allan, and Paul F. Cadman. *France and New England.* Yale Street Trust Company, 1925.

Land evidence Records, Town of Portsmouth, Rhode Island.

MacKenzie, Frederick. *The Diary of Frederick MacKenzie.* Cambridge: Harvard University Press, 1930.

Maps, plate numbers 108 & 109. Town of Middletown. Scale: 200' = inch. Published by Mount Vernon Graphics, Inc., Mount Vernon, NY, 1958. Available at Tax Assessors office Town of Middletown, East Main Road, Middletown, RI 02840.

Marryat, Joseph. *Concessions to America, the Bane of Britain.* London: Kessinger Publishing, 1807.

Peterson, Edward. *History of Rhode Island*. New York: John S. Taylor, 1853.

Plan de la Ville et Environs de Newport RADE in Rhode Island, avec le campement de L'Armee francaise pre de cette en 1780. Photostat at Newport Historical Society of original map located at William L. Clements Library, Ann Arbor, Michigan.

Ricardo, David. *On the Principles of Political Economy and Taxation*. London: John Murray, 1821. Library of Economics and Liberty [Online] available from http://www.econlib.org/library/Ricardo/ricP.html (accessed 18 April 18, 2012).

Tax Records, Town of Newport 1772 to 1801 available at the Newport Historical Society Library, Newport, Rhode Island.

Newspapers
Newport Mercury 1758 to 1820.

Newport Gazette 1777 to 1779.

Newport Herald 1787 to 1790.

The Guardian of Liberty 1800 to 1801.

Rhode Island Republican 1801 to 1806 and 1809 to 1820.

Secondary Sources
Amory, Thomas. *Military Services and Public Life of Major General John Sullivan*. Boston, Wiggin and Lunt, 1868.

Amory, Thomas. *Siege of Newport*. Boston: Cambridge University Press, 1888.

Amory, Thomas. *Centennial Memoir of Major General John Sullivan, 1740-1795*. Philadelphia: Collins, 1879.

Andrews, Charles. *The Colonial Period of American History Vol. 1*. Safety Harbor, FL.: Simon Publications, 2001.

Balch, Thomas. *Les Francais En Amerique pendant La Guerre de L'Independence des Etats-Unis.* Translated by Thomas Willing Balch, Porter and Coates, 1891.

Barker, Hannah, and Simon Burrows. *Press, Politics and the Public Sphere in Europe and North America 1760-1820.* Cambridge, UK: Cambridge University Press, 2002.

Barrow, Thomas. *Trade & Empire, The British Customs Service in Colonial America 1660 – 1775.* Cambridge: Harvard University Press, 1967.

Bayles, Richard M. *History of Newport County, Rhode Island from the 1638 to the Year 1887.* New York: L.E. Preston, 1888.

Benn, Carl. *The War of 1812.* Oxford: Osprey Publishing, 2002.

Benninga, Simon. *Finantial Modeling 3rd ed.* Cambridge, MA.: MIT Press, 2008.

Bertram, Volker. *Practical Ship Hydrodynamics 2ed.* Oxford, UK: Butterworth-Heinemann, 2012.

Bier, Vicki, M. Naceur Azaiez. *Game Theoretic Risk Analysis of Security Threats.* New York: Springer, 2009.

Bigelow, Bruce. *Aaron Lopez: Colonial Merchant of Newport.* The New England Quarterly, Vol 4 No4 (Oct. 1931) PP. 757-776.

Borgmann, Albert. *Technology and the Character of Contemporary Life.* Chicago: University of Chicago Press, 1984.

Bower, Bruce. *Simple Heresy, Rules of Thumb challenge complex financial analysis.* Science News, Society for Science and the Public, June 4, 2011. pp26-29.

Brandimarte, Paolo. *Numerical Methods in Finance and Economics 2nd ed.* Hoboken, NJ: John Wiley and Sons, 2006.

Breen, T. H. *An Empire of Goods: The Angicization of Colonial America. 1690-1776.* The Journal of Britiush Studies. Vol. 25, No. 4 University of Chicago Press(Oct. 1986) pp. 467-499.

Bridenbaugh, Carl. *Fat Mutton + Liberty of Conscience.* New York: Atheneum, 1974.

Bridenbaugh, Carl. *Cities in Revolt, Urban Life in America* 1743-1776. New York: Alfred. A. Knoph, 1965.

Buchholz, Todd G. *New Ideas From Dead Economists.* New York: Penguin, 2007.

Budiansky, Stephen. *Perilous Fight.* New York: Alfred A. Knopf, 2010.

Casson, Lionel. *Travel in the Ancient World.* Baltimore: Johns Hopkins University Press, 1994.

Christensen, Clayton M. *The Innovator's Dilemma.* New York: Collins Business Essentials, 2006.

Chyet, Stanley. *Lopez of Newport.* Detroit: Wayne State University Press, 1970.

Clark, Gregory. *A Farewell to Alms.* Princeton: Princeton University Press, 2007.

Coleman, Peter J. *The Transformation of Rhode Island, 1790 – 1860.* Providence: Brown University Press, 1963.

Coughtry, Jay. *The Notorious Triangle: Rhode Island and the African slave trade, 1700-1807.*
Philadelphia: Temple University Press, 1981.

Crafts, N. F. R. *British Economic Growth During the Industrial Revolution.* New York: Oxford University Press, 1985.

Crane, Elaine. *A Dependent People.*:Newport Rhode Island in the Revolutionary Era New York: Fordham University Press, 1992.

Crane Elaine Forman *Ebb Tide in New England,* Boston: Northeastern University Press 1998.

Desmarais, Norman. *The Guide to the American Revolutionary War In Canada and New England.* Ithaca: Busca, 2009.

Doyle, Arthur Conan. *A Study in Scarlet,* London:Ward.Lock&Co., 1887

Ekelund, Robert, and Robert Herbert. *A History of Economic Theory and Method 5th ed.*
Long Grove, Il.: Waveland Press, 2007.

Ferreiro, Laurie. *Ships and Science,The Firth of Naval Architecture in the Scientific Revolution 1600-1800.* Cambridge: MIT Press, 2010.

Fiske, Jane. *Gleanings from Newport Court Files 1659-1783.* Boxford Mass., 1998.

Fremont-Barnes, Gregory. *The Royal Navy 1793 – 1815.* Oxford: Osprey Press, 2007.

Forbes, Allan, and Paul Cadman. *France and New England.* Boston: The State Street Trust Co., 1925.

Goldenberg, Joseph. *Shipbuilding in Colonial America.* Charlottesville, VA: University Press of Virginia, 1976.

Gat, Azar. *War in Human Civilization.* Oxfor: Oxford University Press, 2006.

Gutstein, Morris A. *The Story of the Jews of Newport.* New York: Bloch Publishing Co., 1936.

Harper, Lawrence. *The English Navigation Laws.* New York: Octagon Books Inc., 1964.

Harrison, Eliza Cape, and Rosemary F. Carroll. *Newport's Summer Colony 1830 – 1860.* Newport History Newport Historical Society Fall 2005.

Hattendorf, John. *Newport, the French Navy, and American Independence.* Newport: The Redwood Press, 2005.

Heppner, Frank. *Railroads of Rhode Island.* Charleston: The History Press, 2012.

Historic and Architectural Resources of Middletown, Rhode Island: A Preliminary Report. Providence, R.I.: Rhode Island Historical Preservation Commission, page 36, June 1979.

James, Sydney. *The Colonial Metamorphoses in Rhode Island.* Hanouer, MA: University Press of New England, 2000.

Jefferys, C. P. B. *Newport: a short history.* Newport: Newport Historical Society, 1980.

Konstam, Angus. *British Napoleonic Ship-of-the-Line.* Oxford: Osprey Publishing, 2001.

Kert, Faye. *The Fortunes of War: Commercial Warfare and Maritime Risk in the War of 1812.* The Northern Mariner/Le Marin du Nord, VIII, No4(October 1998),p1-16.

Kotowski, Maciej. *Hull Clubs and British Maritime Insurance An Analysis of Risk Preferences and Insurance Markets, 1720-1840.* http://webfiles.berkeley. edu/~kotowski. 21 march 2007 accessed 17 Feb 2012.

Kuhn,Thomas S. *The Structure of Scientific Revolutions 3ed.* Chicago: University of Chicago Press, 1996.

Lavery, Brian. *The Arming and Fitting of English Ship of War 1600-1815.* Annapolis: Naval Institute Press, 1987.

Lippincott, Bertram. *Indians, Privateers and High Society.* New York: J. B. Lippincott Co., 1961.

Maffeco, Steven E. *Most Secret and Confidential,* Intelligence in the Time of Napoleon and Nelson. Annapolis: Naval Institute Press, 2000.

Mahan, A. T. *The Influence of Sea Power Upon History 1660-1783.* New York: Dover Publications, 1987.

McClellan, William S. *Smuggling in the American Colonies at the Outbreak of the Revolution.* New York: Moffat, Bard and Co., 1912.

McCusker, John, and Russell Menard. *The Economy of British America 1607 – 1789.* Chapel Hill: University of North Carolina Press, 1985.

McCusker, John. *Colonial Tonnage Measurement. The Journal of Economic History Vol 27Mar. 1967 pp82-91.*

McCraw, Thomas K. *Prophet of Innovation Joseph Schumpeter and Creative Distruction.* Cambridge: Belknap Press, 2007.

Miller, Lawrence. *Barbarians to Bureaucrats.* New York: Clarkson N. Potter Inc., 1989.

Mulvagh, Jane. *Newport Houses.* New York: Rizzoli International Publications, 1989.

Newman, J. N. *Marine Hydrodynamics.* Cambridge: The MIT Press, 1997.

Oppenheim, Alan V., and Ronald W. Shafer with John R. Buck *Discrete-Time Signal Processing* Upper Saddle River NJ, Prentice Hall 1999.

Pencak, William. *Jew & Gentiles in Early America.* Ann Arbor: Universit

Shy, John. *A People Numerous and Armed.* New York: Oxford University Press, 1976.

Sonenscher, Michael. *Before The Deluge.* Princeton: Princeton University Press, 2007.

Sparks, Jared. *The Works of Benjamin Franklin Vol II,* Boston Tappan & Whittenmore, 1836.
Available from Google Books accessed 26 Oct 2011.

Stensrud, Rockwell. *Newport, A Lively Experiment 1639-1969.* Newport: Redwood Library, 2006.

Taylor, Alan. *The Civil war of 1812.* New York: Alfred A. Knopf, 2010.

Terry, Roderick Dr. *The Story of Green End Fort*. Bulletin of the Newport Historical Society, Number 51, page 7, October 1924.

Urdang, Laurence. *The Timetables of American History*. New York: Simon & Schuster, 1996.

Volker,Bertram. *Practical Ship Hydrodynamics 2ed*. Oxford, UK: Butterworth-Heinemann, 2012.

Von EELKing, Max. *The German Allied Troops in the North American War of Independence---1766-1783*. Albany: Joel Munsell's Sons, 1893.

Walsh, Kenneth M., and David S. Walsh. *Memo on Location of Green End Fort*. Newport, Bulletin of the Newport Historical Society, Number 161, Vol. 49, page 1, Winter 1976.

Walsh, Kenneth M. *The Story of the Analysis of Green End Fort*. Newport, Bulletin of the Newport Historical Society, Number 184, Vol. 54, page 113, Fall 1981.

References Supporting Analysis

Allen, Robert. *The British Industrial Revolution in Global Perspective*. New York: Cambridge University Press, 2009.

Arnol'd, V. I. *Catastrophe Theory*. New York: Springer-Verlay, 3rd ed., 1992.

Atkinson, John, and Malcolm Crowe. *Interdisciplinary Research*. West Sussex: John Wiley & Sons, 2006.

Bertram, Volker. *Practical Ship* Hydrodynamics. Boston: Butterworth-Heinemann, 2000.

Breen, T.H. *An Empire of Goods: The Anglicization of Colonial America, 1690-1776*. The Journal of British Studies, Vol.25, No.4, Re-Viewing the Eighteenth Century (Oct.,1886), pp 467-499.

Bronson, Richard, and Govindasami Naadimuthu. *Operations Research 2nd ed*. New York: McGraw-Hill, 1997.

Catz, Elihu. *The Two-Step Flow of Communication: An Up-To-Date Report on a Hypotheses*. Public Opinion Quarterly, Vol. 21(1), 61-78, 1957.

Chapman, Fredrik. *Architectura Navalis Mercatoria*. Mineola, N.Y.: Dover Publications, 2006.

Comstock, John. *Principals of Naval Architecture*. New York: The Society of Naval Architects and Marine Engineers, 1967.

Ekelund, Robert, and Robert F. Hebert. *A History of Economic Theory and Method 5th ed*. Long Grove, Illinois: Waveland Press, 2007.

Gilmore, Robert. *Catastrophe Theory for Scientists and Engineers*. New York: John Wiley & Sons, 1981.

Ginneken, Jaap. *Collective Behavior and Public Opinion*. London: Lawrence Erlbaum Associates, 2003.

Lamb, Sir Horace. *Hydrodynamics 6th ed*. New York: Cambridge University Press, 1993.

Mandel, John. *The Statistical Analysis of Experimental Data*. New York: Dover Publications, 1964.

McCusker, John J., and Russell R. Menard. *The Economy of British America 1607 – 1789*. Chapel Hill: The University of North Carolina Press, 1985.

McGrayne, Sharon. *The theory that would not die*. New Haven: Yale University Press, 2011.

Miller, Lawrence M. *Barbarians to Bureaucrats*. New York: Clarkson N. Potter Inc., 1989.

Neumann, John von, and Oskar Morgenstern. *Theory of Games and Economic Behavior 60th Anniversary Edition*. Princeton: Princeton University Press, 2004.

Nelson, Barry L. *Stochastic Modeling Analysis & Simulation*. Mineola, NY: Dover Publications, 1995.

Preston, Howard W. *The Battle of Rhode Island: August 29, 1778* Providence, Rhode Island State Bureau of Information Historic Publication No. 1, 1928.

Sanders, P. T. *An Introduction to Catastrophe Theory.* New York: Cambridge University Press, 1995.

Root, William L., and Wilber B. Davenport. *An Introduction to the Theory of Random Signals and Noise.* New York: McGraw-Hill Book Co., 1958.

Selby, Samuel M., PhD, J. *Standard Mathematics.* Cleveland, Ohio: the Chemical Rubber Co., 15th edition, 1967.

Tung, K. *Topics in Mathematical Modeling.* Princeton: Princeton University Press, 2007.

Villiers, Alan. *Square-Rigged Ships, An Introduction.* London: National Maritime Museum, 2009.

Wirshing, James, and Roy Wirshing. *Introductory Surveying.* New York: McGraw-Hill Book Company, 1985.

Zwillinger, Daniel. *Standard Mathematical Tables and Formulae.* New York: CRC Press, 2012.

Zubaly, Robert. *Applied Naval Architecture.* Centerville, MD: Cornell Maritime Press, 1996.

Index

Andre, Major John	64
Aquidneck Mill	109, 110, 112
Battle of Rhode Island	62, 63
Bayes, Thomas	19, 123
Bills of Exchange	3, 25, 27
Boston	3, 9, 14, 24, 30, 50, 53, 61, 72, 105, 113, 114, 138, 139, 141
bribery	2, 17, 28, 24
Bunker Hill	49, 50
Burgoyne, General John	52
Business Lifecycle	138
Capitalism	34, 118, 123, 132
captains	6, 11, 23
Champlin, Christopher	56, 64, 79
Chapman, Fredrik Henrik af	19
Charles II	2, 5, 173
customs	5, 8, 11, 17, 22-25, 28, 101, 125
d'Estaing, Comte	57, 69
factors	4, 6, 28, 42, 81, 92
Franklin	67, 68, 126, 140
French POW	17
Fage, Edward	53, 54, 55, 56
George II	1, 22, 140
George III	1, 5, 22, 24, 140
gratuities	24
Greene, Governor William	63
H.M.S. Squirrel	10

Hessian	14, 51
Hispaniola	18
HMS Rose	50
hogsheads	10, 11, 23, 24
Howe, General William	50-53, 57, 61, 63
Howe, John	63
Impressments	95, 96
Industrial Revolution	8, 87, 101, 104, 106, 108, 110, 112, 119, 138
Insurance	103, 104
Jackson, Andrew	100
Jefferson, President	98, 99
Kuhn, Thomas S.	xx
Lafitte, Jean	100
laissez-faire	2, 25
Le Chevalier de Ternay	65
Leicester	50, 75
Lopez Bay	24
Lopez, Aaron	18, 24, 27, 28, 30, 31, 39, 40, 45, 50, 52, 75, 102, 124, 125, 138, 139
Louisiana Territory	93, 97
Malthus, Thomas	82, 106, 126, 127
maritime commerce	7, 34, 74, 90, 92, 99, 103-106, 108, 115, 118, 122, 128-131, 138, 139, 141
molasses	7, 16, 17, 18, 22, 23, 24, 42, 48, 75, 79, 107, 111, 118, 128, 139
Molasses Act	7
Napoleon	73, 93-97, 99-101, 134, 140
neutral merchants	96, 125, 137, 140
Newport Business	6, 115, 122
Newport Capitalism	123
Newport Worth	47, 83-85, 87, 89, 112, 124, 128

Nyquist   16

Peace   68, 94

Perry Mill   109, 110, 112

Pigot, Major General Robert   57, 62

pistole   15

Prescott, General Richard   62

Price fixing   62

Providence   72, 74-78, 81, 87, 90, 91, 92, 104, 105, 108, 111, 112, 113, 115, 121, 127, 129, 130, 138, 139, 141

Quakers   3

Redoubt de St. Onge   15, 73

Ricardo, David   127

Rochambeau   65, 66, 69, 70, 71, 72

Schumpeter   34, 73, 74, 92, 118, 119, 123

scurvy   70, 95

Sherlock Holmes   xviii

Shipping Data   7, 76

Slater Mill   17, 104, 108, 119, 125, 129, 140

Smith, Adam   125

smuggling   17, 24, 28, 124, 140

Stiles,Dr. Ezra   70

stochastic analysis   34, 131

Sullivan, General John   49, 57, 61, 69

Supercargo   6

Taxes   31, 32, 42, 46, 47

Tourist Industry   119, 121, 122, 141

Triangular Trade   48, 111, 118, 128, 139

U.S. dollar   32

USS Chesapeake   28

Wanton, Joseph   62, 63

Whitehorne, Samuel   106, 107, 111

The author Dr. Kenneth Walsh and his wife Mersina.

Mersina was instrumental in the production of this book.

The author is a professional engineer with over 50 years of experience in the field of electrical engineering and acoustics. Upon retirement the author studied history, economics, and other topics resulting in a PhD granted in May of 2013 by Salve Regina University in Newport, Rhode Island.

This book is based on dissertation research conducted over a period of more than two years. In addition to the reviews leading to the successful defense in April of 2013, the book was commented on by Dr. Edward J. Walsh, a noted NASA scientist and the author's brother which resulted in significant improvements in clarity.

The author has published articles in the Newport Historical Society bulletin and helped found the historical society for Middletown Rhode Island. He currently serves on the Board of Directors of that organization.